SPACE IN MIND

East–West Psychology and Contemporary Buddhism

The Editors

Dr. JOHN CROOK is Reader in Ethology (Animal Behaviour) at the Department of Psychology, Bristol University. He first became interested in Buddhism when he was posted with the army to Hong Kong in 1953–4, and, over the years, developed a fascination with the relations between the Buddhist concept of mind and that of Western Psychology.

Dr. DAVID FONTANA is Reader in Educational Psychology at the University of Wales, Cardiff. In 1986 he and John Crook organised a major international conference on meeting points in East–West Psychology. He is the author of a number of important books on psychology and educational processes, and is a frequent broadcaster.

The Other Contributors

Stephen Batchelor, author and lecturer, Sharpham House, Ashprington, Totnes, Devon.

Susan Blackmore, lecturer in Psychology, University of Bristol.

Ven. Ngakpa Chogyam, spiritual Director, Sang-ngak-cho-dzong.

Guy Claxton, senior Lecturer in Education, Kings College, University of London.

Padmal da Silva, institute of Psychiatry, University of London.

Kedar Nath Dwivedi, consulatant Psychiatrist, Northampton Health Authority.

Lynn Goswell, senior Educational Psychologist, County of Avon.

Richard Jones, family Psychiatrist, Wessex Family Psychiatry Unit, Portsmouth.

James Low, psychotherapist, Drug Addiction Unit, Middlesex Hospital.

Paul Thomas Sagal, professor of Philosophy, New Mexico State University, USA.

Martin Skinner, lecturer in Psychology, University of Warwick.

Malcolm Walley, senior Lecturer in Psychology, Nene College, Northampton.

SPACE IN MIND

EAST–WEST PSYCHOLOGY
AND CONTEMPORARY BUDDHISM

EDITED BY

JOHN CROOK AND DAVID FONTANA

ELEMENT BOOKS

First published in Great Britain in 1990
by Element Books Limited
Longmead, Shaftesbury, Dorset

Designed by Roger Lightfoot

Typeset by Selectmove Limited

Printed in Great Britain by
Dotesios Printers Ltd, Trowbridge, Wiltshire

Cover illustration by Martin Rieser

Cover design by Max Fairbrother

British Library Cataloguing in Publication Data
Space in mind : East-West psychology and contemporary Buddhism.
  1. Psychology. Influence of Buddhism
  I. Crook, John II. Fontana, David
  150

  ISBN 1-85230-154-6

Contents

Introduction:
Wordless Views and Viewless Words –
Basic Contrasts in East–West Thought

JOHN CROOK and DAVID FONTANA

The Problem of De-mystification

Although just a place on the far side of the world, the East has long seemed mysterious, other, and inscrutable to the Westerner. He is drawn by the apparent paradox of a people in many ways just like himself, yet holding incomprehensible or strange values and beliefs. And he is bewitched by the mystique created by the whole history of trade in rare and valuable goods – not only silk and spices, but also ceramics, paintings, sculptures and fine furniture, all seeming to spring from another mode of perception.

There is a story which illustrates the contrast between East and West as it shows itself in philosophical ideas. Two monks are arguing. One shows a bowl to the other and asks 'What is the most important thing about this bowl?' His companion answers 'It is the shape of the bowl'. 'Oh no,' says the first, 'how superficial you are – it is the space within it that is all-important.' Just then the Master passes by. 'Neither of you is right,' he says, 'yet both of you have given a correct answer'.

Our story may illustrate a central idea in Mahayana Buddhist philosophy as represented in the famous Heart Sutra: 'Form is Emptiness and Emptiness is Form.' Now, a Westerner, as a result of cultural history and philosophical background, will always tend to seek explanations based on form. Eastern thinkers of many persuasions on the other hand will immediately see the significance of the empty space which is the inevitable companion to all form. This appears in so many ways – witness the spacious landscapes of Chinese painting, the subtle silences in Japanese music. Moreover, the paradigm is a lived experience, not merely some intellectual preference.

In the West, words refer primarily to concrete matters. They rarely open to a view that includes the blank page – the spaces – the experience of punctuation. Eastern words, on the other hand, often seem to evoke experiences of silence or space – the content and the wordy explanations vanish into the view. It seems to us, then, that when East comes West the 'wordless view' meets the 'viewless word'. No wonder the result has often been incomprehension!

In this book we explore these wordless views so characteristic of Eastern thought, with special emphasis on the interpretation of mind. Our exploration is aimed, in addition, at revealing how, at the present time, ideas in the West have moved sufficiently to allow these Eastern paradigms to affect our thinking and to evoke fresh understandings of human life.

But the interaction between Eastern and Western thought isn't exclusively one-way. Just as Western research in physics and linguistics reveals an Eastern-style relativity of form in the universe and in the way in which we represent it in language, so in the East the technological expertise emanating from the West's historical concern with manipulating form has become the foundation of new and extensive economic success. We stand in a period of reciprocal exchange. The problem is there exists scant comprehension of how the contrasting paradigms of East and West can meet and *relate* to each other, thus creating a truly global perspective.

The chapters in this book attempt to enhance this comprehension particularly within the psychological field. Section 1 deals directly with this theme. Section 2 shows how our comprehension of self, mind and meditation can be enlarged by including Eastern perspectives. Section 3 examines problems of personal growth and spiritual development, and examines the social world of Westerners who are attempting to find personal meaning in Eastern practices or viewpoints. Section 4 applies the same line of thought to the study of counselling and therapeutic practice.

Before proceeding, however, we need in this Introduction to highlight certain core ideas that make the 'wordless view' of the Eastern approach so provocative at the present time.

Hinduism, Buddhism and Taoism share a common perspective, namely that within phenomena there exists a 'basis' of which phenomena are an expression. This basis relates to phenomena by way of what we may term *pervasion*. All things are *pervaded* by the Atman, Buddha-nature or Tao – in much the same way that fish in the sea are pervaded by water, or sea-water is pervaded by salt. Eastern thought thus takes a monist position – phenomena are merely representations of contrasting states of an underlying ground. Differences in interpreting this common perspective exist of course. While for the Taoist the Tao that can be expressed remains almost unknown, for the Hindu ultimate reality is conceived positively (much in the same way that a Christian thinks of the Godhead) and for the Buddhist negatively. Contrary to popular belief, this negativism within Buddhism does not imply non-existence. The Buddha endeavoured initially to find his way to the ultimate ocean, but every way he turned all he discovered was the constituent flux of being. This flux, the unending relationship of cause and effect operating in time, is the basis for what he called the 'principle of interdependent origination'. All things are empty of self-nature (*anatta*), everything is nothing other than the process which is the expression of this principle. The Void of Buddhism is thus not non-existence, but rather the absence of discrete entitiveness in a cosmic flow of energy.

The idea was expressed in many ways in Buddhism, reaching its final form in the Madhyamika philosophy of Nagarjuna in which it is applied particularly to language (for detailed discussions see Murti, 1955; Ramanan, 1978; Hopkins, 1983; Komito 1987; Crook and Rabgyas, 1988). No term represents an entity separable from other terms in language which relates to it. The subtleties of this position reveal close similarities to Western contemporary deconstructivist thought as expressed by Wittgenstein (see Gudmunsen, 1977), yet unlike this Western viewpoint, the Buddhist position is not nominalist (i.e. does not believe universal concepts can't represent reality). For Nagarjuna, beyond language is the ineffable, which though not expressible can nevertheless be *experienced*. Indeed it is here that contemporary Christian theology (Cupitt, 1987) can benefit from an examination of Buddhism, for in the latter's wordless view value remains intact rather than emptied of meaning and reduced to the 'here and nowism' of phenomenal existence.

A separate line of Buddhist thought, the 'mind only' school, saw the nature of the underlying pervasive ground as a fundamental stratum of consciousness out of which both subjective and objective states emerged (see Chapter 3). This view has closer similarity to Hinduism than to the radical stance of Nagarjuna, but has nevertheless been important as a major philosophical root for the psychology of mind basic to Zen (Chapter 8).

We can see at once how strange these views seem to mainstream Western psychology, with its reductionism to behaviour, its focus on the mind as agent, and its sharp distinction between subjective and objective. Nevertheless, one of the main endeavours of certain of the chapters in this book is to explore ways in which Western psychological theories *can* be allowed to relate to these Eastern conceptions. These endeavours reveal that the modern cognitive emphasis in psychology does allow a *rapprochement* that is not only of the greatest theoretical interest, but has practical implications for the personal development and spiritual expression of human beings. The authors concerned trace and retrace the patterns that they perceive as particularly important within this rapprochement.

East–West Psychology and Personal Development

Another prime contrast between Eastern and Western psychology concerns the way in which personal development is conceived. Western science considers a person to emerge out of social interaction dependent upon genetic make-up, so that at root psychology remains very much a biological science. It tends to see the individual human life as something finite, beginning at conception, or birth, and ending at the point of physical death. Eastern thought, however, sees each individual as the fresh expression of a former personal condition in a previous life. There are various ways in which this process of metempsychosis or reincarnation is conceived, some strands of Eastern thought taking the straightforward view that personal entities transmit from generation to generation by wandering in space after death until an appropriate conjugation of egg and sperm arises – to which conjugation the external agent is then attached. In this way of thinking, a biological body is simply a vehicle for a transmigrating entity, the character of which is the result of its own 'ignorance'. Other views are more subtle in their examination of the nature of transmission, and of what it is that gets passed down through time.

Buddhism again takes a particularly striking position. That which is transmitted is the shadow side of life – the unresolved negative karma of an earlier life. As James Low (Chapter 9) forcefully expresses it, the entire process of being a person belongs to the realm of pathology. The person *is* the package of negative karma descended from the existence of its previous vehicle in an infinite regression of past lives. Only radical awakening can dissolve such negativity, and allow the total dissipation of such karma. Some Buddhists, however, retain the notion of the awakened being as retaining some sort of personhood, though it may be that such ideas amount to a theodicy – ideas giving support to religious adherents who cannot take on the ultimately impersonal universalism of the Buddhist philosophical perspective.

The way in which East and West may come together over this contrast remains in doubt. Some contemporary Westerners find the more sentimental versions of metempsychosis well suited to their security needs in the face of death, and more credible than simple ideas of a Christian heaven or hell. Psychologists, however, may see in the Eastern view a powerful metaphor of the way in which the concerns of a generation become introjected into those of the next – much as the neuroses of a grandparent can reverberate down several generations of family life. Personal identity itself is so often the expression of a need for acceptance established by the pressures imposed by demanding parents. The Eastern metaphor emphasises the significance of time in the re-creation of selves on a model of previous selves in earlier generations – whether by empathic absorption or reformulation following resentment and rejection of a parental way of life.

Buddhism and the Western Psychologist

We have spoken broadly of the Eastern tradition of Hinduism, Buddhism and Taoism, yet most of the chapters in this book refer to Buddhist ideas. The fact is that the viewpoint of Buddhism and its sophistication has a special attraction for the West. Buddhism is notably undogmatic in its philosophical presentation and, within a wide range of alternative presentations, reveals a marked flexibility. The ultimate nature of mind–matter remains undefined – an apophatic stance that can be experienced as especially relevant in a scientific culture in which success in research only leads more and more deeply into a mysterious universe. Since the mind is itself of the universal nature, the cosmos can never be precisely defined apart from mind. This relativity finds significant resonance in Buddhist philosophy, and is perhaps at the root of its contemporary intellectual popularity.

The chapters in this book are in most cases based upon material presented at a conference on 'Eastern Approaches to Self and Mind' sponsored by the British Psychological Society in Cardiff in the summer of 1986 and organised primarily by David Fontana. But the contemporary fascination in Britain with the idea of relating Eastern to Western ideas in psychology began earlier with its first public expression in a symposium convened by Guy Claxton for the annual conference of the British Psychological Society in 1983 on the topic 'Buddhism and Psychology'. Under the chairmanship of Martin Skinner, papers were presented by Guy Claxton, John Crook, David Fontana and Joy Manné-Lewis. It was expected that these papers would express a minority interest, but in fact the audience was a packed one, the discussion animated, and the interest enthusiastic. It appeared that many clinical and educational psychologists, psychotherapists and psychiatrists had been contemplating East–West problems, and this was their first opportunity for a get-together. The small core group of psychologists responsible for this meeting, all of whom have practical experience of Eastern thought and disciplines, then began to have regular meetings together, initially at John Crook's home in Somerset and later at venues in Avon and in South Wales. This withdrawal to the countryside with log-fires and conviviality enabled us not only to sustain a high level intellectual discussion but also to meditate together and to try out various experiential techniques. The members of this group, Susan Blackmore, Guy Claxton, John Crook, David Fontana, Collette Ray, Myra Thomas, Martin Skinner and Michael West, found much mutual support in these interactions, and further public events were initiated in conferences on Buddhism and Cognitive Science, and in British Psychological Society colloquia on meditation, the social dimensions of meditation, and related topics. The group's interaction and sharing of ideas has already led to two publications prior to this volume: Guy Claxton's edited collection *Beyond Therapy* (1986) and Michael West's *The Psychology of Meditation* (1987). These publications join with two other important works published in the USA (Katz, 1983; Welwood, 1983) which together with an excellent survey of ideas on cognitive science, brain research and consciousness (Blakemore and Greenfield, 1987), and the survey of Asian psychology edited by Peranjpe, Ho and Rieber (1988), provide an initial literature from which we hope to see an expanding field of studies.

SECTION 1

Psychological Perspectives in Eastern and Western Thought

INTRODUCTION TO SECTION 1

The four chapters in this first section indicate some of the ways in which Eastern, specifically Buddhist, psychology may be related to contemporary Western psychological thought.

John Crook stresses the experiential contrast between two types of knowledge, 'knowing how' and 'knowing that', the first essentially discriminative and analytical, the second passive and apperceptive. Both are essential components of the human experience of knowing, but they can and often do appear in opposition to one another. Since Western philosophy is primarily concerned with 'knowing how' and Eastern thought with 'knowing that', it follows that an integration of the two should produce a more holistic perspective. John then develops a historical account of the way in which Western and Eastern thought diverged from contrasting initial premises in Greek and Indian ways of being. He points out that Christianity in particular, due to its insistence on the historicity of its central myth, has been notably subject to crises in credibility, while the contemporary non-religious hedonism of the Western world provides individuals with no certain sense of the meaning of life in a vast impersonal universe. In this context, Eastern ideas, with their profound psychophilosophical background, have impressed themselves deeply on a culture marked by intellectual sophistication and high educational achievement. John concludes by discussing the way in which an East–West dialogue can do much to meet the need for meaning in a global culture increasingly dominated by Western-style entrepreneurial technology.

Stephen Batchelor introduces us directly to Eastern thought in a brief yet comprehensive account of the nature of Mahayana spirituality. He outlines the two complementary philosophical positions of the Madhyamika and Cittamatra schools respectively, which in broad perspective have similarities to the Western viewpoints of the linguistic and deconstructive philosophies of Wittgenstein and Derrida, and of the 'mind-only' perspective of A.N. Whitehead. Each perspective is associated with ways of progressing from merely conceptual to experiential and intuitive insight into the meaning of the key ideas. Stephen proceeds to discuss two of these ways – Tantric Vajrayana and Ch'an (Zen). In spite of the surface differences in practice and orientation, both can be seen to be anchored in the fundamental Mahayana philosophy of the essential emptiness and relativity of all things.

Martin Skinner examines certain parallels between Buddhist and Western ideas on the nature of self. In particular, Martin discusses G. H. Mead's interpretation of the self as a social object. Mead, argued that the mind creates symbols for events and actions, and that these symbols are derived from the social experience of the individual. The idea of one's self is therefore a 'symbol' derived from social interaction in personal development. Communities sharing significant symbols are thus the context within which the mind develops the notion of self. There are very clear similarities between Mead's view and the ancient conception of the illusory nature of the 'self as object' in Buddhism. The relating of Buddhist practice to the theory of 'symbolic interactionism' can thus become a creative contemporary perspective on the processes of mind.

David Fontana looks further at the difficulty Westerners experience with the Buddhist conception of self. David's important overview of Western and Eastern attitudes towards self emphasises that the self is not an object like a table or chair but rather an internal process of attribution. The quality of this attribution is thus subject to many influences that can have personally destructive or beneficial effects. The basis of mind lies as it were behind the process of attribution – that which does the attributing is the fundamental root of personal minding. To become aware of this aspect of mind below or beyond the mere attributing of self is thus a matter of profound insight at an unusual experiential level. Only when self-assertion is related to a perceptive self-negation can a deeper self-affirmation which lies at the root of wisdom begin. Western psychology is just beginning to examine the implications of this Eastern perspective, and the potential of this examination at both the intellectual and the personal levels is indeed the prime motive for the preparation of this book.

JOHN CROOK
DAVID FONTANA

CHAPTER 1

East–West Psychology:
Towards a Meeting of Minds

JOHN CROOK

Introduction: What is the Use of Knowledge?

I awoke this morning with a question. What is the use of
knowledge? And I recalled vividly an occasion, years ago, when
I was a student doing an animal behaviour project on the foraging
and roosting behaviour of the gulls of Southampton Water. I was
attempting to understand the patterns of movement of the birds
as they flew inland up the rivers Test and Itchen to forage after
a night on the salty mud-banks and shallow tidal waters of the
estuary. Their movements seemed to vary with the state of tide
at dawn. I was counting the numbers of each species as they
passed before me on their evening return flight. The light was
beginning to fade, the glow of an early winter's evening lit up
the mud-flats, waders called and some wild duck were moving
about. The long skeins of gulls came out of the darkening
sky inland and flew past in silhouette before me. Every five
minutes I took a count, thus building up a statistical record.
As the time went by I experienced considerable irritation as each
five-minute period arrived – not that I disliked counting, but
the fact of doing it interrupted the depth of silent appreciation
I was experiencing in the beauty of the scene. There was this
sheer wonder going on before me in a totality of relatedness
that made the mind pause wonderingly – and then suddenly
the necessity of counting dark shadows in the air and asking
questions – What bird was that? Where was it going? Why was
it flying in that manner? I was in a conflict between here/now
experiencing and the application of discriminatory intellect. The
'opposites', as the thirteenth-century Zen master Dogen termed
them, had arisen.

Reflection shows that what a scientific observer, an experimenter or a counter of birds is doing, is attempting to understand. Whatever the wonder of 'knowing that' – the immediate moment in the estuary with its sense of intuitive comprehension – this experiential awareness in itself is not an understanding. We are not designed by evolution merely to gaze out of our eyes but rather to internalise 'reality' as a model from which we can make predictions as to our security or success (Crook, 1980). So the questions arise – What? How? Why? And gradually we attribute meanings to events and their relationships – 'knowing what' 'knowing how' and 'knowing why' gradually take shape as 'understanding that'.

In modern Western culture, based as it is in a philosophy that is both critical and science-orientated, education's main aim is to foster a way of thinking that creates constructs through which we can control the world. We are experts at it. No other culture has had such specialised experts in this art of building workable scenarios from inference. And the result has been a material success that has become a treadmill as the need to maintain it has increased with our attachment to the resultant high standards of living. The experience of 'knowing that' – the 'bare awareness' as Krishnamurti has called it – is set aside for poets and mystics, the rejects of our conventional world.

But if you stay with the simple awareness of the moment – whatever it is – a remarkable series of changes in consciousness can appear. The simple witnessing – the staring at what is (Chapter 15) – does not raise the question as to whether you are doing it well! And this simple shift away from an objective self-consciousness (Duval and Wicklund, 1972) means that objects appear simply as objects, feelings as feelings; and, since a special sort of indifference has arisen, the process unwinds before us and the tensions of dualism (Chapter 2) which self-reference entails (Chapters 3 and 4) simply dissolve. The mind becomes a mirror. Now it is the exploration of this capacity, a basic potential in each of us, that Eastern psychology has taken seriously – positing philosophically indeed that this way wisdom lies.

Eastern and Western Perspectives

It is of course simplistic to draw up contrasts between East and West
as if this were an easy matter, because differing Eastern traditions
are exceedingly diverse in their approaches and philosophies. While
they share some basic roots, the philosophical explorations of
experience and the paths of practice to which the various Eastern
systems lead can be very different indeed. I think, however, it is
fair to suggest that at least within the philosophies and systems
of practice of Buddhism, Hinduism and Taoism there is a broad
agreement on the value of life that differs greatly from that of
the Christian and post-Christian European world (see Northrop,
1946).

In the West, the revolution of thought that took place in ancient
Greece led to an awareness of the problems of life in a way that
sought solutions by generating changes in the environment. These
first Western scientific endeavours and technological applications
had their origins in the use of intellect in changing the world. The
result was a growth in power combined from the beginning with
the sense of hubris – that in assaulting nature there was a danger
of overplaying one's hand. The figure of Prometheus appeared
along with the insights of early Greek science and philosophy.
As science gained strength after the Dark Ages, Renaissance
man began to generate undreamed of material power through
developing formal-process technology. The world consisted of
the human doer and the natural done-by. Explanation of the causal
determinants of natural events led to an especially marked dualism
– Man as distinct from Nature and his attempt to explain himself as
an object. In this world of explanation, description generated the
materials for thought and experiment and modern cosmology, and
Neo-Darwinian evolutionary theory and Post-Freudian systems of
psychoanalytical explanation have emerged as among the main
pillars of our world-view today. The basic dualism persists –
Man versus Nature, Rich versus Poor, Doctor versus Patient,
Employer versus Labourer, and the prime mover is always control
over money in a monetised and competitive social world.

In Eastern thought, the aim in facing suffering became the
attempt to release oneself from pain, not so much through an
effort to alter the environment but through the understanding
of self. And this too developed into the creation of powers – the

inner powers of self-control and self-emancipation. The changing
inner attitudes were sometimes found to contain the seeds of being,
bliss and love which might transform the lives of individuals. In a
deliberate denial of the importance of environment, the religious
virtuosi of the East cultivated the non-dualism of integrated being
in which the split between subject and object was set to one side.

These powerfully contrasting trends in thought yielded very
different social psychologies. Western thought naturally tends to
a psychology of identity, an emphasis on the *entity in the id-entity*
– as I first put it some years ago. The self in such an approach
is treated as a reification of a cultural, personal and emotional
historical process. It is a *thing* to be analysed with the methods
of hypothetical deductive logic by scientists trained in the analysis
of objects.

In Eastern thought, the focus on consciousness and the denial of
significance to the environment meant that the ineffability of non-
egoic states became the central focus, goal and philosophical basis
for ways of life. The absence of any outer exploratory quest other
than conformity with a sacred status quo meant that such views
were often ahistorical and lacked historical criticism. For example,
Mahayana traditionalists assert that the Buddha taught both the
Sutras and the Tantras personally, while historical scholarship
shows quite clearly that Buddhist philosophy and practice has
undergone a progression over many hundreds of years. The idea
of scriptural criticism in Buddhism is a Western notion based in the
work of biblical scholarship, and not one indigenous to the East.

Words descriptive of mental states need collective agreement as
to their usage by a community of practitioners who, in following
the manuals of the gurus, can manifest similar or identical states
of mind. Such collective agreement becomes the basis for an
orthodoxy, and for lineages of transmission that necessarily involve
hierarchies of acceptance and learning very different from the
dialectical progressions of argumentative Western thinkers. The
East has produced paradigms that spiral around each other – as
in the emergence of the Madhyamaka from earlier interpretations
of *Sunyata* in Buddhism – circles that always focus in on the basic
experience of non-egoity at the hub of the mandala. Imputations
from experience are impacted into relatively simple all-embracing
notions such as karma, the detailed processes of which may never
be experientially or experimentally explored, but merely asserted

according to traditional authority. The constant return to the 'one' that is the pivot of so much Eastern thought has thus tended to fossilise viewpoints, so that many of the ideas that are interesting Westerners today are actually hundreds of years old and largely undeveloped since the final form of a system emerged.

Peter Berger (1973) has discussed the emergence of Western thought from another perspective. Unlike other major religions, Christianity, in common with Judaism, insisted on the presence of God in history detectable in acts of involvement with the world. The theodicy of Christianity in particular focused strongly on the historicity of Christ. Eastern religions, by contrast, are anchored in psychological perceptions relating the human microcosm to the universal macrocosm which is the deity. The theodical rationalisations for these latter beliefs are not subject to the same acute crises of credibility to which historical assertions are prone. Furthermore, in Christianity, and especially in Protestant Christianity, a man's moral relationship to the transcendent personhood of God provided, as it were, a single hot-line to the Almighty which bypassed Man's relationship with the rest of Creation. Indeed, these other works of God became the preserve from which Man could derive his means of livelihood, justifying his exploitation of the natural world through his special relationship to an other-worldly ruler. The world of nature lost its sacred quality, which has been sustained to a much greater degree in Eastern thought.

It was this freedom to explore nature that led to the emergence of science and technology and which, at the same time, produced a sophisticated, increasingly secular, bourgeois society in which progress in material developments produced critical thinking and novel ideas. The credibility of the old man in the sky was, not surprisingly, soon called in question, giving rise to a struggle for power and influence between Church and humanists from the time of the Renaissance onwards.

The eventual triumph of secularisation has left the majority of Westerners without a mythology, a deeply based symbolical view of the meaning of life. While some still adhere to fragmented churches experimenting with emotive religiosity or social reform, the break-up of the once monolithic structure of Christianity is far advanced. Secularisation has created a world-view in which the principal goal is material success – but such success does little to answer the ultimate questions of meaning, and those centred upon the fact of personal death (Cupitt, 1987). The world-view of science brings no relief either, for here we come up against the smallness of man in an inconceivably vast cosmos. The whole show is a vast system in which man plays a tiny part on a speck of a planet lost in space-time – a system moreover which seems to have no particular interest in human beings. Death is just a meaningless inevitability – much as it comes to dogs or sheep.

This aching void of ultimate meaninglessness is one that most of us struggle to avoid: the rationalisations of religions, the theodicies, have in the past protected us from it. Indeed, as Berger points out, theodicy maintains our alienation from the confrontation with the possibility of personal meaninglessness. Secularisation, however, provokes a confrontation with religious pretence that forces us back naked into the fires of original stone-age questions. Like Zen koans, these demand a ruthless examination of the nature of self in the universe, and a coming to terms with the illusion of entity-in-identity. The strange fact is that had Christianity focused more on the psychological dimensions revealed in its own mystical tradition, the writings of the Desert Fathers, the Athonite tradition, and works such as the *Cloud of Unknowing* for example, the severity of the personal crises, particularly those perhaps of priests functioning in a world where some of their own number proclaim 'God is Dead!', might have been much less, and the need for Eastern alternatives less demanding.

As we have seen, the traditional Western philosophical position has been to stress the role of consciousness as the means whereby an agent discriminates between objective and subjective aspects of experience in order to act effectively in the world. Such a view focuses therefore on individual identities taking reasoned action in the world. 'Action' theory (Bailey, 1986) is based very much in these traditional views and, in so far as human beings actually do perceive themselves as agents, so an action psychology must contribute importantly to human understanding. The work of Mario von Cranach and his associates (1982) emphasises the role of conscious attention in discriminating appropriate action by individuals in social situations – these acts of attention being very much those of agents perceived as entities in a social world.

There is, however, an alternative Western perspective closer to that of Eastern philosophies which plays down the significance of particular entities and focuses more on the processes underlying their interaction. This view, known as 'Motion' theory to Bailey, crops up in a variety of forms. Within philosophy it was championed by Hobbes who, in his *Leviathan*, conceived a totally materialist universe in which the behaviour of human beings is viewed as an expression of the same laws of physics as govern other natural phenomena in the world. Any theory which reduces focus on the entity in identity in favour of a focus on the processes of intersubjectivity and communication tends to reject the traditional Western view of self-controlling consciousnesses in subject–object relationships. In motion theory, the dualism is replaced by a more or less monistic view of process which pervades the merely analytically useful distinctions between artificially separated personal processes in interaction. Thus a number of social psychologists view individual behaviour as occurring within a communication system of intersubjectivity rather than as a result of personal intentions (Birdwhistle, 1959; Watzlawick *et al.*, 1967). Individuals, in short, are seen as having a hallucinatory view of themselves, perhaps due to the way language both reifies and separates their concept of mind from others, and as being in ignorance of the actual interconnectedness of their relations with the environment (see also Chapter 16).

The discovery in physics that an object of observation could not be measured without considering the activity of the observer, has also had mammoth implications for the traditional view that ultimate explanations of matter and cosmos are possible in the form of 'objective' knowledge. The observer now has to be treated as a part of the universal process being observed. One extreme response has been a move towards a new idealism, the view that everything is after all in some sense mind. Whitehead's philosophy (1929, see also Thorpe, 1978) in many ways parallels the philosophical idealism of the Yogacara Vijnanavadins in Buddhism (see Chapter 2), whose description of psychological process emphasises the pervasion of the universe by a principle that makes the distinction between mind and matter purely nominal – all is process in which the appearance of identity is an illusion of conventional utility rather than a true perception.

A number of authorities have also noted the similarity between a science dominated by concepts of indeterminacy, relativism and process, and Eastern cosmological speculation (Capra, 1975; Zukav, 1979). Bohm (1980), in particular, suggests that in addition to the fragmented 'explicate' order of things appearing in their distinctiveness there is also a holistic 'implicate' order of unitary, interconnected process which pervades the universe. For the human subject it is the subject-verb structure of language that forces individuals into the illusion of personal separateness. Bohm sees explicate and implicate orders as complementary, and has been strongly influenced by the philosophical perspective of Krishnamurti (for example, 1954). Other writers such as Daisetz Suzuki (1962) on the Mahayana, and Radhakrishnan (1953) on the Upanishads, have advocated similar positions from an Eastern starting-point.

The implication of these shifts in Western thought away from traditional action theory to a stress on the pervasion of process throughout phenomena is to remove the powerful stress on individualism as the key element in social thought. Yet, since in the conventional world, whether Eastern or Western, people still act as individuals and may do so for well-founded economic and sociobiological reasons, it would be unwise to move to a thoroughgoing transcendentalism whether materialistically or spiritually conceived. Conventionally, people see themselves as agents. Only on reflection does a profounder view arise and influence the values people hold. We are thus dealing here with perspectives rather than with antinomies. For certain types of enquiry and activity in the world an action theory is appropriate while, for others, motion theory will provide greater insight. This has indeed been the view of some outstanding Eastern thinkers. Thus Tsong·kha·pa, the founder of the Gelugpa order in Tibet, remarked that one of the most difficult aspects of Buddhist training was to see the world, at one and at the same time, both in the perspective of the conventional entitiveness of things, and in the perspective of their ultimate emptiness of selfhood in a world of interdependent origination (*pratitya samutpada*). Models of mind which examine the co-occurrence of these perspectives in human life need a new contemporaneous development.

These themes relate furthermore to contemporary views in the sociology of knowledge and an emerging new philosophical paradigm within Western psychology. It is certainly true to say that the prevailing paradigm of a science reflects in large measure the social concerns of its time. While detailed scientific experiment utilises standards of empirical objectivity that are internally impeccable, the entire drift of a field of study may be influenced by forces that lie outside the academic concerns themselves. This discovery of the relativism of scientific enquiry has opened the way to an extreme view arguing that the sciences comprise no more than a prevailing myth of our time. This reaction against an empiricist construction of reality has encouraged the re-emergence of a contemporary 'expressionism' (Taylor, 1975), a term referring to a reborn romanticism that focuses on subjectivity rather than objectivity, on self-expression and personal feeling and on self-awareness as a path to self-realisation (Markova, 1982, p. 105). The emphasis is on the elucidation of meaningful action and the fulfilment of human being, rather than on Kantian or Cartesian satisfactions with rational understanding. The great philosopher of expressionism was Hegel who 'helped to develop a conception of freedom as total self-creation' (Taylor, 1979, p. 167). But Hegel also criticised the notion of self-dependence, thus helping us to relate critically to our lives as embodied and social beings.

Some contemporary writers, in their enthusiasm for a neo-expressionism, have seen 'reality' as no more than a mental construction arising from imaginative attributions from experience, and doubt whether any objective form exists, or if it does then it remains for ever unknowable. For others an even more radical position argues against any reality at all. What we call reality, such writers argue, is simply created in a realisation that arises out of cognitive relationships between essentially mental perspectives.

There are of course built-in limits to these extreme forms of cultural relativism. Not all beliefs or theories about the world are determined by fantasies arising purely from cultural contexts. The claim that all knowledge is social is itself relative to a particular social context in reaction to a previous paradigm. It contradicts itself, because it claims to be true of all knowledge. If it were true, no knowledge could then be validated, for everything would collapse into mere relativism and solipsism (Glover and Strawbridge, 1985).

It becomes clear that ways of investigation and modes of modelling 'reality' each have their realms of meaningful applicability. Thus a model of the universe that works (in the sense that atom bombs are exploded, a plastic industry created or computers made to infer repeatedly confirmable outcomes) clearly has validity within its own terms. Yet models of human existence and value are not bound to models of scientific empiricism, and have a creativity the focus of which becomes their own validation for those for whom they are meaningful. We are unlikely, however, to live meaningfully if we conceive of the universe as merely arbitrary; we need the insight of Tsong·kha·pa if we are to make any reliable or validated sense of our worlds and of those of others.

Meeting the Need for Meaning

Many of us are probably interested in Eastern thought because of a personal search for meaning and a need for integration. Certainly this was true of my own discovery of Ch'an Buddhism as a young army officer doing National Service in Hong Kong during the Korean War. Yet today, when I survey the extraordinary spread of Buddhism in the West, I am saddened to see the progress of that meaningless fragmentation and divisiveness that Krishnamurti asserted to be the result of any form of institutionalisation and sectarian allegiance. Just after World War II, when Christmas Humphries was completing his influential book *Buddhism*, he travelled to the East and obtained the assent of many leading Buddhists to twelve principles that all held in common (Humphries, 1951, p. 74). This almost ecumenical document focused on the centrality of core ideas in Buddhism. As the years have passed, we now have representative teachers of the numerous branches of Tibetan, Japanese and South Asian Buddhism jostling for followers in London, Paris and California. To a young newcomer the scene is one of complex confusion. Unless one is prepared to adopt one line on trust and forget the others, it becomes essential to read widely in order to see more clearly the central core that still remains. Similar difficulties arise for those with wider interests in the East. The kaleidoscopic whirl of teachings and practices produces a fragmentation of common need into factions, followers of chosen gurus, who view one another's affiliations with distrust if not distaste.

For the most part this fragmentation is consequence of the desperate Western need to cultivate distinctive identities, for the disputes are of relatively little interest to the teachers themselves. The best of them know they themselves are only facilitators attempting to help puzzled people to personal insight – and that the varying routes are only paths to a basic goal. Yet, there are dangers here for the unwary; without a path there may be no way forward, but attachment to a path may do no more than create another identity with all its needs for exclusiveness and self-justification. The way forward can only lie in a hard self-examination that few are willing to attempt.

I would like to see this book as an attempt at creating a new procedural paradigm. If you believe, as I do, that the psychological system of the human being has emerged on planet Earth as an adaptation to the natural environment of our evolutionary origin, we can expect all members of our species to have many basic properties of mind in common (Crook, 1980). We have seen that historical study shows that Eastern and Western viewpoints are the expressions of contrasting cultures responsive to differing patterns of environmental origin and cultural adaptation. Today we need to go beyond the duality of East and West (and the devisiveness of sectarianism) to create a genuine East–West psychology which, both in academic study and through practice, can yield a better understanding of the human mind as a species-wide phenomenon.

Such an approach needs an understanding of:

1. the nature of systems of knowledge, their function, their historical and cultural relativity and their content;
2. the way in which systems of belief relate to personal and collective action;
3. the way in which scientific knowledge and model-building can benefit from comprehending the praxes of Eastern systems and vice versa;
4. the way in which we may construct a view of human nature that is universal – in the sense that it is built from the experiences of all cultures and not merely some of them;
5. the way in which we can use such understanding in building sustainable relations between our species and our planet that may secure a future for life on earth.

Models of mind are central to such an understanding. We are only at the beginning of the exploration here, for the way in which Western approaches to consciousness and identity can be related to Eastern understanding is as yet largely unexamined.

New paradigms arise in many different quarters. We have been examining the contrasting perspectives of traditionally Eastern and Western psychologies. I believe there is implicit in this examination the possibility of creating a new view of human consciousness and intellect which is less exclusively focused on the reified self and the performative potential of intelligence (Crook, 1988). The cultural tendency to maximise material gain, so clearly a corollary of the Western capitalist system of environmental exploitation, is so obviously disastrous in a world of limited resources that any critical examination of the mentality which sustains it must open a door to hope.

We know from socio-ecological studies of mammals and birds that where an environment has inbuilt constraints that limit population growth, individuals of species are naturally selected in such a way as to show increases in collaborative, mutualistic or altruistic ways of life. Interestingly these do not eliminate individual initiative and selfish behaviours, but rather provide a wider social context which shifts individual performance away from maximisation in the direction of optimisation and collective benefit. The human race, likewise, must find ways to optimise its use of its own resources and those of nature. And individual nations and cultures must give up their attempts to exploit resources at the expense of their rivals. No appeal to an idealistic future in the stars will bring an answer – such ideas are merely evasions or excuses to maintain a short-term advantage involving the exploitation of others. The answer can only be in a world-wide examination of the global problem and a willingness to solve it together.

The structural changes (*perestroika*) now being developed in the economic systems of states until recently inflexible in their political philosophy and social controls need to lead on into a planetary re-evaluation carried through with a comparable optimism. Through hard work and intelligent endeavour it may yet be possible to rescue the planet from the ecological mistreatment of the last century. If a philosophy and a practice for a sustainable future is to be created, the merging of the contrasting wisdoms of East and West will be essential.

CHAPTER 2

Mahayana Spirituality

STEPHEN BATCHELOR

Historical Introduction

Historically, Mahayana Buddhism has emerged from the original Buddhist traditions through formulating its understanding in terms of the prevailing religious, philosophical and cultural situations in which it has found itself. More than being a *school*, it is really a trend or movement within Buddhism. It stands for the creative and innovative thrust of the tradition combined with a love for the world in which it is active. It is unfortunate that the term 'Mahayana' has become used as a tool in creating sectarian division. The well-known Hinayana/Mahayana split has been wrongly identified as a conflict between two schools of thought, two quasi-institutional bodies. In fact, it describes a conflict in spiritual attitude which only has real meaning on the level of the individual. A person who proudly belongs to a Mahayana school of Buddhism may have a thoroughly Hinayana outlook. Likewise a Theravadin monk meditating in a cave in the forests of Thailand may exhibit a most genuine Mahayana attitude.

It is unimportant whether or not one calls this dynamic movement which is found in all forms of Buddhism 'Mahayana'. Perhaps it would be best to drop this label altogether because of the negative charge it has acquired over the centuries. What is vital in the present situation is not to preserve any particular school of Buddhism but to sustain the creative drive of Buddhist insight, allowing it to find forms of expression which are significant for the time and place in which we live. We do not have to worry about 'schools' and 'traditions': they will look after themselves.

Mahayana Philosophy

Philosophically, there have been two principal movements of thought within the history of Buddhism which have been characterised as 'Mahayana'. These were both highly original ways of thinking which were deeply rooted in the traditional Buddhist experience, yet adopted a manner of expression peculiar to their own time and place (not the time and place of the historical Buddha). The first of these movements called itself the Madhyamaka, which means 'the Centre', and the second the Cittamatra, which means 'Mind Only'.

There are two key terms in Madhyamaka philosophy: emptiness and relativity. The illusion under which people labour is that of believing, both intellectually and instinctively, that they and the world that surrounds them are neither empty nor relative. Instead it appears to them that everything has its own intrinsic reality which seems to exist disconnected from anything else. We encounter everyone and everything as separated and self-sufficient. Yet so deeply ingrained is this tendency that it is extremely difficult to recognise it, let alone dispel it. The Madhyamaka is a concerted attack upon this fixation, the cure for which it sees as the recognition, appreciation and insight into emptiness and relativity. Emptiness is the mere absence of this sense of separation and isolation. It is not some mystical void in which the world disappears. It is the death of a deep-seated fiction at the heart of conventional human experience. And it reveals the pervasive and magical interrelatedness of everything. There is nothing which exists apart from an infinite nexus of causal conditions, constituent parts and mental organisations. Thus relativity, both as a principle of what is, as well as a description of each process we call a 'thing', is the creative counterpart of emptiness.

The Cittamatra, 'Mind Only', philosophy was particularly concerned with the role played by mind in the construction of reality. It conceived of a fundamental stratum of consciousness serving as the ground out of which both subjective mental states as well as the appearance of objects external to consciousness sprang. The foundation consciousness is beyond the subject/object duality which characterises conventional, samsaric consciousness. For the Cittamatra thinkers, the origin of suffering is more than mere craving: it is our unthinking assent to dualism. As long as we assume that what appears to consciousness is intrinsically different from consciousness itself, we will remain bound to a nightmare which will continue to terrorise us until we wake up. Indeed the normal human condition is repeatedly compared to that of a dream. Just as the dreamer is convinced of the separate reality of what he dreams, so is the deluded person convinced of the separate reality of what he experiences. To wake up is to realise that subject and object, mind and matter, are rooted in a common ground which experientially is felt to lie in the depths of the human heart.

Both the Madhyamaka and Cittamatra philosophies are views of the world which serve as indicators of a liberating truth which needs to be realised through practice. In the traditional Buddhist context in which they emerged, they are invariably accompanied by methods which can actually translate their theories into experiences. It is constantly affirmed in the Buddhist tradition that such philosophies are not the product of speculation, but the result of meditative experience subsequently articulated in a rational form.

The Five Paths

One of the classical Indian models used to describe this progression from conceptual to intuitive insight is that of the 'five paths'. Here the broader path from delusion to enlightenment is divided into five principal phases, starting with the phase of accumulation and culminating in the phase of completion. The accumulation phase entails the preparation of the spiritual ground. The ethical steadfastness, supported by mindfulness, concentration and joyous perseverance contained in this phase provide the psychological context necessary for the sound development of the subsequent phases. The second phase is that of application. At this stage one focuses on the cultivation of those faculties of mind which will sustain and heighten insight to the point where the conceptual element is dissolved to be replaced by the first shattering glimpse of reality. These faculties, which create the immediate matrix which allows this shift from the conceptual to the non-conceptual to take place, are trust, energy, mindfulness, concentration and wisdom.

The non-conceptual insight brought about through such application is the third phase, that of seeing. Although it only lasts for short moments it has a profoundly transforming effect. It alters one's entire understanding of the world and the meaning of one's life within it. At this point one 'enters the stream to enlightenment': although the habitual patterns of samsaric life will reassert themselves, there is no turning back from the pursuit of the spiritual path. Such seeing leads one into the penultimate phase of meditation. This involves the repeated acquaintance with what was initially seen in the first moment of non-conceptual vision. Through deepening and sustaining this insight one progressively eradicates the latent tendencies which run counter to enlightenment and keep one subtly enmeshed in untruth. The phase of meditation is a gradual process of purification culminating in a diamond-like samadhi which finally breaks one free of whatever residual bonds still tie one to samsaric existence. At this point one enters the phase of completion, and the transformation from an ordinary being to a Buddha is realised.

This model of the five phases in spiritual evolution holds true for all schools of Buddhist thought and practice. They only diverge in what they philosophically consider to be the nature of the reality understood at the moment of seeing, and the different methods they employ to gain insight into that reality. The Madhyamika, for example, uphold that emptiness, in which there is not even the slightest trace of intrinsic being, is what is realised during the phase of seeing. The Cittamatra maintain that the fundamental non-duality of subject and object is the truth penetrated at this moment of insight. But they both would agree that the stages which lead to this realisation and the stages which bring it to completion are the same. In other words, irrespective of how one philosophically conceives of truth, the spiritual realisation of that truth depends upon the cultivation of a sound basis of ethics, a clear conceptual understanding, mindfulness, concentration and so forth. Having developed and integrated these faculties to the point where they allow the vision of insight to irrupt, one must continue to deepen it in order to erase the psychological patterns and tendencies which run counter to it. Completion of this process occurs when a pervasive transformation of one's sense of self, world and others is actualised.

Practice

Neither the Madhyamika nor the Cittamatra philosophy has produced a specific form of spiritual practice peculiar to its own particular way of thinking. For practitioners, these philosophies have served more as maps drawn up according to different systems of cartography which describe the same terrain. They are both seen as fingers pointing to the moon: the Madhyamika indicates the new moon while the Cittamatra refers to the full moon.

Although there are many forms of practice used in Mahayana Buddhism, the two systems which most vividly characterise the tradition are those of Vajrayana and Ch'an (Zen), and I shall look at them separately in a moment. Both of these methods are products of the Mahayana spirit: ethically, they are rooted in an active concern for the world rather than a longing merely to transcend it; historically, they are creative adaptations of the original insights of the Buddha. The Vajrayana was the form principally assumed by practitioners of the Indian Mahayana tradition and later continued in Tibet (as well as in the Japanese Shingon school). Ch'an was one of the main methods adopted by followers of the Mahayana in China and later in Korea and Japan. While particular proponents of these practices have shown preferences for either Madhyamika or Cittamatra philosophy, the traditions as a whole have clearly been informed by both ways of thinking. 'Emptiness' and 'Mind' are key terms in both systems. Moreover, both the Shingon school as well as the later currents in Ch'an are strongly influenced by the Hua-yen philosophy, a Chinese school of thought based on the poetic and epic *Avatamsaka Sutra*, which seeks to harmonise the main ideas of the Madhyamika and Cittamatra thinkers in the all-embracing net of Indra.

The experiences reached by the practitioners of Vajrayana and Ch'an have revealed not only a deep recognition of the emptiness and relativity of phenomena but also a rootedness in a non-dual spiritual foundation which is referred to by a number of terms: 'clear light', 'original mind', 'ground of everything', (in Vajrayana), and 'heart', 'original face', 'true man' (in Ch'an). (See Chapters 4, 8 and 15.) It seems that the philosophical demand for logical cogency is overriden by the supra-rational nature of deep meditative experience. None the less, both the Madhyamika and Cittamatra frames of reference have been maintained and used as relatively appropriate means of description.

The Vajrayana

The practices and philosophy of the Vajrayana are described in the four divisions of Buddhist *tantra*. These treatises contain a vast amount of material covering a wide range of spiritual disciplines. Yet the key to them all, perhaps, is found in the word *tantra* itself, which means continuity. In contrast to the earlier schools of Buddhism, where a discontinuity between the unsatisfactory state of samsara and the transcendent realm of nirvana is emphasised, the Vajrayana asserts the presence of a common ground in which both samsara and nirvana are rooted. Moreover, this common ground is not a static basis but an unceasing rhythmical movement. Thus the ground is a continuity which expresses itself in every phase of the life/death process as well as in each gesture of enlightenment.

In the *Supreme Yoga Tantras*, a threefold structure of psycho-physical existence is taught.(See Table 2.1.) At the gross level which we experience during the waking state of consciousness, mind and body are presented as separate entities. At the subtle level which is activated during dream consciousness, mind and body are more closely interwoven. And at the most subtle level, which occurs only during dreamless deep-sleep, mind and body are essentially identical. Thus the rhythm of day-to-day existence is one in which we proceed from a gross level of waking consciousness, collapse into the most subtle level when we fall into deep sleep, rise from that into the subtle level of dream consciousness, and finally awake again into the gross state. The process is a cyclic movement leading from psychophysical unity to duality and back to unity, passing through an intermediate phase of neither complete unity not complete duality.

This very same pattern is also found on the larger scale of birth and death. From the moment of conception until the moment before death we exist on the gross plane of birth; upon dying we enter the most subtle plane of death; and between death and the next rebirth we proceed through the subtle intermediate plane. 'Birth' corresponds to 'waking consciousness', 'death' corresponds to 'deep-sleep' consciousness, and the 'intermediate plane' corresponds to 'dream consciousness'. This cyclic movement from birth to death to rebirth is traditionally described as the samsaric condition: one in which beings are propelled from birth to birth by the force of their accumulated actions.

Table 2.1   Levels of Equivalence in the Vajrayana view of
psychophysical existence

Mind–body relationship	Day-to-day existence	Life-to-life existence	Buddhahood
Separate	Waking consciousness	Birth	Emanated Expression (*Nirmanakaya*)
Merging–interweaving	Dream	Intermediate plane (Bardo)	Archetypal expression (*Sambhogakaya*)
Non-dualistic identification	Deep-sleep	Death	Dharma-origin Clear-light or *Dharmakaya*

Yet in the *tantras* this pattern is not something to be rejected or
transcended in nirvana, but to be transformed into Buddhahood.
For the same rhythm can also be detected in an enlightened mode of
existence. Buddhahood is often spoken of in terms of its 'threefold
presence': namely a dharmic presence, an archetypal presence and
an emanated presence. The dharmic presence is the spiritual core
of enlightenment: a state of indestructible harmony with what is.
The archetypal presence is that of the universal images and ideas
which represent the qualities of enlightenment; and the emanated
presence is that of physical men and women who embody the
workings of enlightenment in their lives and times. The aim of
Vajrayana practice, therefore, is to change deep-sleep/death into
a dharmic presence, dream/intermediate-plane into an archetypal
presence, and waking state/birth into an emanated presence.

The goal of the Vajrayana is to transform the unsatisfactory
pattern of samsaric existence into the meaningful pattern of
enlightenment. By means of the methods employed to utilise
the deep-sleep and dream states of consciousness one can prepare
oneself for death and the intermediate plane. For if death is
consciously experienced for what it is instead of unconsciously
being passed over, then the subsequent phases which unfold from
out of this ground are likewise capable of being transformed.
Instead of the intermediate plane being an uncontrollable nightmare, it can become a spontaneous play of the archetypal images
of enlightenment. And instead of being thrown into birth through
the force of karma, one can select the kind of rebirth most suitable
for spiritual practice and the enactment of the welfare of others.

Through tantric practices it is possible to simulate the death process in meditation and reach the most subtle level of body/mind. Here the yogi is able to become conscious of the ultimate mind of clear light and absorb himself in this direct understanding of the ground of samsara and nirvana. Upon rising from this absorption he can proceed to simulate the experiences of the intermediate plane and transform them into an archetypal presence of a Buddha or a bodhisattva. He then concludes his meditation by re-entering the waking state of consciousness suffused with the presence of an enlightening emanation.

Ch'an

The ground of life and death which is reached in the Vajrayana by means of arduous yogic practice can, according to the Ch'an masters, be suddenly awakened at any moment by simply maintaining one's consciousness in the correct state of meditative awareness. The earliest Ch'an teachings set out to portray the nature of such meditative awareness and, without giving any technical aids such as instruction on posture, breathing or koans, directly challenged the listener to adopt such an attitude here and now. In describing 'sitting meditation', the sixth patriarch Hui-neng declares that 'sitting' means that without any obstruction anywhere, outwardly and under all circumstances, one refrains from activating thoughts. 'Meditation' means internally to see the original nature, and not become confused.

The psychology of Ch'an rests on the insight that consciousness is not solely characterised by temporal continuity. This notion of consciousness as a continuum, which through training can be transformed from an inferior to a superior state, is characteristic of most Indian ways of thinking. The Chinese adepts of Ch'an practice, however, understood consciousness as not merely linear but multi-dimensional. Human beings are for the most part 'locked' into a particular mode of consciousness and unaware of other modes which, as it were, 'co-exist' alongside the present mode. The purpose of Ch'an practice is to cultivate the attitude of mind which is most prepared and receptive for the sudden irruption of that mode of consciousness called 'enlightenment'. To quote Hui-neng again: 'Unawakened, even a Buddha is a sentient being, and even a sentient being, if he is awakened in an instant of thought, is a Buddha. And thus we know that the ten thousand dharmas are all within our own minds.'

The Ch'an attitude is not, however, a state of mental inactivity. It is one in which one is no longer caught up in the compulsive rush of thoughts but makes no effort to suppress them. There is an element of patient detachment which entertains no expectations about what might happen. One listens with a calm, almost childlike openness. Yet a certain tension is present in the form of unknowing perplexity. It is this perplexity which acts as the trigger for shifting consciousness into its enlightened mode (see Chapter 8).

The whole idea of proceeding along a graduated series of stages by applying certain techniques is regarded as just another symptom of the mode of consciousness in which we are fixated. Assenting to such a model of the path only reinforces the kind of consciousness from which, through Ch'an, one is seeking to break free. The kind of guidance received in Ch'an training is consequently more concerned with breaking down our conventional habits of thought, and making provocative and often paradoxical challenges to the ways in which we see ourselves and the world.

No technique, however time-honoured and subtle, is capable of producing the meditative attitude of Ch'an. This attitude is the interface between delusion and enlightenment. It cannot be reached by the devising of any strategy.

The Mahayana Quest

In trying to define afresh the thrust and relevance of Mahayana spirituality, one needs to be open to the challenges and needs of the present situation, and non-dogmatic in one's relation to the tradition. What is of importance in any genuinely creative movement is the quest itself rather than the adherence to any particular philosophy or method of practice. Even among many who call themselves 'Mahayanist' there is often a marked attachment to a particular position, a wariness of other schools and beliefs, and a tendency towards isolation rather than interaction. The traditional Mahayana philosophy of the essential emptiness and relativity of all things is rarely applied to one's own point of view. It is precisely this that Western Buddhists need to learn to do.

CHAPTER 3

Spontaneity and Self-Control: G. H. Mead and Buddhism

MARTIN SKINNER

Introduction

When comparing Eastern and Western approaches to self and mind it is immediately clear that Eastern approaches have evolved over long periods of time in very different traditions of thought from those in the West. Both traditions are empirical, but one is essentially intuitive and experiential, telling us to beware of thought or even that thought is to be avoided, while the other is carried out using methods to ensure the most objective and publically scrutinisable thought possible.

The Western psychologist would say that knowledge can only be based on communicable observations which can and must be opened up to public examination. The Eastern psychologist would say that the definition of knowledge as 'that which can be shared objectively' rules out certain types of understanding and ignores the possibility that the means by which we create and share knowledge shapes and limits it at the same time. The Western psychologist, while not exactly believing that facts exist in and speak for themselves, is likely to be guided by the belief that as a scientist he or she plays practically an invisible part in their emergence into awareness. The Eastern psychologist on the other hand is likely to be guided by the belief that facts are both terms and acts of measurement and that we should not confuse any experience we may have with our description of it.

Both approaches have their merits. During the last two decades the conviction has grown that there may be something valuable to be achieved by setting the two approaches side-by-side to see how each illuminates the other. The conviction can be seen to have grown as a result of people in the West becoming aware of limitations of and dissatisfactions with the Western view. Whether or not the convictions are mistaken and the view valid there have certainly been many attempts to develop the East–West traffic. The view from the East, however, is that views are to be distrusted. We are offered a programme of private, personal practice, koans, instructions to meditate, to achieve without intending to achieve. The message is that, methodologically speaking, we're on our own. If there is a goal then the one sure way of never achieving it is to want it or to look for it.

Such a view is so different from that which forms the basis for Western scientific enquiry that I believe it is important to look for any way of moving to meet the Eastern view from within the terms of the Western view. For a psychologist interested in self and mind one needs to look for theories of these two phenomena which can, at least in some respects, be mapped on to the theories of the same phenomena coming from the East. Finding such theories will facilitate a synthesis of ideas by providing a vocabulary with which to bridge the apparent gap between the two views. This leads me to the point of this chapter: to outline briefly a school of thought which comes from social psychology which would seem to go some way towards making such a bridge between Western and Eastern approaches to self and mind. The school of thought is 'symbolic interactionism', which focuses on the essentially symbolic nature of human interaction and which proposes that this exchange of symbols between people also goes on within the individual as the thinking mind.

I would like to advance the possibilities of bridge-building by focusing on two concepts which seem central both to Eastern approaches to mind and self and to symbolic interactionism. These are 'spontaneity' and 'self-control'. They are opposite poles of the same phenomenon. Eastern approaches recommend and give guidance towards the achievement of the former, while symbolic interactionism, by providing an explanation of self-control has, by implication, much to say about spontaneity. So, firstly, I wish to say something general about spontaneity, then symbolic interactionism will be introduced before returning for a look at their relationship.

Spontaneity seems to be at the heart of the process of enlightenment in Buddhism. In discussion of enlightenment, terms such as 'renunciation', 'detachment', 'selflessness', and 'original self' are sometimes used in descriptions of processes of disidentification from our idea of ourself. This disidentification is seen in turn as a necessary and sufficient precursor to a calm, peaceful, and natural state of mind where some natural, true ability will find unhindered, *spontaneous* expression.

Spontaneity is defined by the Shorter Oxford English Dictionary as 'voluntary or unconstrained action, acts without deep thought or premeditation. Proceeding or acting entirely from natural impulse without any external stimulus or constraint'. I would only, from a psychological point of view, take issue with the word 'voluntary' in the above extract. Voluntary action is *willed* action, willed by the self, and what the self wills to happen and therefore intends cannot be spontaneous. The most interesting part of this definition for my purposes is the inclusion of the idea of constraint; that spontaneity represents in some way a release from constraint. From an Eastern perspective, too, spontaneous action means action without constraint, particularly that produced by the self. Spontaneity is seen as the direct expression of impulses without reference to the self or any other conventional object.

If, then, spontaneity is freedom from constraint, what are the constraints under which we normally operate? Here a lead can be drawn from White (1959), who discusses four distinct levels at which organisms may respond to their environment. Each of these levels provides a qualitatively distinct mode of recognising and responding to objects and thus provides a hierarchy of different modes by which organisms can be constrained by their environments. White's analysis suggests at least three modes of responding to objects and thereby producing constraint: those which are written into the physical and biological bases of life; those which are the result of habits formed by conditioning; and those which are the result of the social objects which human beings create in the course of social interaction. It is to the third of these categories that I would like to draw attention but first I will elaborate a little on the other two.

With regard to constraint and the physics and biology of life we can say that anything not random is lawful and that anything lawful is constrained. At a biological level we have and, of course, *are* (see Fromm, 1978) an inherent integrity the maintenance of which is both an aspect of life and life itself. The myriad life-supporting processes which go on within us, do so as if creating and recognising boundaries and categories of events. For individual survival there has to be a recognition of boundaries essential to the physics and biology of being as well as the important contours of physical surroundings. Individual existence and integrity depends upon an ability to categorise, or at least recognise, features of the internal and external environment and to respond differentially to them. Thus they are recognised as objects. This is a prerequisite for and thus a property of life in all sentient beings.

Then there are objects which arise out of an organism's capacity for conditioning. Certain formerly irrelevant and unnoticed features of the world about us may come to be categorised and constrain our behaviour because of continued association with an object or event which we do recognise. The organism which can be conditioned in this classical sense is just as much constrained by these *signs* of objects and events as by the object or event which the sign has come to represent.

For human beings there is a third kind of object towards which we act and by which we are therefore constrained. These are objects which exist by convention, purely as it were by agreement between consenting adults. Of course, nobody knowingly gives consent as the agreements are part of the cultural package which we internalise in the course of socialisation and their origins, as Berger and Luckmann (1967) point out, are lost from the individual's perspective.

These, then, are conventional objects with conventional meanings. There are many objects which we know as abstract nouns towards which we orientate our conduct and by which we are, accordingly, constrained. While the objects implied by our 'built-in' recognition of boundaries described above are associated with patterns of sensation from our five senses, these conventional objects, which exist only in as much as people continue to orientate their conduct towards them in agreed ways, exist only in the imagination or minds of those party to the agreement. (Note that in Buddhism the mind, which is the Western description of this imagining, is considered to be a sixth sense.) In any case, prime among this third class of objects is the self.

Since this third class of conventional object cannot directly be detected by any of our five senses and consequently has no physical existence, we need a special mechanism to bring such an object simultaneously into the experience of two or more interacting individuals so that they may agree on its presence even though they cannot directly perceive it. This mechanism is language in the most general sense of the word. A symbol which evokes the same experience in two or more people we can call, as indeed they are in symbolic interactionism, a 'significant symbol'. I might have a mixture of attitudes towards the country in which I live concerning expectations of loyalty, obligations, rights, etc. How could I be sure that these were your experiences too? I could utter a sound, a *vocal significant symbol*, which stood in an agreed relationship to these feelings and attitudes, a sound like that which we write as 'patriotism'.

Now that we are talking about symbols, the path to symbolic interactionism is clearer. A sign is in some way related to what it stands for, while for a symbol the connection is arbitrary and conventional, depending solely on a consensus among a community which has internalised the relationship.

The basic tenet of symbolic interactionism is that human social interaction is effected through the exchange of symbols, the most important and sophisticated of which are the vocal ones of spoken language. The roots of symbolic interactionism lie in at least two places. First there is the intellectual climate following Darwin who had introduced a phylogenetic perspective on human beings and a tendency to think in terms of the evolutionary function of our behaviour. Second they can be seen in the work of American pragmatist philosophers such as William James, John Dewey and W. I. Thomas working at the turn of the century, whose ideas were developed into sociological and social psychological explanation in the first thirty years of this one. Perhaps the most important of these sociologically orientated social psychologists was G. H. Mead and it was a student of Mead, Blumer (1969), who subsequently coined the term 'symbolic interactionism' to capture this emphasis on the role of symbols in 'inter-' and 'intra-personal' interaction. In Mead's analysis significant symbols are necessary for the creation of conventional (what he would call *social*) objects and the creation of selves depends on the ability to create social objects because the self *is* a social object, formed in the same way as any other.

It follows that if Mead is to explain the evolution of mind and self he needs to be able to explain the evolution of significant symbols, and this he does by starting with the analysis of social acts and examining the role played therein by gestures. In Mead's explanation the origin of significant symbols is to be found in gestures which are seen to arise in the course of normal practical co-ordinated activity in animals. When one animal makes a move which initiates an act and a second animal moves in such a way as to co-operate in the completion of the act on the basis of seeing just the initial phase of that act, the second animal has responded to a gesture.

Gestures, then, are the initial phases of acts and are by definition as much of the act as the responding animal has to experience in order to complete the act. By responding to the gesture the perceiving animal contributes to the act, thus creating its consequences. The consequences of the gesture become, for both animals, its *meaning*. A gesture becomes significant when every member of a community recognises what a certain movement represents in terms of the act to follow and is thereby able to make the response appropriate to the completion of the act as anticipated by both interactants. When it becomes unnecessary for the act to run its course for the completed act to be experienced and taken in some agreed way to have been effected, gestures become a useful abbreviated way of co-operating. Gestures may then become abbreviated, stylised and abstract. When they no longer share any of the physical, temporal or spatial properties of the act which they stand for they cease to become significant gestures and become significant symbols.

One may speculate as to why we have settled on vocal significant symbols rather then visual ones even though it seems likely that many if not most gestures were originally visual and obviously still are. Certainly talk can go around corners and so we can co-operate with people whom we cannot see, so we do not have to be looking at them to be interacting. Another possibly important point is that the hands are far too valuable for other practical activities to be continuously occupied in creating symbols for communication. But perhaps the most important reason and certainly that emphasised in symbolic interactionism is that we can hear and respond to our own vocal significant symbols as others do and this cannot be said of visual significant symbols. The corollary of this, as many proponents of symbolic interactionism have pointed out, is that we can entertain a completely reflexive representation of ourself through the audio-vocal channel in a way that we cannot in the visual gestural.

An explanation of significant symbols is crucial for the explanation of self and selfhood as emerging through evolution. Symbols permit us reliably and predictably to refer to objects which are not 'actually there' and to interact with other people as if they were. From the beginning of our life those who have cared for us have acted towards us as an object, and one with special symbolic significance. They have initiated acts involving us and we have co-operated in their completion. They have referred to the physical thing which we are to them, referred to our conduct and referred to the joint acts which we have created. From the start of our life they have used words both for the physical object that we are to them and for the social object which we are to them with all its conventional qualities, properties, rights and obligations. We internalise their definitions of our conduct in the same way that we internalise the rest of their definitions of an experiential reality which is initially subjective but soon becomes cast in the same network of interrelated objects as theirs. It would appear an important observation that children typically first refer to themselves in the third person, mimicking exactly the designations of their conduct which others are making. Recently, Harré (1987) has discussed the way in which the self is organised through the grammar of language, a theme continued in several chapters of Shotter and Gergen (1989).

While Mead published no comprehensive account of his social psychology and its relationship to mind and self, one exists in the posthumous edition of his lectures on these subjects by C. W. Morris (1934). In these lectures Mead sees self-conscious acting as having two phases, much in the tradition of William James (1890) before him. Firstly, there is the spontaneous impulsive phase which represents the biological momentum of the living, growing organism and secondly there is the phase which represents the casting of recognition of that behaviour in terms of social objects. The former phase is referred to as the 'I', the organism as subject, the latter as the 'Me', the organism as object. The 'I', when recognised in terms of the social object *it is on the point of creating*, is resolved with the 'Me' to form, in the next instant, the ground for the next 'I'. Mind is thus seen as a continual interplay between subjective and objective experience or between the spontaneous and the constrained. So the 'I' can never be known directly because the knowing of it depends on its becoming 'Me', in fact the knowing of it *is* its becoming 'Me'. When this process is going on that which Mead refers to as mind is present and he means by mind what most people do: the faculty of self-conscious thinking.

It follows from this analysis that what we call 'self' and 'mind' are an internalisation of the social process going on around us. We come to know our experience (in the sense that we can point to it and talk about it and in Mead's terminology 'take an attitude towards it') by designating it as objects. We acquire the means of doing this by copying the designations which other people around us are making. Indeed the only way we can make sense and be made sense of is to be able to cast the flux of our sensory experience into objects tradeable with those around us. Thus there is for Mead no mind without self, and nor is there mind without society – without, that is, a community sharing significant symbols.

So what of self-control and spontaneity? The thinking which we are advised from the point of view of the Eastern model of thought to beware of and even to avoid is seen by Mead as an internal dialogue between the impulsive, natural organism and the 'generalised other', this being Mead's term for the generalised societal position from which we act towards our impulses. We recognise these impulses in terms of the acts as objects they initiate or threaten to initiate. It is this imaginative completion of acts which allows for the control of behaviour and hence self-control. Self-control because the control is usually carried out in terms of the imminent object's relevance to the especially important object with which bodily sensations and a sense of worth are uniquely associated: the self. The control is essentially *post hoc*, while at root, action is spontaneous.

Outside such an analysis as this it is difficult to discuss self-control without getting into an infinite regress. If an action were a product of self-control because it was preceded by a decision to do it we should then have to enquire whether or not the decision to do it was preceded by such a decision which merely pushes back the question a stage, and so on. Eventually there has to be a point where there is either a homunculus, as is indeed implicit in many otherwise serious psychological accounts, or there is an infinite regress which would result in the immediate cessation of behaviour in any self-controlled mode.

Buddhism seems quite clear about the spontaneity underlying all actions: there is nothing but spontaneity. Indeed one only has to try meditation to realise our helplessness when it comes to trying to direct our attention towards the counting of our own breaths. When we attempt to count we find our attention wandering; when we attempt to forget our breathing we find we can think of nothing but our breathing and the counting. To this important extent mindfulness and mindlessness are descriptions of the same process: they are beyond self-control and all we can do is let them happen.

Mead's symbolic interactionism, offers, of course, no guidelines or description of how an organism with the capacity for creating objects out of experience could cease doing it. Indeed why should one want to? However, the *possibility* of the cessation of self-control is implicit in his theory, as is a clear indication of why it could not be achieved by intention, for intending is described as part of a process involving the control of action by the recognition of objects including the self. It is interesting to note the association between the words 'object' and 'objective' with the latter's connotation of 'intention'. We frequently use the words 'object' and 'objective' interchangeably to denote intentions.

A case could well be made that of all the accounts from Western psychology which discuss 'self' and 'mind', Mead's is that which is most able to link the terms directly to the world of behaviour while at the same time being mappable onto the teaching of Buddhism on these same terms. Symbolic interactionism would appear to provide a strong and useful link between Western psychology with the traditions characterised at the start as Eastern approaches to mind and self. For those who wish for illumination each is capable of illuminating the other.

CHAPTER 4

Self-Assertion and Self-Transcendence in Buddhist Psychology

DAVID FONTANA

Introduction: Buddhism and the Concept of Self

From the work of Jung (see 1962, 1978, for recent editions of earlier relevant writings) to that of Wilber (1982a, 1982b, 1983), a succession of psychologists and philosophers have busied themselves with interpreting Buddhist thought for the Western mind, and with indicating the implications of this thought for our concepts of human change and development. Parallel to this movement within the West, a number of Eastern scholars, of whom D. T. Suzuki (1969, 1970, 1971) is the best-known example, have also been rendering Buddhism into a form that the Westerner can use, and have revealed (for those who care to look carefully enough) the similarities between the insights that Buddhism contains and those taught by Western mystical traditions.

One of the greatest problems faced by the Westerner when studying Buddhism, however, and when attempting to use its psychological and spiritual techniques, is the concept of the 'self' that it appears to contain. Many Western writers interpret this concept as a form of nihilism, which denies the reality of individual existence and is, therefore, of dubious help to those in psychological distress, since all too frequently this distress appears to be due to a confused and underdeveloped sense of self-identity and validity . . . to be due, in fact, to the very failure to develop an inviolate awareness of that existential self whose existence Buddhism appears so intent upon refuting. Such an interpretation does less than justice to the richness of Buddhist philosophy or to its capacity for helping the fragmented personality and providing it with a meaning and a direction that embraces individuality as well as the unity that underlies this individuality.

To understand the Buddhist conception of the self, we must first of all understand that Buddhism at base is an essentially practical undertaking. It is concerned first and foremost not with abstract philosophising but with the development of practical techniques that allow the individual to lead what we in the West would call a psychologically balanced and successful life. It lays emphasis not upon accepting things upon the authority of other people, but upon employing techniques for discovering these things for ourselves. As such, we could say that it teaches a scientific method, although a method that, unlike Western science, directs its attention first toward the inner world and only after toward the outer. This is not a question of priorities, with the inner world being emphasised at the expense of the outer, simply a realization that what we discover outside ourselves must inevitably be conditioned by (in a sense be *a consequence of*) what we discover inside.

By examining this inner world, it becomes abundantly clear to us, Buddhism argues, that we each have a 'self,' in the sense of a set of ideas and feelings that arise from our personal experience and that we use to give that personal experience unity, coherence, and individuality. At this practical level, therefore, the self is a fact, and a highly relevant one since without this self, the ordering of our individual physical and psychological lives would appear to be an impossibility. Since the existence of such a self is clearly evident and can be put to the test of experience, no amount of philosophical speculation and verbal subtleties can alter it, far less abolish it as a fit object for scientific exploration. Thus the Buddhist is likely to be greatly amused at the problems that Western philosophers have with the notion of a self (see, for example, Ayer, 1973), problems that are shared to a greater or lesser extent by many Western psychologists.

This clear acceptance of the self as an empirical reality gives the Buddhist, in fact, a clear advantage over those Westerners who find philosophical and psychological difficulties with the concept. It also allows him to question the preference shown by certain Western experimental psychologists for always making other people the subject of their research. How can we hope usefully to investigate others until we have learned to investigate ourselves? Without self-knowledge, we have no model of the self that we can offer up as a research paradigm or as a way of guiding others in their exploration of personal space. Since only the self can experience the self, all worthwhile experimentation into the self must begin not with other people but with the experimental test-bed that we each of us carry with us throughout life. Only by first looking within can we learn how to start the process of looking without.

There is an interesting methodological similarity here between the Buddhist approach and that of the Freudian psychoanalyst, who also has to complete a course of inner discovery before being qualified to psychoanalyse others. The consequence of this Buddhist emphasis on self-investigation is that the Buddhist is not asked to take anything on the authority of others, however eminent. Put things to the test for yourselves, the Buddha reminded his disciples. Enlightenment can never be a second-hand experience. Life has to be lived and interpreted in the first person. Simply to base one's understanding of the self upon the teachings of others is to mistake their experience for one's own. It is, to draw an analogy from Bruner's (1966) writings on education, to deal with the 'middle language' of a subject, with the facts and formulas derived from other people's work, rather than with the discoveries of one's own investigations. Although branches of the Church have sometimes chosen to ignore it, we find the same emphasis upon personal discovery in the teaching of Christ ('Seek and ye shall find,' 'Seek ye first the Kingdom of Heaven'). We find it also in Vedanta, which is not organised on the basis of conformity to a creed or dogma but 'expounded as a quest' (Ranganathananda, 1978) and in the 'know thyself' of the Delphic oracle.

On the basis of this practical, firsthand approach, Buddhism recognises that we each have a self in the sense that we each have ideas and concepts and feelings that we use to define ourselves and that give our individual lives coherence and form. Indeed, this self is essential as a means of physical preservation (Govinda, 1969). By fixing the limits between self and not-self, the individual defends himself against the world. If we wish to survive, then certainly we must accord the self 'reality' status. And because the self is real, then the world is also real, since the self relies upon this world (the environment) for sustenance, and also needs to protect itself against the dangers and perils the world presents. Essentially, the ideas, concepts and feelings that go to make up this self stem from inborn temperament and drives, together with those learning experiences and memories that allow us to experience coherence and continuity in the way we experience ourselves and our relationship to the world around us.

Something of the practical nature of this notion of the self can be conveyed if we take an analogy from modern physics, and from a humble article like a house brick. In terms of physics, this house brick may be a very strange item, not at all what it seems to the ordinary senses. Far from being a solid object, the physicist tells us that it is predominantly empty space and that only a small fraction is substance (which substance in turn is really only a form of energy). Yet this knowledge is of no use to us at all if someone chooses to throw the brick at our head. On the brick-throwing level, the only sensible response is to take the brick for what it seems, a hard and dangerous object hurtling towards our cranium, and one that demands some prompt evasive action on our part if we wish to escape injury. On this level, both brick and injury are real events, and ones that we need to learn about and incorporate into our knowledge of the vulnerability of that equally real event – the self.

Physical survival, therefore, depends upon our seeing within both the brick and the self the operation of a reality. And by the same token, *psychological survival* depends upon our seeing within both the demands made upon us by other people and our own legitimate wishes and needs, the operation of a reality. The balance between other people and the self has to be maintained, just as the right relationship between the brick and the self has to be maintained. We live, in other words, in a life space composed of the not-self and the self, and our existence as effective human beings demands that we treat both as if they are real. From the cradle onwards, we thus need to build up workable concepts about the not-self and the self, concepts that to a large extent depend upon exploration and discovery, and upon what we might call a process of self-assertion. We assert our individual wishes, our individual needs, our individual feelings and ideas, and we test both the reactions of others toward us and our internal responses to these reactions.

Through self-assertion, we build up the concept of a separate, real, individual self, a self that seeks to maintain itself in the face of the various levels of challenge presented by the external world. It is to this self that we refer when we stress the importance of self-esteem, self-acceptance, and self-knowledge. Psychological health demands that we come to know the legitimate needs and aspirations of this self, that we come to value it and recognise its personal and social rights, that we come to know its strengths and weaknesses, and come to anticipate its likely reactions to the events of daily life. There are similarities here between the Buddhist concept of the self at this level and Jung's concept of development towards the differentiation of the ego. The ego comes to see itself as a unique, coherent, valid structure, a structure that can be understood, expressed, and guided by the conscious willing of the individual.

A large number of psychological problems stem from difficulties in developing self-assertion. The individual, perhaps because of a process of invalidation imposed by parents and teachers, fails to generate the necessary sense of personal identity and personal worth and the strategies of self-guidance and management that go with self-assertion. Instead, he experiences identity confusion, fragmentation, guilt, self-rejection on the one hand (aggression turned inwards) or defensiveness, hostility, self-centredness and antisocial behavior (aggression turned outwards) on the other. Either way, or with any combination of these conditions, there is little chance of what Maslow (1968) calls self-actualising getting underway. To use Maslow's terminology, the individual is denied satisfaction of the range of *basic needs* upon which the early stages of this process depend.

Sadly, then, many psychological problems (probably the great majority, at least in the first phase of life) stem from failure to master the self-assertion aspect of development. I say sadly, because this aspect is really only the first step in the individual's development. And here we come to a higher aspect of the Buddhist teaching on the self. Because essential as self-assertion is, once it has become fully realised, it can quickly develop into a threat, not only to the individual's relationship with others but to his own psychological and spiritual progress. Again this is something that we can put to the test for ourselves. It is self-assertion that can lead to a disregard for the rights of others, to a failure to show compassion to those less fortunate than ourselves, to an unwillingness to curb our own ambitions or to abandon our own life goals where these conflict with the needs of those around us. This negative behaviour differs from the aggression turned outwards to which I referred above in that it stems not from a need to defend and revenge a painfully fragmented self, but from an over-identification with the asserted self and with its wishes and plans. The individual is psychologically 'healthy', and well-integrated and organised at the ego level, but he or she is now mistaking the reality of the asserted self for ultimate reality, and is devoting psychological energy to its maintenance and its gratification.

At this point, we come to the difficult Buddhist concept of *anatta* or no-self, a concept that has caused many people to see Buddhism as an essentially negative or life-denying psychology. Part of the problem lies in the accurate translation into English of the Pali term *anatta* (*anātman* or *anātmā* in Sanskrit). Further confusion is also caused by the fact that in Hinduism (although not in the Hinduism of the *Bhagavadgita* and other important texts), the term is often used to apply to the not-self to which I referred earlier in this article, that is, to all the things that are 'not me'. Perhaps the best way of understanding something of the real meaning of anatta is to see it as indicating that true human nature is not conceivable by what we usually call the human 'mind'. This mind is only capable of knowing objects; therefore what I usually call my 'self' is not really me at all. This 'self' consists of objects in the sense of ideas and concept and feelings (defined in Buddhism more closely as the five *tendencies*, that is, form, habit, emotions, perceptions, and discriminations), and, therefore, cannot be my true nature. This true nature is what we refer to when we talk of anatta. It is me, yet it is not the me that I talk about when I discuss my 'self'. We cannot conceptualise the true nature in words, since words are objects. We can only experience it. It is not nihilism or extinction, as some people who misunderstand Buddhism claim. Instead, it is true reality, a reality against which the reality of the self and of the external world that I have been discussing up to now is seen as purely relative.

One helpful way of trying to illustrate this is to go back to our example of the brick and modern physics. At one level, the brick is certainly real in the sense that it is a hard solid object, and physical survival demands that we treat it as such. On another level, however, it is wrong to regard this solidity as having anything more than a limited, temporal range of convenience. To the physicist, working in the laboratory, this solidity is an illusion, and the stuff of which the brick is composed has a quite different kind of underlying reality, an underlying reality of empty space and violent subatomic motion. In terms of this underlying reality, the crude external distinction between the brick and other apparently solid objects disappears, since all are seen to be composed (if we can use such terms) of the same energy.

To the physicist working at the subatomic level, belief in the brick as ultimately a solid, separate object would be an insurmountable obstacle to progress. At this level, the whole notion of the solid brick turns out to be something that must be transcended if the theory and practice of physics are to be allowed to advance (see, for example, Zukav, 1979; or Capra, 1975, 1982). So with Buddhism, the idea of the self as ultimately a solid, separate object is an insurmountable obstacle to progress. To use convenient labels, having achieved *self-assertion*, we now need to move towards *self-transcendence* if we are to continue with our psychological and spiritual progress. But, and this point must be clearly stressed, the achievement of self-assertion is actually a prerequisite of our moving towards self-transcendence. Unless we have first realised the self, then we cannot move beyond the self. I am indebted to my friend Guy Claxton of the University of London for pointing out to me that in oral teachings, Bhagwan Shree Rajneesh sums this up in the words 'Give God your ego, but make sure it's a good ego!' For the Buddhist and for Shree Rajneesh, the message is the same. The self is created as a way of allowing us to go beyond the self. The same message is given by Christ ('If any man will come after me, let him deny himself . . . For whosoever will save his life shall lose it').

Without self-assertion, self-transcendence is beyond us. The insecure person, desperately trying to hold together the fragmented elements of an immature self, cannot undertake the processes involved. Perhaps paradoxically, someone who has been prevented by early experiences from developing a satisfactory sense of personal identity finds the prospect of the complete *loss* of personal identity that anatta seems to imply quite terrifying. It is said that the person who is afraid to live is also afraid to die, and perhaps this is equally appropriate when it is the death of the self rather than the death of the body that is being discussed. Yet unless the death or transcendence of the self takes place, there can be no further psychological or spiritual development. There can be no realisation of the true nature, no enlightenment, as the Buddhist would put it.

But – and this is crucial – death or transcendence of the self is not *death* in the sense in which we usually understand the term (extinction, annihilation) since there is nothing actually to 'die'. The self is analogous to a concept rather than to a fact, and self-negation is simply the outgrowing of this concept. Put another way, it is negation of the exclusive identification with a limited view. With self-negation comes the knowledge that there is nothing permanent or substantial about the self, and to imagine the contrary is merely to hold a view of reality clouded by *avijā* (ignorance or 'not-seeing'). Such a view leads us to value everything from the egocentric standpoint of personal desire. It generates a longing for pleasures with which to gratify this egocentricity, and leads inevitably to *upādāna*, or attachment ('clinging' might perhaps be a better translation) to these pleasures, to a craving for them if they cannot be obtained, and to aversion and often hatred towards the things that stand in the way of this attainment. And both clinging and craving lead to the same inevitable result: disappointment. For when we possess things, our possession is only temporary. Nothing lasts, and the individual is left with the suffering that comes from seeing the things to which he is attached change and pass away, or be left behind as he grows older and changes in turn.

On a social level, avijā, or ignorance, causes equal if not greater suffering. For it is this ignorance that leads to crime and warfare and exploitation, with individuals and whole societies striving to eliminate the people and things that stand in the way of their craving. Note that far from being theoretical or unworldly, Buddhist psychology is thus eminently practical, and works towards a more just and compassionate society. It also, incidentally but perceptively, warns against the all-too-common form of social concern that has nothing to do with altruism but everything to do with personal aggrandisement and personal power. Such quasi-social concerns use other people for the user's own ends, with the satisfaction of their needs important only so long as they serve towards the gratification of the user's needs. Social concern of this kind is simply another way of feeding the cravings of the self, whether these cravings have to do with feelings of self-righteousness on the one hand or with social or political power on the other.

From the foregoing discussion, it will be seen that the person who achieves self-assertion but fails to move beyond is in a sense just as much of a psychological problem as the person who fails to achieve self-assertion in the first place. True, he or she will be able to cope much more effectively with life than will the person who has not achieved self-assertion. But the self-centered tendency to relate things to one's own interests instead of examining them in their proper context, and the tendency to crave self-satisfaction, will, in Buddhist psychology, represent insuperable barriers on the path towards the release from psychological suffering. The person who has achieved self-assertion may enjoy apparent happiness, and may become an outstanding success in career terms, but unless self-transcendence is achieved, there will be no ultimate satisfaction in anything, because both the self and the things that gratify the self are doomed to impermanence and the sorrow of parting and loss.

It is worth noting at this point that in our child-rearing practices, we in the West often go directly against Buddhist psychology (see Chapter 9). Buddhist psychology maintains that in life we should first pass through the phase of self-assertion (which need only be relatively short) and then move on to the phase of self-transcendence. In the Western world, however, we find that these two phases are often reversed. In childhood, particularly during the formal educational process, the social and cultural constraints generally demand self-transcendence from the child. He or she has to conform to the patterns laid down by adults, to learn the workings of a complex social and economic system, to live up to the expectations of others. Self-assertion is often interpreted as insolence or insubordination, and is suppressed rather than guided and understood. In adult life, however, the emphasis is upon self-assertion. The self-assertive person is valued and rewarded, and obtains key positions in industry and politics and the professions. And for those self-assertive people who fail to gain this kind of power, society allows a range of other outlets where self-assertion can be exercised: the ill-treatment of minority groups, for example, or of foreigners, or of the poor and needy, or through identification with 'patriotism' or some other emotive cause. And if all else fails, men and women can misuse their self-assertion on each other and on their children.

Realising Anatta

Whereas the path towards self-assertion is relatively easy to understand, the processes involved in the realisation of anatta are much more elusive. As we have already indicated, anatta is the individual's true nature, and as such cannot be defined in words, only experienced. Yet, if we must attempt some sort of verbal description, perhaps the best one would be that it is pure awareness, an awareness in which the distinction between the person who is aware and the object upon which awareness is focused disappears. There is no more self, no more fragmentation between the myriad things of which the universe appears to be composed, only a sense of unity and bliss. Various terms are given to this experience in the literature, but in Zen Buddhism it is usually referred to as *satori*, and the attempts to give some inkling of its real flavour are so well-known that no further elaboration is needed here (see for example Suzuki, 1980). It is the final stage in self-transcendence, where the avija, or ignorance, that has led us to believe that the self represents anything more than relative reality, falls away.

This description of anatta, imperfect as it necessarily is, gives some clue as to the processes by which it is realised. These processes must all involve a way of forgetting the self, of discarding those mental activities that operate to sustain this self. One useful contemporary description of certain of these processes is that by Wilber (1982b). Wilber's account is particularly valuable, since he writes from direct experience, and with the advantage of a thorough knowledge of Western psychology. In his account, Wilber tells us in fact that even the term *experience* is inadequate, since the ultimate state (anatta, the true nature) is

> not a particular experience among other experiences, but the very nature and ground of *all* experiences, high and low. . . . *In itself*, therefore, it [is] not experiential at all; it [has] nothing to do with changes of state. . . . The ultimate state is what I am before I am anything else; it is what I see before I see anything else; and what I feel before I feel anything else.

Wilber makes it clear that to achieve this state (or more correctly, to realise that we are already in it), some form of inquiry into 'Who am I?' is and 'has always been held to be the basic path, perhaps the sole path'. This form of self-inquiry is probably most widely known within the context of Zen Buddhism but it is equally apparent in the teachings of Hindu sages such as Ramana Maharshi (see Osborne, 1971) or Vivekananda (see Toyne, 1983). The object of this inquiry is to strip away, layer by layer, the concepts used in self-assertion.

Each of these concepts is seen, in turn, to be nothing more than a label, with a purely temporary and limited range of convenience. None of these labels is the ultimate state, the anatta that cannot be conceptualised or reduced to mental objects such as ideas and memories. Writing from the standpoint of Ch'an Buddhism, the Chinese tradition from which Zen is a development, Lu K'uan Yu (1971) talks in terms of the 'host and the guest'. The guest, by definition, is a temporary resident, the host the permanent occupier. Everything in our lives, therefore, that is temporary is part of the guest. Self-assertion is the guest, and the task that faces us is to bid farewell to the guest and realise the host.

But the constant 'Who am I?' question ('Who is it who is happy?' 'Who is it who is angry?' 'Who is it who is fearful anxious/jealous/bored/upset/self-satisfied/thinking/doing?' 'Who is it who is meditating/seeking enlightenment?') can be a daunting experience (Chapter 13), as I intimated earlier in this article, for the person who has failed to develop a reasonable level of self-assertion as a preliminary requisite. Unless one is fortunate enough to have found the right teacher to take one through this exercise, the total loss of identity that it *seems* to imply can be too much to face all at once. This is one reason why the need for the right teacher during the stage of self-transcendence is so often stressed. But even without such a (physically present) teacher, progress is still possible. In fact, in some ways, the role of the teacher is dramatically changing in the modern age. Now that so many of the secret teachings and traditions are available in print, the student can, as it were, turn to the last page in the book before reading the earlier chapters. Whereas at one time the teacher would lead the student on, step by step, revealing simply what was necessary at that point of their development, the student now has access to virtually the entire body of the teachings. Like finding answers to questions one has not yet learned to formulate, most of this advanced teaching is meaningless at all but the most superficial intellectual level to the aspirant, but nevertheless it is available. And the result is that much more is allowed to, and demanded of, the aspirant, who is now much more constrained to become his own teacher.

With or without a teacher, then, with or without satisfactory self-assertion as a preliminary, the individual can start loosening the artificial bonds of the self. Both Christ and the Buddha taught how this can be done: by loving one's neighbour as oneself, by taking no thought for the morrow, by seeking the Kingdom of Heaven (enlightenment, salvation) before all things, and by stilling the mind. These teachings can perhaps best be summarised in three words, *view*, *action*, and *meditation* (see for example Sogyal Rinpoche, 1979). Right view implies that we come to understand at the knowledge level that the self does not represent our true nature, that love, compassion, and the unity of all things are true, and that hatred, dissension, and division are false, and that there is a way to realise this truth within ourselves rather than simply to 'know' it with our minds. Right action implies that we put this view into the way we live our lives, that we seek to purify the mind by loving and compassionate behavior to all living beings, that we reject pride, status, selfishness, defensiveness, aggression, and immorality as simply ways of gratifying and sustaining the small self or ego, and that we seek and attend to the teachings given to us by enlightened men and women over the centuries. Right meditation implies that we practise techniques for stilling the discursive chatter of the mind, a chatter that fatally distracts us from the search to realise our true nature.

Teachers of meditation and books about meditation abound these days, and the subject is too large to tackle here. But the emphasis in most cases is upon sitting in meditation, with the mind focused upon the breathing or a mantra or a mandala or upon some other point of concentration. Less attention is given to the fact that meditation can and should also be an integral part of everyday life. The term sometimes given to this is *mindfulness*. It implies that whatever one is doing, the attention is placed gently and naturally in that activity, instead of on the train of thoughts that chase through the mind. Most of us, in our daily lives, are rarely actually doing the thing upon which we are supposedly engaged. While ostensibly occupied with it, we are in reality thinking about other matters, with the mind only paying minimal attention to what it is we are supposedly undertaking. The process tends to get worse as we grow older, as more and more thoughts and the obligations that they represent clamour for our attention. Absent-mindedness is not the prerogative of the university professor, but is in fact the universal malaise of our complex and pressurised way of life. And the more we try to be mindful, concentrating fiercely upon whatever it is we are trying to do, the harder it all seems to become and the more readily thoughts start crowding back. The secret of mindfulness, if secret it is, is simply to turn from one activity to the next without allowing the mind to stay behind in the last activity or in the train of thoughts that it sparked off. Kennett (1972) gives detailed accounts of the training in mindfulness undertaken by the Zen practitioner, but perhaps the best account of all is given by the Zen master Kenzo Awa (see Herrigel, 1953). When instructing his pupil in the art of archery, Kenzo Awa places great emphasis upon releasing the bowstring without the jerk of the fingers and wrist that indicate a mind preoccupied with thoughts *about* loosing the arrow rather than a mind resting egoless and without tension in the activity itself. You must hold the drawn bowstring, says Kenzo Awa,

> like a little child holding the proferred finger. It grips so firmly that one marvels at the strength of the tiny fist. And when it lets the finger go, there is not the slightest jerk. Do you know why? Because a child does not think: I will now let go of the finger in order to grasp this other thing. Completely unselfconsciously, without purpose, it turns from one to the other, and we would say that it was playing with the things, were it not equally true that the things are playing with the child. (Herrigel, 1953, p.45)

Whether we can act 'without purpose' in the way in which Kenzo Awa means may be debatable, certainly at first, but the image of the small baby turning its attention so completely and so joyously from one activity to another, totally absorbed in the activity itself rather than in thoughts about it or about the previous activity or about any other extraneous matter, is as helpful as it is beautiful.

Mindfulness is, therefore, not something that demands tremendous efforts of concentration. Instead of involving an effort to *do* something, it involves simply a relaxation, a letting go of the stream of thoughts that usually dominate the mind. As in sitting meditation, when these thoughts arise, one refrains from the process of discursive associations that they usually spark off. The attention remains gently fixed upon the activity in hand, and then turns from that activity to the next activity as naturally as the small baby turns from the finger it has just been grasping to whatever else comes into awareness.

Mindfulness of this kind, if practised patiently, even humorously, without discouragement at the constant early failures and without any sense of annoyance or striving, begins to show gradual but unmistakable results. One begins to notice more of what is happening, to appreciate one's surroundings, to notice subtle sensations of sight, touch and sound, and to become more aware of one's own body and the beauty of the world it inhabits. Memory improves (half the time we forget things because we are not really attending to them when they happen). Concentration improves. And the mind becomes less readily dominated by the anxious, fearful, or angry thoughts that so often occupy our thinking. And if mindfulness is practised as part of a programme that also includes sitting meditation, then the two exercises feed and help each other, gradually easing one away from the identification with the small self that usually rules our lives. Even when negative emotions arise, it now becomes increasingly possible to view them with the same relaxed awareness with which one views everything else that is happening. Thus instead of *being* angry or upset or frightened, one is simply aware of the physiological symptoms that accompany these states, almost as if one is observing them as an outsider. This capacity to observe the emotion rather than become it means that the emotion begins to lose its power to overwhelm and control the individual, and without the constant resonance between physiological symptoms and mental states, after a time even the former begin to lose something of their potency.

Return to the Self

For many of us, however, whether we have achieved a satisfactory level of self-assertion to begin with or not, there is an understandable reluctance to attempt self-transcendence and the state of anatta. This may have little to do with the desire to be selfish or to seek personal gratification or to dominate others. It may simply be a feeling that if we lose the self, we face annihilation. There will be nothing (in the nihilistic sense) left (see Chapter 15). I have already indicated, when the term '*self-transcendence*' was first introduced above, how mistaken this feeling is. Just how mistaken is demonstrated by the lives of beings such as Christ and the Buddha who have provided us with examples of this state beyond the self. Such beings can hardly be called nihilists, either in their lives or in their teachings.

In Zen Buddhism, such teaching is contained particularly in the well-known declaration that before enlightenment, mountains are mountains and rivers are rivers; then one gains the first initiatory experience and mountains cease to be mountains and rivers to be rivers, but when one obtains ultimate understanding, mountains are again mountains and rivers are again rivers (see Suzuki, 1971). Related to the self, these three stages of mountains/rivers, no mountains/rivers, and a return to mountains and rivers could be represented as self-assertion, self-negation, and a return to self-assertion. However, as Suzuki points out, although after enlightenment mountains and rivers become mountains and rivers again, 'innerly or spiritually there is [now a difference] as great as it is between heaven and earth.' In fact, the mountains and rivers of the first stage and the mountains and rivers of the final stage 'belong to altogether different categories'. To remind ourselves of this difference, we should, therefore, describe the return to the self not as self-assertion but as *self-affirmation*.

Suzuki, in his usual gentle and helpful way, tries to get us to see this by using the example of a circle. A circle has a point and a circumference. Realisation of this centre and this circumference is the stage of self-assertion. The self is both the point and the circumference, with the latter representing the boundary between the self and the outside world. With self-transcendence, both the point and the circumference disappear, to be replaced by a oneness between the individual concerned and the rest of creation. Returning after this enlightenment, however, one returns to the realisation that this disappearance, in its own turn, is not the final truth. The point now reappears, but as Suzuki tells us, it now 'finds itself to be at the centre of a circle with no circumference . . . The circle now ceases to be the threatening wall. The point is now everywhere, filling as it were the whole area of the circle which has no circumference.' As a consequence, the 'Self-point is shorn of its fictitious contents which are now replaced by an infinite number of Self-points overflowing the circle. Every one of such Self-points is my Self – the Self in its original just-so-ness.'

Although some Buddhists query whether the ego ever gives up entirely, for Suzuki the final state of self-affirmation is now achieved without any further effort. It is natural consequence of returning from the experience of *satori*, the experience of unity, back into the world of forms and diversity. Thus the world of forms and diversity is in its way just as much a part of the final enlightenment experience as is the experience of the reality that underlies these forms. Both are necessary, because both go to make up the one thing. We could not have experienced unity, and known it for itself, unless we had first experienced diversity. And having experienced unity, we now see it as the reality that underlies diversity, or more accurately, as the reality that in its true nature diversity actually *is*.

At a practical level, self-affirmation differs from self-assertion in that it encompasses this reality. It is still anatta in that it is not identified with the limited self that we experience during self-assertion, but it is an anatta that knows that the same reality that quickens me quickens the rest of creation. In place of identification with the limited self, we have *awareness* of the limited self, an awareness that sees this self for what it is, a necessary expression of true reality, something that helps me to survive in the physical world and to realise this true reality, but no more. It is, therefore, no more to be asserted or defended or enhanced for its own sake than is any other means to an end.

With this awareness comes a tremendous release from the petty concerns of self-assertion. Something of this release can be savoured long before we reach the actual stage of self-affirmation, simply by acceptance at the right *view* and right *action* level that self-affirmation is what actually is. The importance of right view and right action was discussed earlier in this article, but it should be emphasised that they do not imply blind faith. As I have tried to make clear, the Buddhist approach is a practical one. Right view and right action are not sustained by faith or by the dictates of those in authority over us. They are sustained by the immediate psychological rewards that they bring for the person who really tries them for him- or herself.

Self-affirmation differs from self-assertion also in that it allows for genuine compassion towards others. In self-assertion, one may give to others, but the giving is primarily a way towards self-satisfaction. In the practice of self-transcendence, before we have realised the true self-transcendence of anatta, our giving is much less selfish than in the self-affirmatory stage, but it still contains an element of selfishness, even if this is only the desire to subdue the self. In self-affirmation, however, there is no thought of the limited self, because the distinction between the one who gives and the one who receives has disappeared. This is the true meaning of seeing Christ in everyone, and of loving one's neighbour as oneself. Giving, therefore, contains no element of sacrifice, or of do-gooding, or of obedience to an external moral code. It is done, quite simply, because it is the natural thing to do. (Note that this is not to denigrate moral codes; like the self, they are essential as a way of helping one reach the stage where they are no longer necessary.)

Conclusion

Ken Wilber (1982b) sums up the reality that is self-affirmation when he writes that this reality 'is actually what all states have in common, and what all states have in common is not itself another state, much as the alphabet is not another letter.' Reality is 'the totality of everything arising moment to moment. . . . That is why it is both the great mystery and the perfectly obvious.' He also describes his personal experience of the transition from a state of self-negation while in meditation to a state of self-affirmation as he emerged from the meditation, using language that parallels some of the points I made in the last section. In his description, he makes it clear that when in the self-transcendence state there is no 'I' there to experience it. Paradoxically, therefore, the only way of experiencing the state is to move out of it. 'To experience that state, I had to separate myself from it.' This interdependence between the self-transcendence and the self-affirmation states is, it seems to me, what Govinda (1977) means when he writes that unity and individuality are 'two sides of the same coin.' A coin cannot exist (be experienced) unless it has two sides. Both are the coin, yet the coin is neither one nor the other but a reality that comprises both.

This reminds us, of course, that although I have treated the three states of self-assertion, self-transcendence, and self-affirmation as if they were chronological, this is not, in fact, the case. The small child, even while learning self-affirmation, will also be introduced by parents to aspects of self-transcendence (sharing, thoughtfulness towards others, waiting one's turn, and so on). And when true self-transcendence is achieved, it can only be fully realised in self-affirmation. And once self-affirmation is achieved, its continuance may depend upon a regular return to self-transcendence in meditation, just as the true expression of self-affirmation in daily life will involve continual self-transcendence.

Similarly, of course, we cannot conceptualise one of these states without having also conceptualised the other two. We need all three if we are to approach an understanding of the Buddhist interpretation of the self. An interpretation, incidentally, that remains remarkably consistent whichever of the main Buddhist traditions we choose to explore; and an interpretation that has rich implications for the way in which we experience ourselves and the world. The most fundamental of these implications is that reality is not something we have to discover for ourselves 'out there'. Reality is something we carry with us throughout life, if we are only prepared to stop what we are doing and allow ourselves to realise it. We are each of us the answer to our own question, and the techniques we use on the path toward self-affirmation are simply ways of helping us learn how to listen to this answer.

Acknowledgement

The original version of this chapter appeared in the *Journal of Humanistic Psychology*, and reproduction is by kind permission.

SECTION 2

Self, Mind and Meditation

INTRODUCTION TO SECTION 2

Readers unfamiliar with the history of Western psychology may be surprised to discover that attempts to understand experience have not been its prime endeavour. At the end of the last century philosophers and psychologists such as William James were well aware of the fact that for most of us an understanding of the nature of self-awareness and consciousness was of the greatest interest. Effective means for objective study were, however, not found, and psychologists focused instead upon overt behaviour which could be directly observed and measured. The excitement and influence of Behaviourism was often intense, and major advances were made in the theory of learning. The edifice so constructed was none the less soon to crack. Tolman and his colleagues studying rat behaviour in mazes came to the conclusion that the animals' performances could not be understood in terms of sequences of behaviour learnt in relation to the environment. Much more was involved; the animals appeared to be creating maps in their heads with which to solve problems. This 'cognitive' idea was gradually to become of major importance in behaviour study generally. In particular Noam Chomsky was to demonstrate the inadequacy of B. F. Skinner's behaviourist approach to language acquisition. The central problem in psychology thus once more shifted to the cognitive processes of mind, rather than to the control of behaviour as such.

This analysis of cognitive processes does not, however, necessarily extend to problems of consciousness. Because although mental performance can be described in machine-like language or algorithmically, the question of what it consciously *feels like* to be undertaking this performance remains a problem. Basically, any activity expressible as performance can be observed and measured, but any activity bounded by inner experience like consciousness cannot; the evidence is essentially subjective.

None the less the relationship between cognitive processing, categorisation, planning and thought on the one hand, and conscious awareness of these processes on the other, has gradually engaged the attention of psychologists – particularly those concerned with social issues and personal development. It is clearly meaningless to discuss the emergence of personal identity, for example, without relating it to the understanding of self-awareness and of feeling.

Already in the nineteenth century the philosopher Brentano and thinkers such as Husserl, who founded the phenomenological tradition in Western psychology, had stressed the point that the essential feature of the mind was that it was 'on about' something. Mental activity is always a reference to some issue. This activity is called intentionality. To be intentional means to hold some representation of an issue in mind, and to work with it in some way to some end. The precise philosophical meaning of intentionality has been much debated, but its emergence in psychological science was emphasised when Kenneth Craik in Cambridge argued that the prime functions of the human brain were to create and manipulate representations. Indeed it is only through representation that the human subject can be said to know the world. We never know the world in itself, we only know our representations of it.

There are two main ways of approaching an understanding of the mental mechanisms responsible for these representations. The fundamental method is to rely on scientific reductionism; to examine the hardware of the brain, to look at neurones, brain structure and neurochemistry and to attempt to construct a picture of mental activity through examining the relations between these components. Popularly such an approach is called the 'bottom-up' method. It is like trying to understand a television set or a computer by pulling it apart and looking at the bits. While advances have been achieved in this way, an understanding of the process as a whole eludes us.

The alternative method is to keep the process intact and observe its functions under different circumstances. This is like characterising the performance of a radio by turning the knobs in all possible directions and then thinking up what design or engineering 'blue-print' could account for what is observed. This 'top-down' approach, which is relatively new in the West, has given us some idea of the complexity of the mind, of the holistic nature of its functioning and of its truly enormous creative potential. As an approach, it has been facilitated by the development of information science (cybernetics and systems theory), but has been powered principally by the failure of the 'bottom-up' approach to answer fundamental questions.

In Eastern psychophilosophy, the 'top-down' approach has always been the method of procedure in attempting to give explanations of mind. The faculties and processes of mental activity are minutely categorised and described, and attempts then made to describe their dynamic interaction. Eastern models focus particularly on processes of *transformation*. Thus one model of mind accounting for worldly behaviour or suffering is matched to a complementary model depicting processes of change, salvation or enlightenment. The focal problem then becomes the practical one of moving personal activity from the negative system to the more positive one.

In this section we consider some contemporary models of mind that depict processes of conscious awareness, self-consciousness and personal awakening. Susan Blackmore discusses the way in which the mind creates models of 'reality', including representations of the place of self in that reality. She discusses mystical experience in terms of alterations in the modelling process, and draws attention to the personal challenges evoked by attempting to view one's own life in this way. Guy Claxton's chapter develops the issue by focusing on the assumptions we carry concerning the fixity and continuity of our 'self'. He points out that the anatta doctrine in Buddhism has always claimed that the 'sense of self' is based mistakenly in the assumption of permanence and thingness. But if the self is merely an idea or a 'model', what then is the significance of life? The notion that we are a process rather than an object is at first frightening, for it means the giving up of basic assumptions. Nevertheless, both Sue and Guy point to the remarkable sense of personal freedom and expansion that can develop from such a cognitive re-evaluation of the idea of self.

Kedar Dwivedi provides an account of the model of mind and its transformation found in the approach to Vipassana meditation of the Theravada school of Buddhism – representing the earlier psychological thought of the Buddhist Sutras. He is particularly concerned with the process whereby negative emotions associated with limiting views of self can be transformed, and we gain here a direct insight into the intellectual background of a way of transformation based in meditation.

Finally John Crook builds on his description of Zen training in Western Zen Retreats (see Chapter 13) and in orthodox Zen sesshins of the Chinese and Japanese traditions to show that the model of mind and personal transformation in the Lankavatara Sutra of the Vijnanavada School of Mahayana (the Cittamatra of Stephen Batchelor's Chapter 2) has much in common with a comparable model he constructs from contemporary Western premises in cognitive psychology. This model is useful in understanding the process of Zen training, and John argues that it is important for Buddhists to examine the way in which contemporary cognitive psychology can be of value in updating Buddhist psychology without losing the integrity of the ancient tradition.

JOHN CROOK
DAVID FONTANA

CHAPTER 5

Mental Models and Mystical Experience

SUSAN BLACKMORE

An Experience of Strangeness

Mystical experiences, whether originating naturally, as a result of a spiritual practice or as a result of psychedelic chemical ingestion, are the prime focus of my research interests and in this chapter I will attempt to explain or account for them within the framework of Western cognitive psychology. Clearly I am not going to be able to explain all manner of experiences described as mystical. Indeed I am only going to take one very simple example and tackle that, and even here I may fall far short of doing it justice. Nevertheless the example will give you an idea of what it is I am trying to do.

Imagine that I am walking one day through the woods and I stop by a large plane tree. There am I and there is the tree. As I look, I gradually stop perceiving the tree to be separate from me. Suddenly the tree and I are both similar, both just things standing there looking at each other. Then I am not so important anymore. There is me and there is the tree but each is as central as the other. And what of the rest of the scene? Every other tree is just as much there. Gradually the sense of me looking at any of this dissolves. There is just a vast wood, and all the rest of the world, just as it is in that moment. There is no one looking at anything. In that moment everything seems to be just right, just as it is. Time seems not to be. Leaves rustle and branches move, clocks strike and people walk, but everything is still and timeless and joyful. Then that too dissolves. I am re-forming, looking at the tree again. It is the same tree. It looks the same but somehow not the same It is more solid, more strong and tall and tree-full. Its leaves are vividly green and gold and brown and mottled. Its trunk is gloriously complex with its shedding scraps of bark. And so are all the other trees along the path. I walk among these marvellously vivid trees with a little smile on my lips.

This is a simple and undramatic experience, but it is the kind of thing I am going to talk about. I begin by treating it as an altered state of consciousness (ASC). Now as soon as I say that, I have to face the main problem of working with ASCs, which is that we cannot answer the most fundamental question about them – a question which I have been battling with for many years. It is 'what is altered in an ASC and indeed what is it that stays the same'? It does not help to say that consciousness is altered for we do not have any clear understanding of what consciousness is, nor are there any theories with which to deal with it. Nor does it help to say that a 'state of consciousness' is altered, for again we have no useable theories.

I suggest that most research on ASCs has worked at levels of explanation which drastically limit the progress that can be made. For example, there are two main approaches. One is highly reductionist. It assumes that what is altered in ASCs are things like pulse-rate, brainwaves, blood-flow, sweating and so on. Of course these things are altered, and it is important for our further understanding that we know about them. Indeed, I would be most interested to know what happened to various physiological variables when looking at that tree. However, it does not provide anything approaching a complete answer as to what is altered. It says nothing about the changed perception of the tree, the changed perception of self, or the changes in time. Most important, it has nothing to say about that little smile.

The other general approach has been quite the opposite and comprises occult and paranormal-type explanations of what has altered. These explanations often include mysterious substances, ideas of consciousness as some kind of 'stuff', or 'other worlds' and 'higher vibrations'. I find most such accounts internally inconsistent and unworkable. Certainly I have yet to find any that can be effectively related to cognitive psychology. I therefore suggest an alternative approach, one which has it that while reduction to underlying physiology is conceivable, the best place to start is at a much higher level of explanation. I choose to begin with the model of the world which a person creates with experience, let us call it the personal model of reality.

Central to cognitive psychology is the assumption that the brain is basically a model-builder. Perception is a process of building models of input; thinking, remembering, planning and deciding all involve constructing models of the world and of ourselves in it. It is perhaps odd that models of the external world are generally treated by the psychology of perception, and models of self are studied in social psychology. Nevertheless the two kinds of model are inextricably linked.

At any time we have some kind of model of the world apparent to us in experience. Crucial to this model, for most people and for most of the time, is that it all organised around a self. There is always someone who is doing the perceiving or remembering. There is a self at the centre of my perceived world. In this way we live within what I would call our 'me-now model'.

The 'me-now model' is a model of myself doing whatever I am now doing. For example, it may include the room here, the table, the sky outside and everything else of which I am currently aware. It is a very complex and stable mental model. It is me now. But there is perhaps only one kind of model of reality.

It is by thinking about these models that we can progress, for it is at this level of explanation that I suggest we can begin to understand the nature of consciousness and its changes.

Viewing Consciousness as Mental Modelling

I am going to make three suggestions about consciousness. The suggestions are these:

1. Being conscious is what it is like being a mental model.
2. People are self-conscious because they construct a model of self in the world.
3. Altered states of consciousness are best understood as changes in a person's model of reality.

I want to discuss these suggestions from two different points of view. First there are what we might call the objective consequences; the logical aspects about which we might disagree; from which we might draw testable predictions or argue about scientific merits. Then secondly there are the subjective consequences. What happens to one's view of the world if one actually takes these suggestions seriously? How does this view affect one's model of reality?

Being conscious is what it is like being a mental model. I would like to point out that the wording is carefully chosen. I do not mean that mental models in some esoteric way produce consciousness, or that consciousness is some kind of different stuff from the models. I mean only that being conscious is what it is like being a mental model. And I mean any mental model. When any information-processing system constructs representations of anything, then there is consciousness – consciousness of whatever attributes, distinctions and divisions, which that system has constructed in order to build the model.

I have explained this idea in more detail elsewhere (Blackmore, 1986). You might try asking yourself what it would be like to be various things or various mental models. It does not make much sense to imagine what it would be like to be this table. At least one can imagine that it would not be like anything much. The table does not respond to events or construct representations of them. Being a table would be still and changeless. But perhaps you can imagine what it is like to be an ant's model of the table. In whatever way the ant models the table, that is what the table is like for the ant. If the ant constructs concepts such as heavy or solid, smooth or warm, then the table is like these concepts.

Humans, of course, construct multiple models of their world, from the simple models in the periphery of the visual system to the complex models in central processing. What they do supremely well is to end up with a model of self in which a vast amount of diverse information is brought together into a model of self-now – or the me-now model. And we can certainly imagine what it would feel like to be such a model of self. I am suggesting that that is all we are.

You may still be unhappy and want to ask questions like – if all mental models are conscious, why am I not aware of all those other models my brain is constructing? Or indeed – if this is what being conscious is, then who is conscious of what? Perhaps I can try to answer these questions, but to do so I need to go on to the second proposition.

That is – people are self-conscious because they construct a model of self in the world.

I have already outlined the kind of model of self with which most of us live most of our waking life. I would say that we are this model – or rather that our normal conscious experience is no more and no less than the changing contents of this model. What it is like being human, is what it is like being this model of a person. This forces us to see that we often talk about self in two quite distinct ways. We talk about the whole conglomeration of body and behaviour and memories and so on – much as other people might see us. But we also talk about 'I' the subject of experience. It is this 'I' which is the model – ever changing and constructed. We may say that I (the system) constructs 'I' (the model).

From this we can answer the first question. It is now clear why 'I' am not aware of all the other models going on in the system. After all 'I' am only one of those models. When any information in the system is represented in such a form that it makes sense to, or becomes part of, the model of self, then 'I' will become aware of it. (And you might just as well say that it becomes aware of me!) But anything which is not part of this model is outside of 'my' awareness. We can also see how changes in the model lead to changes in what 'I' am aware of. 'I' attend to something when it becomes incorporated into the me-now model.

All this may seem counter-intuitive, but I think it only does so because we are blinded by the normal set-up. We are so used to having constructed just one main model of self, that we are unable to see that it is just constructed, and that life would go on without it. We are so used to tying every experience in to this self, that we cannot conceive of their being experience without it.

We also cannot easily conceive of there being more than one self, but this is perfectly possible if more models are constructed. Indeed this may be exactly what happens in cases of multiple personality, or in some forms of hypnosis in which there is 'divided consciousness'. Of course only one model of self can be used to control behaviour at any time, and so the others have to go into temporary abeyance. None the less, these unusual states can give us insight into our normal constructed state.

It is also useful to think about changing models of reality in sleep, which we take quite for granted, but which in fact involves quite bizarre changes in experience. Every morning we wake up; a new model of self is constructed, and it is sufficiently like yesterday's for us to carry on as though nothing has happened.

Now the other question I asked was, 'Who is experiencing what?' This now becomes clear. There is no need for any sort of homunculus in the system. If I construct a model of self experiencing a world, then that is how it will be and there will necessarily be a split between self and world. But the system might alternatively construct a model in which there was no separation of self and world. In this case there would be consciousness of whatever were the contents of the model, and no one would be conscious of anything. There would be no subject–object dichotomy. Of course self-less modelling might not be very good for the co-ordination of behaviour, but it is certainly possible, as many people would probably testify. So the question of *who* is experiencing *what* only arises because we are so used to constructing models of self. All 'our' experience is the experience of a constructed self, and we find it hard to imagine experience otherwise.

I would also add that if you accept both of these proposals, then it becomes interesting to ask such questions as whether computers are conscious, or dogs or cats. Most computers do not construct models of self – or of the system itself. They do construct models and to that extent there will be consciousness of whatever is represented, but there will be no self-consciousness. Some robots do construct representations of self and their environment. They need to in order to co-ordinate movements and actions. So to this extent they could be said to be self-conscious. Similarly most animals construct rather well-defined models of self. They have to in order to behave and respond to their world. In this way we can easily imagine what it is like to be a cat (the model) – so long as we know enough about the kinds of models of the world which that cat (the system) constructs.

We can now see that if we accept these propositions we have to accept that our experience, and what we usually think of as our deepest self, is no more than a process of modelling. Every momentary model gives rise to its successor. From this it becomes clear that by changing the models, profound changes in experience will come about.

That brings us to the last proposition, which is that ASCs are best understood in terms of changes in a person's model of reality, rather than in the system which constructed them. In other words we need to understand how 'I' (the model) have changed rather than how I (the system) have changed (even though we may accept that one is totally dependent upon the other).

This means that I can answer my original question about ASCs very simply. I would say that what is altered in an altered state of consciousness is a person's model of reality. I have previously used this approach to develop a theory of out-of-body experiences (Blackmore, 1984), of lucid dreams (Blackmore, 1987) and of experiences near death and in meditation (Blackmore, 1986). I would like to apply it to the experience I described at the outset.

Interpreting the Strange Experience

We may ask – what happened to my model of reality when I stood and looked at that tree?

Well – first of all it was a perfectly normal model with a tree constructed on the basis of sensory input and a self constructed, as usual, out of all that remembered stuff about what I think of myself. But then, for some reason (and I am not speculating here about the many possible physiological or psychological reasons), that distinction began to break down. I stopped building separate self and tree models. I (the system) just constructed a model of tree and person standing there, each looking at the other. Then the person disappeared, or became insignificantly trivial, in a general model of the world at that time, with all its actions going on unobserved by just one particular self. There just was whatever there seemed to be. Any sensory input that was processed led to a general model with no viewpoint, no centre and no observing self. With no self there was no wishing it to be any way rather than other. Things are just as they were. With no self-related plans and predictions time became no more than a sequence of events. Without a model of self the tree and everything else could just be whatever was modelled. 'I' was no more. I (the system) had ceased to construct 'I' (the model).

Then the model of self was reconstructed. The system began to put back together the familiar self, and 'I' reappeared. 'I' saw the tree again and went on my way through the woods. But now all the trees looked brighter and realer. Some vestige of letting them be remained. And more than that, I (the system) had learned that it could do away with 'I' (the model). One can never quite be the same after that. And one is left with a little smile as a reminder.

After such an experience there are many things that can happen and I would like to add a few comments on these. It is possible to forget the experience entirely or to remember it well and let it illuminate the rest of one's life with developing clarity. This relates to the functioning of state-specific memory. It is well known from experimental evidence that things are easier to recall if they are recalled within the same state of consciousness in which they were first learned. For example, the drunkard can remember where he hid his last bottle when he is drunk but not when he is sober. It is very hard to remember what it was like taking LSD until you take some again, or in some other way achieve a similar state.

The propositions given above allow one to see state-specific memory as being related to the model of reality which a person has. I can remember past experience better when I construct a similar model of self in the world. Now to the person who has a rigid and unbending representation of self, the mystical experience with the tree will be hard to recall. It is too far from the normal model of reality. But to the person who has some flexibility in modelling reality, it will be easier to recall. He (the system) can construct varied models of self and even come close, perhaps, to constructing no model of self.

This also tells us something about the sense of 'realness'. This is something which constantly fascinates me. I find nothing more unpleasant than the feeling that things do not really seem real – an undefinable and awkward sense of being out of touch with everything. It is important to understand this sense. At one end of the spectrum are pathological states of derealisation and depersonalisation in which nothing seems real. At the other end of the spectrum are the mystical experiences in which it is constantly said that things seem extraordinarily real and 'as they are'.

This also begins to make sense now. In the normal state the model of self is central to everything. And it does not just rest still. The model is constantly one of planning for how things might be, wishing they were otherwise, trying out possible responses to things and looking at things in terms of value to the self. Taken to extremes this results in a model which has drastically reprocessed and distorted the input. Nothing is let be. Everything is attacked from the top down and turned into something else, for incorporation into the me-now model and its plans.

At the other extreme there is no greedy model of self. There is therefore no need to assess things for value to the self, to like or dislike, to imagine things otherwise than they are, or to try to change them. They might as well be as they are, simply processed from the bottom up, uncluttered and real. Normal life can be seen as reaching a trade-off between processing things enough, and going too far and destroying them.

Conclusion

I am not here making an ontological statement about any external reality. I am only suggesting that if being conscious is what it is like being a mental model, then the contents of that model will seem more real when they are not cluttered up, or distorted by manipulation into a model of self.

All of this leads to one simple way of looking at self. 'I' am no more and no less than a model of a person in the world. 'I' am, if you like, an illusion. That is not to say that 'I' am unreal, only that 'I' am constructed, and in some sense might just as well not be.

Now, I said at the beginning that I wanted to consider both the objective and subjective consequences of this view. Everything I have said so far is part of the objective consequences. We might all argue about this. We might bring up logical objections or try out crucial experiments to confirm or falsify it all, and we might end up at some kind of agreement.

However, there are some subjective consequences. If you genuinely believe in the viewpoint suggested here then it changes your experience of being in the world. I can affirm this because I have been trying to do so now for several years. It is hard to accept the theory on more than just an intellectual level, but it is possible. The changes are slow but quite powerful. And they are positive as well as negative.

On the negative side it is disorientating and terrifying. If you really believe that you are no more than some construction of a brain, then self-importance vanishes. This might be a 'good thing', but it is mighty scary. There is also a sense of terrible instability. If there are only arising and disintegrating models, then where is my familiar persisting self? Help! It is not there to prop itself up. If there are only models it is easy to lose all sense of direction and of any continuing solid self who is 'in control'. All this can be pretty unnerving and, I believe, arises from seriously trying to accept the propositions I have put forward here.

On the other hand there are the positive aspects. Accepting this view provides a wonderful freedom. If 'I' am only a mental model, then I know that I don't have to cling to myself in the same old way. If I accept that there is a new model every morning, or even every moment, then I can let go of my sense of permanence and all its guilts and constructions. In letting go it also becomes easier to change models and hence to remember altered states; to remember what it was like taking LSD, or being hypnotised. Meditation is also easier. If you accept that experience is just a flow of models, then the experiences which arise in meditation can more easily be released.

I don't know whether these consequences would be the same for everyone. Indeed, above all else I hope that some of you may be sufficiently interested in the ideas I have put forward here to try them out for yourself, and to let me know how you get on. I hope that for you the positive consequences will outweigh the negative ones – or perhaps better still that you will be able to reach some kind of integration. And, of course, the viewpoint I am presenting here has a direct application to the understanding of experiences uncovered in the practice of Eastern religions. The way in which this viewpoint matches the intellectual comprehensions of their meditations by Eastern sages is a further and fascinating story.

CHAPTER 6

Giving Up the Ghost: Why Selflessness Seems So Dreadful

GUY CLAXTON

Introduction

At the beginning of the sixth chapter of his *Madhyamaka–vatara*, Chandrakirti says: 'Should an ordinary person hear about *sunyata* and immediately experience the surging of such great joy that his eyes become moist with tears and the hairs of his body stand on end, such a person has the seed of the mind of 'buddhahood' (Geshe Rabten, 1983, p. 52). The question I want to consider is why most 'ordinary people' have quite a different reaction. Buddhism after all tells us that everyone possesses the seed of buddhahood. Why then should the most common reaction to the ideas of *sunyata* (emptiness) and *anatta* (no-self) be disinterest, disbelief, apprehension or hostility? For most people these notions seem to threaten loss rather than to promote liberation. If Buddhism brings Good News, why is it so often received with blank or despondent faces?

The central Buddhist doctrine of *anatta* or 'no-self' is often initially understood by people to imply a loss of free will, and this is something about which people typically feel most strongly. Daniel Dennett (1984) explains why. 'If having free will matters, it must be because not having free will would be awful, and there must be some grounds for doubting that we have it . . . But what exactly are we afraid of? . . . Anyone who dreads the prospect of not having free will must have some inkling about *what that terrible condition would be like* . . .' (p.5). Thus the solution to the problem of why selflessness seems so dreadful must be sought by uncovering people's intuitive beliefs about what it *means* to be (or have?) a self and about the kinds of threat that are raised by the suggestion that one might, or even should, give up this conception. What do we suppose we would be losing if we were to lose our selves?

At heart Buddhism is not concerned with conduct or with understanding. Its focus is on *perception* and its aim is a shift in perception, specifically in the way we perceive ourselves, that, once made, brings spontaneously in its wake other shifts in how we feel, think and act. We must start therefore with an introduction to what the Buddhist view of perception is.

The Computer Metaphor

People are not computers, of course, but it may be helpful here to utilise the computer metaphor. I have a small computer on my desk that is a 'personal word processor'. This is the main function for which it is sold. But to say that it 'is' a word processor is to misrepresent matters somewhat. It does not 'know' what kind of a computer it is until it is told. Whenever I want to use it, I have (after switching it on) to insert what is called the 'Start-of-Day' disc, which is what tells the computer to be a word processor, and *how* to be a word processor. Once this set of programs is loaded, all functions of the computer become those of a word processor. Every tap of a key or movement of the 'mouse' is interpreted by these programs. The computer perceives everything through eyes of its word processor programs, and, while it is being a word processor it cannot perceive in any other way, nor conceive that any other way is possible. Likewise, it can only react as a word processor.

Thus, by loading into my computer its Start-of-Day disc I have both mobilised and immobilised it. I have given it a sophisticated way of perceiving, processing and responding. But I have had to tell it that, for the time being, this is the only way, so that *everything* has to be construed in this light, and anything that doesn't fit will be either misconstrued or ignored. Of course I can use my word processor to write poetry or prose, gibberish or genius: it has great flexibility and power. But the ground rules are set.

Interestingly, while the computer is functioning as a word processor (that is, while the program is *running*), it cannot at the same time display (or *list*) the program itself. The instructions that the program contains are not capable of being scrutinised directly: yet they are manifest in the way the computer interprets and responds. We can observe their effects but we cannot, whilst the program is running, observe *them*. Thus if the program contains bugs or errors, these too will not be observable directly: they cannot be perceived by the computer, for they are determining how the computer perceives. If my word processor seems to be producing unhelpful or even bizarre displays, I can do one of two things. I can either try to cope with them or compensate for them, using the resources that are inherent in the program itself. Or I can stop word-processing, switch into an entirely different mode that will enable me to inspect the *contents* of the word processor program, and try to find the error and correct it or edit it out.

In Buddhist psychology we are something like the computer, and 'Self' is the Start-of-Day program that tells us what kind of a computer we are to be. It tells us who we are, what we need, what counts as a threat, what is to be sought and what avoided. Within the parameters set by the Self program our perceptions and reactions are many and varied, but the whole play has to be conducted on the stage, and with the backcloth, that the program constructs. Like the word processor we are (usually) not aware of this program but only of its effects. But when these effects are dysfunctional, upsetting or weird, our habitual response is to seek solutions in terms of the capabilities that the program permits, rather than to look for 'bugs'. Because we have lost sight of the distinction between computer and program, we take the Self 'mode', unthinkingly, as the only possible one, and the perceptions it generates as therefore being inevitable, right or 'real'. Thus, reflexly, our attempts to remedy unhappiness are produced by the same flawed program that produced the unhappiness in the first place, while new experiences and ideas that 'do not compute' can only be reinterpreted in the standard way offered by the program, or allowed to pass unnoticed.

Imputations of Selfhood

What does the 'Self' program tell us that we are? How does it define our nature, our capabilities, and our priorities? If we were to 'list' it, rather than 'run' it, what instructions would we see?

1. **'I' is a kind of 'thing'.** The most basic question is 'what kind of thing am I?'; and the answer that the program provides is 'a "thing" kind of thing'. As John Crook remarks on page 15, it puts the 'entity' into 'identity' and instructs us to relate to ourselves as if we were some kind of object. Next, the program spells out what this means – what it means to be a 'thing'.

2. **'I' is separate.** A self is bounded in space, says this instruction. What is inside the boundary is 'I'; what is outside is 'not-I'. What is inside is my business to defend and preserve. What is outside matters only in relation to what is inside. Can it hurt me? Can it help me? Does it confirm me?

3. **'I' is independent.** A self exists in and of itself. I may interact with other things; I may even need some of them from time to time. But basically my existence is independent and autonomous.

4. **'I' is persistent.** Events come and go, but things persist. It is in the nature of a thing to continue with its 'identity' through time as well as through space. Although I was born, and will die, in between I have a degree of permanence. Memories become 'real' records of my past, and so confirm it.

5. **'I' is a collection of characteristics.** Instructions (1) – (4) create the *container* of a self, and (5) gives it a *nature*. What is it that is localised and persistent? It is my character or personality. I define my self as a collection of attributes, like height, sex, colour, occupation and history. An important sub-set of these characteristics is my preferences and ambitions – the likes, dislikes and intentions that I can rely on my self to display.

6. **'I' is coherent.** Because I am *one* thing, all my characteristics must be compatible with each other. I am 'all of a piece'. I cannot be both 39 and 10 years old, nor can I be both 'intelligent' and 'dim'.

7. **'I' is a reflection.** Though my nature is my own, and exists independently of what 'not-I' is up to, yet paradoxically the Self program sets great store by what others think and say about me. If enough people treat me as X for long enough, I shall become X to my self, too.

8. **'I' is standards.** The Self program tells me not only to construe my nature in terms of other people's reaction to me, but also to

allow them to set conditions for my 'worth'. My self-esteem is set to become conditional on certain standards of thought, feeling, speech and conduct.

9. *'I' has needs.* Who I am determines my basic goals and priorities. Not only *do* 'I' persist – 'I' *have to* persist. So I become defined in terms of the conditions I seek or cling to, and those I avoid or escape from.

10. *'I' has things.* Although my basic identity occupies more or less the same area of space as my body, the Self program has me set up 'outposts' of my self that I am also committed to defend. These are my possessions, which include the people and geographical areas I become attached to, as well as 'my' car and 'my' savings. 'Mine' reinforces the premises of separateness ('mine' versus 'yours'), persistence (ownership continues over time) and control (I can do what I like with 'my' stuff).

11. *'I' can instigate.* As well as defining the expressions 'I am', 'I need' and 'I have', the Self program also tells us how to construe 'I *can*'. Sometimes I am pushed about by 'not-I', but on other occasions, very important for my identity, I am a source or instigator of action. I do not only respond: I initiate. This is the instruction that tells us we have 'free will'. It has to come a little way down the list for it relies on my seeing myself as separate from the world. Having distinguished 'I' and 'not-I', we can attribute authorship of action to one or the other. 'She made me angry' gives responsibility away. 'I walked the dog' claims it back.

12. *'I' can control myself.* This ingenious instruction applies the previous kind of interpretation. Just as 'I' splits off from the world, and can then exert (partial) control over it, so 'I' can split my self in two and perform the same trick. 'I'd stay in bed all day if I didn't force my self to get up.' 'I had to restrain my self from hitting him.'

13. *'I' can deliberate.* The Self program leads me to identify my self most closely with a particular kind of control or instigation – that which is preceded or accompanied by a congruent train of thought. We are instructed to notice such episodes and to construe them as obvious evidence in favour of the executive power of the self (expressing its self through its most influential medium – conscious deliberation).

The Escape from the Self

One could go on to show what elegant variations the Self program
spins on these central themes. But the framework is sufficient to
allow us to begin to construct an answer to the question with
which we started. Selflessness cannot but seem dreadful to a being
that deeply believes itself to be a Self, for the Self program can
only either ignore the teachings of *anatta* or misconstrue them as
implying real loss, rather than as the dispelling of a concept that
has never referred to any actual, existing thing. It is impossible
for such beings to see *through* their selves precisely because they
see *with* their selves. Any experience or any idea that is contrary
to the specification of the self is thus transmuted into a *threat* to
self and is liable to give rise to anxiety, aversion or an ostrich-like
unconsciousness.

Each of the components of self that have been brought into
being by the Self program is a hostage to fortune. Losing
our *separation* from the not-self becomes dangerous. Welwood
(1979), for example, speaks of psychologists, though he might
have included people in general, when he says:

> The great difficulty that most Western psychologists have with the
> Eastern notion of transcending the self stems from their assumption
> that self-transcendence would lead to one of two states, neither of
> which our culture regards as wholesome: (1) psychosis or regression,
> the loss of one's boundaries, such that one lives in a continual
> state of panic and insecurity about threats to one's existence; or (2)
> asceticism, in which one totally abandons the demands of ordinary
> life, including passion, pleasure, and successful participation in social
> and economic realities' (p.60).

We shall return to the second in a moment.
To lack *persistence* is a possibility that seems to strike at the root
of self. The idea, for example, that memories are not accurate
records of a real past but back-projections that owe as much to
present needs as to verifiable history, can be unsettling if seriously
entertained. Not to have a fixed, reliable *set of personal characteristics*,
but instead to recognise one's openness, unpredictability and lack
of definition, also seems like a loss of self. Yet psychologists as

well as Buddhists are beginning to throw doubt on this fixed reliability: 'I believe we must call into question . . . especially those concepts which stress a precise demarcation, the kind of fixity and permanence of the self that is usually implied by such terms as 'character' and 'personality'. (Lifton, 1970, p.38)

To experience one's self as not being *coherent* is also a threat: one may, while the Self program is running, feel 'invaded', or as if one's personality is coming 'unglued'. Curiously the commitment to seeing our selves as coherent, when we in fact contain many 'sub-selves' which may speak with quite different voices, is maintained by identifying exclusively with these selves in turn, so that none has to acknowledge the existence of others. As Needleman (1983, p.12) says:

> Beneath the fragile sense of personal identity, the individual is actually an innumerable swarm of disconnected impulses, thoughts, reactions, opinions and sensations, which are triggered into activity by causes of which he is totally unaware. Yet at each moment the individual identifies himself with whichever of this swarm of impulses and reactions happens to be active, automatically affirming each as 'himself', and then taking a stand either for or against this 'self', depending on the particular pressures that the social environment has brought to bear upon him since his childhood.

To be unable to see your self defined as a *reflection* in other people's reactions and habitual forms of interaction is also rendered as a threat by the Self program. It is for this reason that 'solitary confinement' coupled with sporadic, unpredictable and unintelligible interactions with others, is so frequently used as a form of psychological torture. To a self, such treatment constitutes a dramatic and disorientating attack on identity. The threat to self experienced as shame, guilt or loss of self-esteem, and brought on by experiences of failing to meet *standards*, is more common, though sometimes no less intense.

We are all familiar with the distress caused by loss of *possessions*, a distress that is normally out of proportion to the physical hardship involved. Pre-eminent here is the actual or threatened loss of people with whom we have become identified. Behind jealousy, for example, lies the particular belief that 'I need you' – my survival is dependent on your staying around. The repercussions of attachment, aversion and delusion that Buddhism identifies as the main causes of suffering are nowhere more fully evident than in the anxiety, entreaties, threats, promises, sulks and paranoia of the unfortunate person in the grip of jealousy.

And there are also threats from experiences and suggestions that run counter to our instructions to see our selves as instigators, controllers and deliberators. It is here that people often seem to be most vulnerable, for as we have seen the most frequent misconception of *anatta* is as a denial of free will. The fear that lies below the surface is that, if my will is 'taken away', I shall be left actually handicapped, and in several ways. Firstly, I shall become paralysed: *anatta* will have stolen my motive force, and without it, nothing will happen. Secondly, I shall become fatalistic: without free will there is no point in caring about my fate as I cannot influence it, and apathy will inevitably ensue. Thirdly, I shall become a puppet: at the mercy of external forces and events. In this context, it is interesting that challenges to our belief in the power of self-as-instigator are by no means new in the West. For example Thomas Hobbes wrote:

> A wooden top that is lashed by the boys and runs about sometimes to one wall, sometimes to another, sometimes spinning, sometimes hitting men on the shins, if it were sensible of its own motion would think it proceeded from its own will, unless it felt what lashed it. And is a man any wiser, when he runs to one place for a benefice, to another for a bargain, and troubles the world with writing errors and enquiring answers, because he thinks he doth it without other cause than his own will, and seeth not what are the lashings that cause his will? (Molesworth, 1841, p. 55). Or more recently:
> . . . the whole of man's psychic life is the product of suggestions coming from different sources, some immediately external and others stored in the mechanisms of memory. And this whole process . . . is constantly screened from our awareness by the belief, also conditioned in us, that we are acting, individual selves. Our so-called 'freedom of the will' is only an *ex post facto* identification with processes that are taking place 'all by themselves' (Needleman, 1983, p. 14).

Finally, the anticipated loss of control arouses fears that I shall become unpredictable: there will be no 'chief executive' to ensure the continued smooth and orderly running of the show, and internal anarchy will break out. Also I shall become dangerous: it has only been the 'self-control' that my self has been able to muster that has prevented me from acting out my worst fantasies and most hostile thoughts. Flawed though it is, it is my 'will-power' that has kept me out of gaol so far.

To a being that believes itself to be a Self of the kind described, the fears of madness, evil, apathy and the rest are real and justified. To abandon the Self is not to give up a ghost but heedlessly to disconnect the most vital functions on the life-support system. It is only from *outside* the confines of the Self program that it is possible to entertain with some equanimity the possibility that this so-vital system has actually been a dysfunctional encumbrance, and that without it life would not only go on, but would be immeasurably improved. Through its teachings and through meditation, it is Buddhism's first job to pry loose our grasp on the idea of Self, so that we can begin to find a vantage-point outside the program from which we can inspect it. As Wilber (1979 p. 19) puts it, speaking of these programming instructions:

> . . . the fact that (a person) can comprehensively *look at* them means
> that he has ceased using them as something *with which to look* at,
> and thus to distort, reality. Further, the fact that he can look at them
> means that he is no longer exclusively identified with them. This
> identity begins to touch that within which is beyond.

Only when this first hurdle has been cleared can selflessness shrink in dreadfulness and expand in possibility.

Conclusion

I have quoted several Western psychologists and philosophers of religion in order to show how the monopoly of the Self program on our way of perception is being challenged from many quarters, not just from the Eastern spiritual traditions. But we might close by returning to Buddhism and the eminent contemporary monk Nyanaponika Thera (1986, p. 176):

> When encountering something higher, animals and undeveloped
> men, whether 'primitive' or 'civilised', usually react by distrust,

fear, flight, attack, resentment, hostility or persecution; for they can view that higher form of life only as something different, alien, and therefore suspect. It is the sign of a truly developed human mind that it meets the higher with due respect, with admiration, and the wish to emulate.

To practise 'listing' the contents of the Self program may help to open a chink that can lead towards such development.

CHAPTER 7

Purification of Mind by Vipassana Meditation

KEDAR NATH DWIVEDI

Introduction

If someone makes an insulting or hurtful remark to us, we often
find ourselves feeling angry. Within split seconds our hearts begin
to race, our blood-pressure goes up, our breathing becomes
shallow and rapid, our skin conductance shoots up, and our
blood chemistry becomes spiced with a cocktail of sugar, fatty
acids, steroids and adrenalin. Moreover, this happens without
our permission and usually without our knowledge. According
to Buddhism, this happens because of our false *ditthi* or view.
False ditthi means a kind of cognitive distortion which is almost
universal and which arises due to the illusion or delusion of self or
ego. This illusion is considered to be a fundamental problem, and
is described in Buddhism as *kilesa* or impurity or defilement.

With the passage of time the anger may subside, but a little
later we may remember the insulting incident, and once again
we start fuming with anger; the heart races, the blood-pressure
shoots up again, and so on. This can happen without warning,
even though we may be at the time with a group of congenial
friends, experiencing only their kindness and good fellowship.
Our physiology is reacting therefore to memories, ideas, images,
fantasies and constructs *as if* they were real, substantial, here and
now. Such an emotional involvement ignores the distinctions
between reality and fantasy. The faculty of discrimination is
weakened and blurred. It is as if *real* New York and *thoughts about*
New York are confused and treated as one and the same thing.

This dissolution of the faculty of discrimination is a common occurrence. If we watch a horror film many of us are scared stiff. Similarly an erotic film can produce physical excitement. Yet in both cases we are only seeing electronically produced images on a screen.

Our emotions involve not only this kind of autonomic arousal and cognitive impairment, but also stimuli to vocal and physical action. Thus in the case of anger, for example, we may shout, use abusive language, or even become physically violent.

The Buddhist Model

The Buddhist model of this pathogenesis proposes a three-tier operational system (see Figure 1 on the following page). In this model the universally prevalent illusion or delusion of self leads to disturbing thoughts which, in turn, can lead to damaging mental, vocal or physical actions. The basic defilements leading to the delusion of self are called in this model *anusaya* (latent predisposition). In the presence of weak discrimination and of contact with mental objects, anusaya leads to disturbing or unwholesome thoughts known as *pariyutthana* (obsession), and pariyutthana in turn leads in the presence of poor volitional control and contact with physical objects to unwholesome actions or *vitikkam* (transgression).

The three tiers of this model were explained by the Venerable Ledi Sayadaw (a Burmese Buddhist monk who lived from 1846 to 1923) by means of the analogy with a box of matches (1981). Sayadaw pointed out that it is possible to discern three levels of 'fire' in the matches. The first is the subtlest level of latent, implicate fire inherent in the entire live box of matches. The second is the fire that is created when one or more of the matches is struck, and the third is the transference of the fire from the match to another object by bringing the two objects into contact with each other.

The Removal of Defilements

Just as there are three levels of defilements, so there are three levels to their removal. The Buddhist Noble Eightfold Path represents these levels as *sila, samadhi* and *panna*.

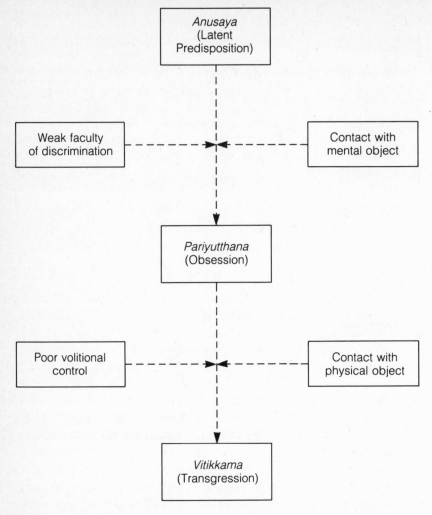

Figure 7.1 Pathogenesis

Sila means moral conduct or volitional control or virtuous living, and is practised by taking moral precepts and suppressing physical or verbal manifestations of the defilements (that is, of unwholesome or *akusala* actions). The five basic moral precepts are abstinence from killing, from sexual misconduct, from stealing, from lying and from the use of intoxicants. *Samadhi* (also called *samatha*) means mindfulness or concentration (for example the concentration upon breathing) and starts by:

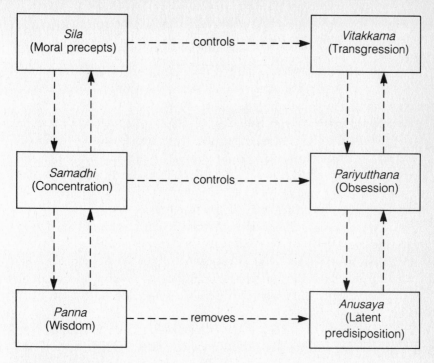

Figure 7.2 The Path

1. focusing or applying the attention;
2. remembering to come back to the object of meditation, when the mind drifts away, by discriminating between thinking and reality;
3. sustaining attention on the object of meditation for longer and longer periods, thus controlling mental involvements with the defilements.

Vipassana Meditation

If the latent predispositions are not properly eradicated, our control over defilements will only be temporary. We therefore need *panna*, which means wisdom or experiential insight, in order to eradicate these defilements altogether. Panna is cultivated by Vipassana meditation. Vipassana deals with false view, that is with the false notions we have about the real nature of things (in particular about the existence of a 'self' and about subject – object distinctions), and thus purifies the mind and leads us towards enlightenment.

Let me explain the difference between this experiential insight and ordinary, second-hand knowledge, the kind of knowledge that comes from reading about the nature of things from the scientific viewpoint. From this scientific viewpoint, as expressed for example in quantum physics and relativity theory, we learn that we are made up of insubstantial empty phenomena, a flux of everchanging quanta of energy producing the illusion of solidity, and that special illusion of continuity and permanence which we describe with such terms as 'I', 'ego', 'self' and 'my body'.

This learning has its value, but it only scratches the surface of our lives. It makes no real difference to the way in which we actually experience the world, and of course no real difference to this special deep-rooted illusion of 'self'. The ideas of emptiness, of transitoriness and of selflessness derived from such abstract learning are certainly fascinating and intellectually stimulating, but they evaporate when our sense of solidity and continuity comes under attack.

We can draw an analogy with the cinema. Films are made up of a series of still photographs. But when we watch a film, we see only clear movement, an illusion of continuity produced by the rapidity of change. Cognitive processes have the same rapidity, and give birth to the same kind of illusion. If you aren't convinced of this rapidity, it is worth noting that when using electroencephalographs to record electrical activity in the brain, neurophysiologists observe that evoked potentials occur in milliseconds. Approaching the subject from a different angle, Buddhism describes the cognitive cycle as taking only seventeen mind moments, there being 17×10^{21} such mind moments in the wink of an eye.

In contrast to abstract learning, vipassana is an *experiential* method of acquiring knowledge, and thus leads to panna. It is a meditative technique that requires a fine, sharp, steady and penetrative concentration, and that examines the mind–body phenomenon and discerns the true nature of subtle experiences. It leads to a gradual purification of mind, to the eradication of latent defilement, and finally to enlightenment. To be practised correctly, however, vipassana requires adequate accompanying practice of both sila and samadhi. Without sila there would be inadequate volitional control, and without samadhi there would be inadequate concentration.

Training in Vipassana

The life-style of a monk or nun is of course particularly conducive to the practice of sila, samadhi, panna and therefore of vipassana. But the practice is suitable for laypersons as well. Even in the Buddha's time, twenty-five centuries ago, many householders practised vipassana as a way to enlightenment. Similarly today: there are a number of vipassasna teachers and centres catering specifically for lay-people. They may differ slightly in that they may place varying degrees of emphasis upon one or other of the three inherent and interconnected characteristics of our experience, recognition of any one of which leads naturally to the recognition of the other two: *anicca* (the impermanence of all things) *anatta* (the non-existence of the self) and *dukka* (the basic unsatisfactoriness inherent in human life). None the less their stress upon sila and samadhi will remain the same.

An example of a centre currently operating specifically for lay-people is the International Meditation Centre at Splatts House, Heddington, Wiltshire, where practitioners follow the tradition of Sayagyi U Ba Khin under the guidance of Mother Sayama and of Saya U Chit Tin. During the ten-day course at the International Meditation Centre at least the five basic precepts of sila (abstaining from killing, from sexual misconduct, from stealing, from lying and from the use of intoxicants) are observed throughout. Samadhi is practised for the first four days by a steady focus of attention upon the breathing (*anapana*), and this together with a rule of silence leads to a considerable degree of control over the attention. From the fifth day onwards vipassana is practised by minutely examining the illusory but experiential solidity of mind – body formations in order gradually to dissolve the cognitive distortions produced by latent defilements. Thus the practitioner is enabled to tread the path to purification.

CHAPTER 8

Mind in Western Zen

JOHN H. CROOK

How are we to understand the unity of ourselves and the Buddhas? First we must understand the practice of the Buddhas. The practice of the Buddhas is carried on with the whole world and together with all sentient beings. If it is not universal it is not the practice of the Buddhas. Therefore, from the time we first aspire to the way until we attain Buddhahood both practice and attainment must be one with the whole world and all beings.
Dogen Zenji: Shobogenzo

Introduction

How are we to understand the nature of Zen training? A spontaneous answer to such a question might be the one given me by a Ladakhi yogin in Zangskar when asked about a similarly academic issue.

'Since you have had the good fortune of receiving instruction in meditation why don't you go and do it? After a while you will have no need of asking such a question.'

Shamefacedly perhaps, I would have to reply that Buddhism is full not only of methods but also of explanations. Understanding a map can help a puzzled explorer, and communication of ideas must be one of the activities of a Bodhisattva. In Buddhism the intellect is not to be rejected – it is, however, to be kept in its place.

The experience of 'enlightenment' and the path to it have received a great deal of analysis in Buddhism. While developing the practice of Western Zen Retreat (Chapter 13) I became interested in the implications it held for an understanding of the human mind. Buddhist psychology provides more than one clear model of mind with which to understand the personal changes associated with training. Until recently, however, it has been impossible to relate such models to matching Western endeavours. The renewal of cognitive enquiry in the West, the new focus on consciousness (Blakemore and Greenfield, 1987, for example), and the new interest in meditation (see West, 1979, 1987) has led to fresh perspectives and new orientations that reveal a remarkable similarity in approach to the Buddhist thinking of centuries ago. The result is that today it is possible to relate Buddhist and Western thought to give us an overview of mind that provides greater and more comprehensive understanding. Such an overview can serve as a map for those Westerners exploring personal development in the context of Zen or Tibetan yogic training. This chapter summarises my preliminary attempts to relate Buddhist and Western psychology within this overview. The attempts continue.

The Purpose of Training in the Psycho-Philosophical View of the Mahayana

Buddhist thinkers claim that their methods provide an insight into the nature of the mind that is generally hidden from us by our pervasive individual and collective ignorance. This ignorance (*avidya* = not seeing) is based in attachments to our mental representations of experience of the self – attachments that necessarily lead to uneasiness and anxiety (*dukkha*) because such representations are impermanent (*anicca*), lacking the quality of sustained entity. Training provides direct contact with the non-discursive basis of mind through methods that deconceptualise the processes of experience. This leads in turn to a way of life based in an openness of process rather than in the restrictiveness of self-conceit. The result is inner freedom. That which has now been perceived is called the 'unborn mind', because it is that state of awareness which is present before ideas arise within it. We may see this as a process in time – as when reference is made to the original mind before one is born, or, more deeply, as an underlying pervasive state that is always both present and available but which is obscured by the process of categorisation. According to this view, experiences may occur therefore in either a dualistic or a non-dualistic mode (Joshu Sasaki Roshi, 1983). Vijnanavada philosophy – one of the main Mahayanist doctrines basic to Zen thought which developed between 300 BC and AD 500, puts it that *knowing* (vijnana) always indicates the co-occurrence of subject and object, but the *manner* in which subject and object relate to each other depends upon our mode of viewing.

This mode can be either non-discriminative awareness or discriminative experience. The two modes can alternate with each other, because to function in the world a capacity to discriminate objects is necessary. However, in the state of 'ignorance' a person is entirely unaware of the non-discriminatory mode, and remains bound and caged within a network of projected discriminations. Training consists therefore in the development of 'skilful means' whereby the trainee looks, listens and distinguishes things while yet being aware of the pervasiveness of their interdependent relationship. The perception of object and self as interdependent arises when the object is traced back to its source – it appears as a mere reflection in a process of mental mirroring. Centring one's awareness within the mirror is to lose the sense of discrete positioning in space and time. The non-dual participation in this profound vision delivers one from the fears rooted in concepts such as 'permanent' versus 'impermanent', or of 'I' versus 'not I'. Awakening is thus the release of a conceptualising mind into its pre-conceptual 'unborn' state. A person who has recognised this knows who he or she *is*, and becomes free to construct a life less confined by earlier defensive illusions.

In the *Lankavatara Sutra*, the Vijnanavada view is expressed in a psychological model which is further developed in the psycho-philosophy of Vasubandhu (D. Suzuki, 1932, 1953; Wei Tat, 1976). Three main processes make up the terms of this model (see Figure 8.1):

1. *Alayavijnana*: the unborn mind or 'suchness' of experience, the womb or embryo from which every discriminable thing emerges, the storehouse consciousness which is the pervasive basis of phenomena.
2. *Manovijnana*: the cognitive world of subject – object relations in which all sensations, perceptions and cognitive discriminations are rooted.
3. *Manas*: attention, cognitive discrimination or thought, which separates subject or object for the purpose of analytical understanding and thereby creates the known world of separate objects in their logically defined and imputed relationships

(*manovijnana*). When *manas* focuses upon *tathata* (the experiential continuum of personal life) without the involvement of *manovijnana* a direct experience of uncategorised truth happens.

In the Western Zen Retreat (see Chapter 13) two main methods for producing this direct experience, the Communication Exercise (CX) and Zazen, are applied, both based in traditional devices. The CX makes use of a koan or paradoxical question. To seek to answer the question 'Who am I?' is to confront an evident absurdity because of course one knows precisely who one is. Yet, to respond in such a way is at once to reveal an uncertainty, for what kind of a knowing is this and what is it that is known? The use of a paradoxical question functioning in this way is characteristic of Rinzai Zen.

Much of the time of the retreat is spent exhausting the mind of its conceptual schemes – exhausting the capacity of thought. As disidentification proceeds (see Chapter 13), the mind 'enters the desert' – a 'dark night of the soul' in which all attempt to answer the question is abandoned, since no verbal or emotional reaction

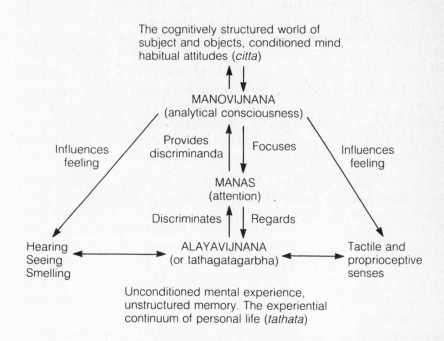

Figure 8.1 The model of mind in the *Lankavatara Sutra*. After Crook, 1980.

is forthcoming, but still no clarity emerges. This approximates to the 'Great Doubt', considered by the eminent master Hakuin of the Rinzai School as an essential stage before koan resolution (Kasulis, 1981, Chapter 8). Crossing the desert is a long and often painfully arid process. It ends when the 'Great Death' occurs. This death is simply a giving up of intentionality – a breaking out of the mode of focused perplexity – not through a rational process but through a sudden realisation that the koan points to something quite other than thought. There is an explosive or implosive quality to this realisation in which the trainee falls out of his thinking.

Prior to this occurrence, a number of misleading states of mind may arise. With low energy in poorly focused states, the doubt transforms into trance, into unresolved but pleasing serenity, or into experiences of bliss. While these are signs of intense meditative concentration, they do not constitute the 'death' to which Hakuin refers. They can furthermore be observed or witnessed by the mind, thereby demonstrating the continuation of dualistic functioning. Often in the Western Zen Retreat this is as far as a participant may get, and if he or she then really wishes to take up Zen training a focused commitment to a further *sesshin*, together with daily practice, will be required.

The background to the CX is the repeated practice of Zazen (see Chapter 13). The retreat begins with Zazen, and Zazen continues intermittently even when the CXs have become the predominant activity. This Zazen is at first without a koan and on the last day – as the koan changes its nature and function and the crossing of the desert appears, it is once more virtually koanless. This focused awarness of being – this 'searching the heart', is characteristic of Soto Zen as well as of other systems such as the Tibetan Mahamudra and *rDzogs·chen*. Its prime characteristic is that here the purpose of sitting is none other than the sitting itself; the realisation that meditation and awakening are not separate, one being used to strive for the other, but that in truth it is illusory to think there is a 'realisation' to obtain. The pervading awareness is already present, but split by dichotomising cognition. The great master Dogen has described the movement of Zazen as involving three steps. First there is 'thinking' – then there is opposition to thinking or 'not-thinking', and finally there is an abandonment of both thinking and not-thinking in a state of 'without-thinking'. It is 'without-thinking' that constitutes the unborn mind.

Zazen should not therefore be used to reach some exalted state, for Zazen itself is already sufficient. To sit is simply sitting, but full understanding of that only dawns in 'without-thinking'. There is thus no particular goal to aim at, nowhere 'else' to go. If 'without-thinking' arises, it does so; if it does not, that also is so. Clarification comes about without premeditation – meditation comprises clarification. The beginner's mind is already enlightened. Indeed, to become attached to 'without thinking' is to make a mistake; eventually thinking, not thinking and without thinking are all seen simply as expressions of the universal principle that pervades all of them.

Ch'an Master Shen-Yen has pointed out to me[1] that a Buddhist practice utilised for therapeutic purposes does not in itself constitute Zen. For Zen to be fully present there is needed Great Doubt (enquiry), Great Angry (that is, forceful) Determination, and Great Vows. In discussion we agree that in the Western Zen Retreat Great Doubt and Great Angry Determination may arise, and produce valid experiences and insights into the basis of mind. However, unless a practitioner undertakes to live a life of preceptual truth through the making of Great Vows, there is no Zen as a Buddhist understands that term. These great vows are basically twofold; an unremitting determination to come to terms with karma, one's own, that of society and that of human existence, and then the undertaking of the quest for enlightenment, not for oneself alone but for the good of all sentient beings. The great endeavour is to live the life of a Bodhisattva – one who uses his or her insight for the benefit of others, so that even if all except one person had attained awakening he or she would not abandon that one for the sake of personal peace until that one too had 'crossed to the other shore'.

Changing Perspectives in the Western Understanding of Consciousness

Awareness and Intentionality

Most Western thinkers regard consciousness as the pre-eminent property of discrete individuals able to distinguish self from others in order to plan and execute reasoned actions. Western attitudes have largely precluded the development of meditative practices and of phenomenalistic philosophy based on the subjective empiricism inherent in the Eastern view (Crook, 1980, also Chapter 1 in this book). Explorations of experience in Western phenomenology and existentialism have remained largely at the level of introspection, and show little awareness of the states of mind discussed in Buddhist philosophy. Recent developments in Western psychology, however, have begun to focus on perspectives which, in examining mental functions more in terms of process than as elements of personal construction, show similarities to the Buddhist analysis.

Traditionally, Western psychologists have associated consciousness with the human capacity for language, speech and thought and argued that conscious events are processed by the language system of the left hemisphere of the brain. The discovery of two modes of consciousness, appositional and propositional, has, however, led to a new appraisal. Watzlawack (1978), for example, argues that we are now led to assume that we have two modes of awareness capable of harmonious and complementary integration, while functioning in ways which under stress can become either split from one another or unbalanced. The mutual functioning of the two modes has a global capacity with respect to personal experience, and consciousness is no longer considered to be associated only with verbal activity (Baars, 1983; Dennett, 1978).

The historical origin of consciousness has also been examined recently within the evolutionary perspectives of cognitive ethology. A distinctive development is to perceive *both* consciousness and intellect as co-emergent properties of the human species consequent upon the natural selection of more socially effective individual performances (in terms of survival and reproduction) within highly complex societies (Humphrey, 1975, 1983; Crook, 1980). As I have argued elsewhere (1983), a range of types of awareness with differing functions may be present in advanced animals as aspects of their ecological adaptations, social complexity and ways of life. From research into their cognitive capacities, an implicit awareness of self is suggested for some birds and mammals, but explicit and meta-cognitive awareness of self as the agent of action may well be limited to animals with language or protolinguistic abilities – namely man and chimpanzee (for further discussion see Griffin, 1980).

Psychologists concerned with human social interaction and communication have, however, often been impressed by the extent to which complex activity can occur without conscious awareness. William James noted that 'actions originally prompted by conscious intelligence may grow so automatic by dint of habit as to be apparently unconsciously performed'. Langer (1978) claims that a very large proportion of communicative behaviours are performed 'mindlessly' – that is to say without awareness, that this appears particularly true of 'scripted' behaviours – those for which conventional forms have been prescribed. There is, moreover, considerable evidence that people are often unaware of their conversational goals (Berger and Kellerman, 1983) and this, together with other studies (see Buck, 1984; Hample, 1986), suggests that social performances often take place with little involvement of higher cognitive reflection (Nisbett and Wilson, 1977). A number of Western thinkers have argued, moreover, that consciousness is merely epiphenomenal, an incidental by-product of brain activity, and that being conscious is indeed sometimes an impediment to action. Jaynes (1976), for example, concludes that conscious awareness is not essential for learning, thinking, logical reasoning or conceptual appreciation. It becomes necessary therefore to delineate clearly the function of conscious awareness on a basis of the contexts of its occurrence.

Baars (1983) lists a number of functions that are accompanied by conscious awareness. These include: formulating intentions and projects; control of project execution; observation of consistency between intentions and actions; checking the outcome of projected action; context-sensitive behaviour adjustment; restructuring unconscious conflicts; access to unconscious motivation; and responses to novelty. While several scholars agree that consciousness is only relevant where new learning is being attempted – the information becoming scripted and used automatically thereafter, others have pointed out that it appears to be present in most responses to novelty, suggesting a link with the arousal elicited together with the orientating reflex. Communicative competence may often develop through a series of stages in which errors are corrected through the application of focused awareness prior to the development of highly skilled but relatively mindless social performances. All these suggestions, and others like them, support the view that conscious awareness is normally present when an individual is being called upon to adjust to a situation arising in his world in a way that requires him to monitor the effect his behaviour is having. While such a context is clearly present in situations of novelty or new learning, psychologists seem to have underrated the need for continuous adjustment in an individual's perception of the world.

Recent research into goal-directed action, furthermore, seems to restate the central position of consciousness. The behaviour of humans is characteristically goal-orientated, verbally reportable and therefore conscious, planned and purposeful within highly diverse social contexts. Such action is furthermore both interactive and intersubjective, and highly susceptible to mutual negotiation based on the empathic sharing of meanings. Mario von Cranach and his co-workers (1982) argue that cognitions become conscious through attention, and that conscious cognitions form an 'information processing system which for certain tasks is superior and superordinate to other systems of comparable functions' (p. 78). Conscious cognition also involves the emotive expression of experienced states and motivation. An actor is considered to be conscious of goal, plan and intention when he is subjectively aware of them and can report this awareness to another. Consciousness is thus especially likely to be associated with needs for intersubjective communication. Since attention is what moves cognition into awareness, the limits to attention span, its voluntary and involuntary control, become central to a comprehension of conscious action. Attention is directed towards conditions that require 'steps and levels of organisation which meet specific difficulties (for example resolutions, evaluations and decisions, etc.)' (von Cranach, 1982).

In my view, consciousness arises together with the process of monitoring for personal adjustment. Such a view would account for the continuous character of the 'stream of consciousness', and its especial intensity in problematic social situations.

The means whereby individuals adjust to their world is through constructing representations of it. Craik (1952) pointed out that this was perhaps the prime function of the brain. The sum of such representations amounts to a model of reality – or more strictly it is the only reality which the subject can actually know. It constitutes his world, and its relation to some external actuality must always be debatable. Representational systems depend upon feedback that allows the organism to compare the outcomes of its actions with those predicted when action was initiated. Monitoring detects discrepancies between expectation and outcome and allows for the incorporation of new information into the model so that the representational system remains updated and stable. It is the temporal continuity of this process that is felt by the subject as 'experience', and this awareness constitutes the subjective basis (ontology) of phenomenal sensing. It is a trick of language that makes us speak of experience as an objective property of information processing. Where such processing engages an issue, it is in itself what consciousness is.

Susan Blackmore (1982, 1984, also Chapter 5) points out that models of reality can become defective through lack of information or through distortions of information. They then become ineffective representations of whatever is 'out there'. A belief in reality requires a stable base so that under such circumstances the mind seeks to recreate one. Blackmore argues that when the brain is disturbed by drugs, illness, emotional imbalance or death it seeks to maintain stability by drawing on memory to replace distorted representations. Under certain conditions, such as dreaming or out of body experience, reality may become attributed to representations based more on recall than on current input. The resulting assembly may often produce bizarre experiential effects.

The processes of reality creation we have been discussing are based in three related processes. First of all there is the basic intentionality (Dennett, 1978) of the monitoring process – the 'aboutness' of experience in its most general sense. The modelling is 'on about' the maintenance of its own stability. This continuous streaming of experience is a basic sort of awareness unfocused on specific objectives. This is not so much what it is like to *be* a mental model (Chapter 5) but what it is like to be *continually creating* one. Secondly, as moment-to-moment deflections from expectation (a dripping tap starting up in a still room, an unintended conversational reference uncomplementary to oneself, a sudden alarming situation) arise, so the mismatch between input and projection leads to a sharp focusing of at-tention. Thirdly, this focused conscious state of experience is often accompanied by a deliberate attempt to make sense of a situation – that is, to fit it logically (Hample, 1986) into a conceptually structured view of reality – one which in the human species is linguistically determined so that it can be referred to in communication with another person.

A fascinating feature of this triple process – Intentionality, Attention and Conceptually constructed reality (Figure 8.2) – is its formal similarity to the model of mind basic to the Vijnanavadan perspective in Buddhism, the prime philosophical basis of Zen (Figure 8.1) which we discussed above. Where now does this similarity lead us? What does it tell us about the nature of experience? To go into this question requires us to examine the way in which human beings attribute meaning to their models of the 'real'.

Meaning, Attribution and Consciousness

Perhaps the most vital characteristic of the human mind is its constant quest for meaning. Meaning is given socially, for the human being's conception of reality is derived through interactions primarily with others and only secondly with the natural world. Social meaning arises in the following of cultural rules which in simple societies are the means whereby a people maintain themselves in their ecology. To act in accordance with culturally prescribed interpretations of reality is thus to live a meaningful life, and this is maintained by monitoring one's performance for correctness as an agent of behaviour (Harré and Secord, 1972). To step beyond those rules or to experience a revelation of 'reality' other than that culturally prescribed, is to go outside the 'sacred canopy' of the culture, to know the 'chaos' of the outsider (Berger, 1967). Since 'chaos' is inevitably cropping up from time to time due to the arbitrary nature of convention, individuals may experience both a fear of deviance and a personal constriction due to the societal requirement for conformity.

One consequence of attributing meaning to action in accordance with culturally prescribed rules is the creation of value. Values become the conditioners of motivation and may assume superordinate control over goal-directed action (Chapter 3). If, however, individual behaviour was based merely upon the norms of cultural contexts and needs for conformity, it is clear that in hierarchical social structures many individuals would soon fall prey to exploitation by others whose values enabled them to assume the rights of mastery. We may suppose therefore that individuals should resist exploitation were it to entail lowered survival and reproductive success. In my view, Vine (1986) rightly supposes that, from an evolutionary perspective, the primordial processes of self-esteem are likely to centre around the performance of strategies which, directly or indirectly lead to at least the maintenance of family welfare, reproductive success and hence genetic fitness. Values for action thus seem highly likely to be constructed ultimately in relation to the basically biological goals of individuals which, within stratified societies, may generate conflict between factions with divergent sources of personal esteem (see Tajfel, 1978). Indeed, research into complex pre-industrial societies suggests that their inherent dynamics do arise in relation to competitive action ultimately focused on family and individual economic success which is usually also indicative of reproductive potential (Chagnon and Irons, 1979; Dickemann, 1979; Crook and Crook, 1987; Crook, 1989).

In summary, therefore, human 'being' consists in monitoring incoming experience for events that are discordant with a current model of reality based upon past experience. I have argued that,

CONCEPTUAL WORLD

The conceptually constructed and logically discrimin-
ated world of events and things to which reality is
explicitly attributed.

ATTENTION

Match-Mismatch detection identifies an Issue – leading to attention being focused on it.

INTENTIONALITY

The maintenance of a representational picture of
'reality' through a fed-forward expectancy of attributed
perceptual/conceptual norms. This is the "streaming
of consciousness".

Figure 8.2 The threefold process of reality attribution: a simple diagram for comparison with Figure 8.1.

104 Space in Mind

in both the Vijnanavadin view and in that of the contemporary psychology of consciousness, a threefold process relating implicit background knowledge, attention and conceptually constructed understanding is engaged whenever someone actively apprehends the world. Yet the meaning given to this apprehended world is not an aspect of the universal process; rather it is determined by the sociobiological and cultural setting into which an individual is born. Furthermore, this setting provides the values against which the individual assesses his own performance and that of others, as desirable, good or bad. If an individual assesses personal performance negatively, the result will be socially induced anxiety due to a lowering of the person's self-esteem. The person is then likely to work to improve this esteem through action in the world of a highly self-conscious kind. It is precisely this unending worry about self-assessment that is a prime cause of *dukkha* – uneasiness or mental suffering in human societies.

William James called the objectified self which is the target of this evaluation the 'Me', and contrasted it with the ongoing awareness of existence – the 'I'. Duval and Wicklund (1972) discuss this distinction in terms of an Objective Self Consciousness (OSC), in which the self is taken as an object, and a Subjective Self Consciousness (SSC) wherein the subject focuses upon an ongoing activity irrespective of the fact of personal agency. OSC operates primarily in a comparative mode – it is socially referred. Comparison raises issues of self-esteem and initiates concern with a personal position on some scale of socially held value. Commonly, OSC is accompanied by a mild negative affect or even anxiety, whereas SSC lacks this characteristic and is often accompanied by an absence of stress. Csikzentmihalyi (1975) discusses the difficulty self-regarding or self-conscious people may have in releasing themselves into the 'flow' of dance, rock–climbing, a sport or a skilled task. Here 'flow' is an aspect of SSC, and of its relative lack of concern with social norms (Crook, 1980, p. 321). It looks then as if a way out of suffering depends upon how one manages experiences of the objectified self. (See also Chapter 11.)

One way of looking at the personal changes that develop within the dis-identification occurring in a Zen *Sesshin* is therefore to argue that these are the expressions of a progressive release from states of OSC characterised by concern over social issues. The release is in the direction of SSC and accompanied by a shift towards a loss of concern with self-justification, an increasing relaxation into flowing with one's process as it occurs, and a relaxation which eventually leads to an empathy with others in intersubjective disclosure.

Modelling States of Experience and the Practice of Training

In attempting to understand this process more clearly, I have argued elsewhere (1987a, b) that subjective experiencing can be usefully envisaged in terms of placing moment-to-moment awareness anywhere on a circular surface defined by two crossed dimensions (Figure 8.3). In this simple model the first of these dimensions defines experience that ranges from being highly intentional (having a purpose or goal in mind) to being highly attentional (focused on here and now experience without goal orientation). The second dimension expresses experience that at one extreme is totally concerned with environment (Extension) and, at the other, focused on interior awareness (Intension). When these two dimensions are crossed, we can define any locus on the surface so formed in terms of degrees of Intention–Attention and Extension–Intension. Broadly described, four quadrants arise:

Top Left: Subject-related thought.
Top Right: Object-related thought.
Bottom Right: Situational awareness.
Bottom Left: Inner state awareness.

The vertical dimension calls for further comment, for it will be clear that high levels of attention often accompany goal-orientated thought and action. What is implied here is, however, the relative degree to which the subject is orientated towards a desirable situation in future time (Intention-expectation, etc.) or, conversely, towards the quality of ongoing present moment experiencing, in which focus on alternative conditions is absent. The dimension defines what is essentially a difference between concern about a desirable or non-desirable state other than in the 'Now', and a non-judgemental observation of the actual passing moment.

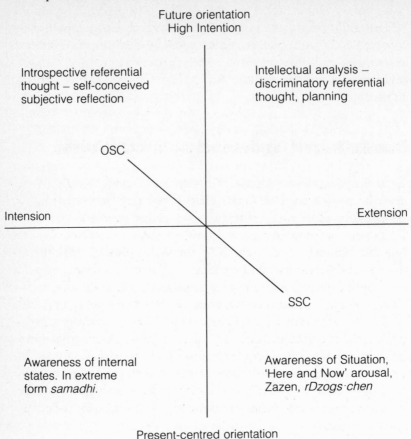

Figure 8.3 The range of states of human awareness as an interaction on three dimensions. See text for explanation. After Crook, 1987b.

During the course of any activity plottable on such a surface, the subject may or may not be consciously or unconsciously self-regarding. Thus in the top right position a subject, although explicitly or implicitly utilising self-conception as the basis for planning, may or may not be synchronously self-conscious in the sense of feeling regarded in whatever way by another. Similarly an introspecting subject (top left) may or may not feel regarded by another at the same time. It thus appears that the OSC–SSC distinction cuts across the two axes of these conditions creating a third dimension. In the bottom left and right states, the increasing loss of intentionality with heightened single-pointedness of attention suggests that the presence of this third dimension becomes weaker as the activity deepens in the downward direction. The result is thus perhaps not a geometrical sphere with three dimensions of equal potency but a shape more like a hot-air balloon.

The positioning of consciousness in top right occurs when one is actively involved in planning action in the world or reviewing past action with a view to improvements. Top left states are often highly objective self-conscious conditions which take the self and its experiences as the topic of intellectual examination and relate them to ideas of personal social effectiveness. These introspective concerns are doubtless significant in producing understanding of feelings in relation to others.

Bottom left states arise when the inward regard continues but without a focus on any problematic issue, direct attention on the inward state deepening without attendant thought processes. In meditation training such states are induced by closing the eyes and focusing attention initially on a repetitive activity which cuts out thought. After a length of time (which varies with the pressure of thoughts demanding attention) the mind settles into a relative silence which deepens into trance and finally a consciousness that has no object, known in Sanskrit as *samadhi*. This inward trance, as in Transcendental Meditation and Autogenic Training, has been found to initiate a 'deep relaxation' particularly beneficial to people prone to anxiety (review in Crook, 1980, pp. 338–51; West, 1979, 1987). Since this condition is not sleep (EEG differences confirm this), arousal from it can be virtually immediate and an unconscious monitoring of the situation seems to be present throughout – although this may vary with the depth of *samadhi*.

As the mind slips into inward meditative trance, a variety of conditions may arise in which disinhibited unconscious material from memory appears out of context, superimposing dream on a semi-alert awareness. This material may often be distorted into fantasy which, however, retains its own logic (as Freud and Jung emphasise in their respective analytical systems). As this logic works its way through, partly repressed personal issues may be resolved in symbolic form – a process also thought by some to be a key function of dreaming. Conditions of awareness on the border between top and bottom left also allow peculiarly direct empathic apperceptions of mental and physical states in others –

such apperceptions again being intuitive or 'heart–felt', rather than intellectually accountable. It is in states of awareness of this kind that the shaman, the *Hla·ba* of Ladakh for example (Brauen, 1980), can perceive the problems of his patient, and evoke a healing state through charismatic influence.

In meditation training, the practised induction of bottom right states leads to experiences in which the boundary between self and situation dissolve – in the 'headless' state (Harding, 1974) there is simply the environment within which a body sits – awareness reaches from horizon to horizon as one undivided experience, self and 'reality' appear as one. In the Tibetan practice of *rDzogs·chen* this undivided openness (unbounded-self-environment-continuum) is called *rig·pa* – a term meaning space; and indeed unlimited spaciousness is the prime quality of mental experiencing in this mode (Namkhai Norbu, 1986, see also Chapter 15 of this book).

The model implies that the stressful states induced in the upper intentional modes in the figure will be relieved by recourse to the private concerns involving low intentionality in the lower half. The system implies a periodic shift between preferred conditions. David McFarland's state space interpretations of cybernetic motivational systems (McFarland and Houston, 1981) suggest that individuals will move towards states (*sollwerten*) of optimum comfort. Even so, when endogenous need states (hunger, thirst, sex) arise, motivational deflections from a maintenance level will occur. Similar patterns of change are likely to influence the cognitive states we have been considering. The relation between states of personal rest and the demands of social action will be expressed in the periodic appearance of intentional behaviour. Self-awareness and the ability to position consciousness appropriately within these dimensions provides a trained individual with the capacity for insight needed if equanimity is to become a personal characteristic.

Conclusion

Our model of experiential states, including those induced by meditation, leads us to an understanding in Western terms of the ancient model of mind basic to Zen and other similar disciplines.

In spite of the immense gap in time and contrasts in initial perspectives, there is no fundamental contradiction between the two. Historically, it seems strange that Mahayana thought, after a long period of philosophical dynamism based on an internal critique leading to an advanced psycho-philosophy, should have fossilised into a fixed form serving merely as a basis for praxis. Excellent though this praxis has been and insightful as the philosophy remains, unless Buddhist thinkers engage today in discourse with the rapidly developing cognitive science in the West, the relevance of their practice may be inadequately perceived by non-practising thinkers and consequently undervalued or dismissed. Just as modern physics and Eastern cosmology are now engaged in fruitful discourse (see, for example, Bohm, 1980) and as Western philosophy takes up themes similar to the no-soul doctrine (*an-atta*) (Parfit, 1984, see Abe 1985 for a comparative perspective) so too can the relating of Buddhist speculation to contemporary psychology have a deepening effect on Western thought and action.

Note

1. This interview was subsequently published in Chinese in *Humanity* 37, 1986. Ta Ye Road. Lane 65–89. Peitou Taipai, Taiwan. See also Sheng-Yen, 1982.

SECTION 3

Psychological and Spiritual Development

INTRODUCTION TO SECTION 3

In Eastern Psychological thought it is axiomatic that humans are in a constant state of development, of change, from the cradle to the grave. This is in fact the teaching that lies behind *anatta*, the absence of a static, permanent self. There are parallels in Western psychology, in particular in the so-called *state-based* approach to personality. As opposed to the *trait-based* approach, state-based theorists argue that the personality, far from being a fixed quality (a set of traits), is very sensitive to the circumstances in which we find ourselves at any given moment in time. Face us with difficult and daunting circumstances, and our experience of who we are is very different from what it is when we are faced by pleasant and supportive ones. Day by day we change, dependent upon our moods, upon the way in which others treat us, upon the ideas and concepts we have about ourselves.

And yet, behind this shifting and changing flux which we call ourselves, each of us holds certain relatively constant objectives. We want to change in desirable directions. We want to experience satisfaction and escape from suffering. No matter how we may define and express these objectives, integral to them is the hope that things can be better than they are now. And this of course is the essence of personal development, at least of that part of personal development which seems to lie within the scope of our conscious will. In the present section, the authors attempt to show how Eastern psychology helps us to take charge of this development, and employ what Buddhism terms *skilful means* in order to achieve our escape towards satisfaction and away from suffering.

As the authors show, however, such an escape is not without difficulties. Chief amongst these are the twin realisations that if we would really achieve satisfaction we must firstly rethink and redefine what we mean by satisfaction, and secondly rethink and redefine what we mean by ourselves. Central to our human problem is a mistaken notion of who we are. In spite of the common experience which shows us, if we study it closely enough, that our personalities are indeed a process rather than a fixed set of qualities, and that just as we change so does life change around us, we persist in believing to the contrary. We persist in believing that we are fixed and inviolable, and that we can hang on to the experiences of life and preserve them, as if in aspic, from the challenges of change and decay and renewal.

James Low plunges us into a view of psychological development almost unthinkable to a Westerner. From the Buddhist perspective, he argues, the entire realm of human experience is pathological, dependent as it is on the working out of unresolved karmic conditioning that arose in previous times. Psychological development is therefore a process of deepening delusion, which if not radically transformed leads on into another life predicated upon the concluding muddle of the last one. James takes us through the arguments of the Nyingmapa view in Tibetan Buddhism, and leads us finally into a discussion of those processes of transformation whereby individuals can become aware of their innate Buddha nature – the basis of mind that is always present however much obscured by the karma-creating effects of ignorance.

Padmal de Silva goes on to discuss strategies of self-management advocated in Theravada Buddhism. He points out that apart from the main aim of uncovering or reaching Nirvana, there are many simple techniques provided for improving day-to-day living. These strategies are primarily behavioural, so similarities with modern behaviour therapy can be drawn. Padmal argues that on a practical level this behavioural approach is quite in keeping with the overall empiricist stance of early Buddhism.

Malcolm Walley examines the way in which the transformations in behaviour and attitude in the process of Buddhist training are conceived, and shows that these transformations can be effectively described in terms of cognitive reversals. Both da Silva and Walley thus develop themes demonstrating important parallels and similarities between the Buddhist path of transformation and two contrasting psychological approaches in the West.

Paul Thomas Sagal takes a more philosophical perspective, emphasising the therapeutic value of scepticism in Buddhist thought – especially in Zen Buddhism. He traces traditions of scepticism in both East and West, noting important similarities and contrasts. The relative absence of dogma in Buddhism, especially in Zen, allows an unusually free relationship between idea and experience, for the latter is not rigidly framed by preconditioned values. Such freedom allows us to use philosophy as a form of therapy, while psychotherapy itself provides the basis for a dynamic personal philosophy.

John Crook describes a recently created form of five-day retreat in which individuals confront themselves in the rigorous manner characteristic of Zen training. The 'Western Zen Retreat' as it is called links the practice of meditation to an exercise in which participants working in pairs share their personal experience of struggle with a paradoxical question (koan) such as 'Who am I?' 'Tell me who you are'. John discusses the retreat experience and its effect on participants; the personal clarification that results from 'dropping the question' is interpreted by him as 'dis-identification' – a letting go of those imprisoning concepts and self-attributions upon which one's identity and sense of personal worth are based. This dis-identification produces results that are not only therapeutic in the Western sense, but provide the basis from which a participant can begin Zen training in earnest.

Finally, Lyn Goswell reminds us of the need to measure our progress by looking at our personal relationships. She does this within the setting of Theravada Buddhist monasticism, looking at the motives and some of the issues faced by people who come to live together in a spiritual community. Contrary to popular belief, monasteries aren't necessarily havens of peace and light. Bringing people to live together in close but celibate communities, and under clear rules and regulations, places inevitable strains upon each individual. In the monastery, there aren't the easy avenues of escape from challenging situations that one often finds in the world outside. And the greatest lesson in tolerance you may have to learn is how to sit at meals day after day opposite a brother or sister whose nose drips or who messily slurps up the lunchtime soup.

JOHN CROOK
DAVID FONTANA

CHAPTER 9

Buddhist Developmental Psychology

JAMES LOW

Development in the Buddhist perspective

From the Buddhist perspective the entire realm of ordinary
human experience belongs to pathology. The consciousness which
perceives entities, identifies them conceptually, responds to them
emotionally and is able to recognise them again, is said to be
a malfunctioning of an innate cognitive capacity. The process
of human development from conception onwards is held to be
one of increasingly complex delusion in which the more sense
one makes of things, the further one is alienated from the true
meaning of existence. This chapter provides an account of the
Buddhist perspective on personal development as given in the
classical literature on the subject.

The Buddhist theory of Dependent Origination (Tibetan:
rTen·ching 'Brel·bar· 'Byung·ba) describes a twelve-stage process
of development for each individual life.[1] Dependent origination is
the notion that on the basis of this present moment of experience
the next moment of experience will arise. It is not suggesting a
simple linear process of cause and effect, but rather a spiral of
increasingly complex interactions. It is a dialectical progression
in which the present moment of interaction between subject and
object contains conflicts and ambiguities which are resolved or
disguised by moving to a further level of complexity.

The first stage of an individual life is that of *Ignoring*, (Tibetan:
Ma·Rig·Pa) in which the consciousness at the end of the previous
life chooses to deny the direct experience of its own noetic being
which has become available with the separation of mind and body.

This is not a conscious choice, for the force of habitual focus on 'other' makes the recognition of pure awareness without otherness very difficult. There is an impulse to ignore the gap in interaction and seek 'other' again. Such a tendency to avoid confronting that which has previously been ignored or repressed is of course also well known to Western psychotherapists.

This stage is often referred to as ignorance, as if it were a fixed state of nescience, a dull nothingness. But in Buddhism it is conceived as a process, a dynamic mode of being, which develops itself and gives rise to a range of modes of experiencing. Ignorance, or ignoring, is both something that 'just happens', and something for which one must take responsibility or 'own'. Texts dealing with Dependent Origination, such as the *Āryasālistam Sūtra*, tend to give a rather cursory discussion of ignorance, so it might be helpful to look at a three-stage model of ignoring often employed by Nyingma scholars.[2]

The first stage is called Co-emergent Ignorance (Tibetan: *lhan·chig sKyes·pa'i·rig·pa*) and is compared to falling down a flight of stairs and then being dazed and disorientated. This is a moment that occurs within the general ground of being (*gZhi*), and the surprise and pain it induces develops a sense that something is happening. The energy of shock, far from relaxing back into its own ground, tightens as a sense of something. This is pre-conceptual, pre-emotional, a moment of 'pure' energy. This energy feeds on the ground and develops into the next level of Ignorance namely Identification (Tibetan: *kun·tu·brTags·pa'i·ma·rig·pa*) in which self and other develop as named entities. Moments of experience are identified and labelled, the flow of experience developing the richness of the categories, which in turn increase the complexity of the experience as conceptual and emotional factors develop. Self and other then develop side by side and the individual comes to experience himself as an entity in a world of entities, a vast array of 'givens'. This is the third stage of ignorance where one is unaware of the Nature of Karmic Causation (*las·rGyu·'Bras·la·rMongs·pa'i·ma·Rig·Pa*). Here the individual is totally unaware that he is continuously involved in creating himself and his world, and so finds it very difficult to assume responsibility for his situation.

The power of ignoring leads to the second stage of *Assembling* (Tibetan: *'Du·Byed*) by which, out of the mass of tendencies, emotions, and potentialities accumulated by past karmic activity, the particular structures and patterns for the coming life start to manifest. The consciousness experiences this unfolding as being swept helplessly along until, if it is to take human birth, it perceives a human couple making love, desire arises and it is drawn towards the genitals and unites with the sperm and ovum in the moment of conception. If desire for the female arises along with aversion for the male, then the gender will be male. If the emotional response is the reverse, then the gender will be female.

This description of the process of assembling resembles accounts of many of the functions of the unconscious in analytical psychology. Its process is not accessible to consciousness and its impulses are difficult for consciousness to handle – indeed the rest of life is seen as a coming to terms with inner and outer realities formed largely by the assembling function. Karma is the power of past experience and unresolved issues, and generates attitudes which influence the choices developed in the coming subject – object interaction. At this stage, meaning and being are seen as hovering in an ambiguous area between the power of past experience and the possibility of present choice.[3] The instructional paths to spiritual freedom in Buddhist teachings seek to relocate meaning and being in direct, unmediated awareness of the present moment.

With conception, the third stage of *Consciousness* (Tibetan: *rNam·shes*) begins. Consciousness here means a particular self-referring cognitive capacity coming in contact with a definite context. The function of consciousness is to know, to understand, to make sense of – and it does this by utilising whatever powers it has, including attention, memory and fantasy. At this stage the context is wholly internal, being the stuff provided by the power of assembling. The particular consciousness of this new life cuts its teeth in the realm of fantasy by struggling to make sense of the past-derived contents of its own mental process. And by so doing it develops its capacity to handle complexity and ambiguity, which in turn enables it to become aware of 'other' as external. It is thus in no sense a *tabula rasa* when it turns its attention on the differentiated environment.

The fourth stage is *Identification* (Tibetan: *ming·gZugs*), in which present experience in the womb is acknowledged, identified and labelled with a private nomenclature grounded in past habits of language use. This labelling makes possible consistent identification, which engenders a sense of structure and stability.

This permits the fifth stage of *Sensory Perception* (Tibetan: *sKye mChed*) to arise. The complexity of the data reaching consciousness is increased by identification, to such an extent that it forces the differentiation of six forms of consciousness in correlation with the development of the sense organs in the embryo. The five senses each have their own consciousness, and there is a sixth consciousness which receives, organises and responds to their inputs. As the embryo develops in the womb, the influence of sensory experience increases and the past-dominated fantasy decreases in importance. The 'assembling' factors have provided a 'deep structure' of patterns and possibilities, and the rules governing their generation into manifest experience are a mixture of past-derived and context-induced factors. But it is important to remember that the context of womb and outer environments have all been 'chosen' by the assembling factors, and in a real sense mirror the condition of the experiencing consciousness. The actual nature of 'other' is not recognised, for it is always seen through the prism of the self.

At birth the sixth stage of *Contact* (Tibetan: *reg·pa*) occurs, in which the baby makes intermittent contacts with objects. This stage is held to be quite traumatic, and is depicted by the image of a man with an arrow in his eye. Contact penetrates the self and draws it into transforming interaction. It is seen as addictive, a process that once started is difficult for the conscious mind to stop. Psychologically, though not socially, no special attention is paid by Buddhist psychology to the role of the mother, and there is no stress on transitional objects in Winnicott's terms. Rather, all contact is seen as both uniting and separating subject and object, and as introducing the anxiety or suffering of impermanence and unpredictability.

Dependence upon object or 'other' is further developed by the seventh stage of *Feeling* (Tibetan: *tshor·ba*). Every moment of contact gives rise to feelings which are said to be pleasant, unpleasant or neutral. It is at this stage that conscious choice starts to be a factor in interactions, and the basic force governing this choice between possible objects of contact is said to be the universal desire to maximise pleasure and minimise suffering. Each infant has his/her own karmically derived pattern of predispositions towards experiences. On the basis of the feelings engendered by contact, the infant starts to invest the various objects of its environment with differing values of attractiveness. The fact that feeling is impermanent forces the infant to try to change the environment in order to create new possibilities for feeling – and this is why the infant seeks attention from other people.

The eighth stage, *Craving* (Tibetan: *sred·pa*), develops as the consciousness becomes habituated to contact and feeling, and so needs more and more in order to be satisfied. This is symbolised by a man getting drunk, and is often said to be like drinking salt-water. There is a yearning for distraction, to get out of the intensity and 'boredom' of the present situation by enjoying a new sensation. It is this urge that leads the child to explore the world and gather a variety of experiences – all of which develop the various faculties of consciousness, which in turn create the demand for more data, more experience.[4] The interaction of self and other is in a loop creating ever greater complexity throughout.

This gives rise to the ninth stage of *Taking* (Tibetan: *len·pa*), in which the child grows up and develops a capacity to take what it needs from life. The systems already established now manifest themselves as *needs* which the individual must seek to satisfy through work, marriage, friendship, etc. In seeking out the things that have already been established as most pleasant, each person solidifies the traits that make up their personality. Yet there is an implicit understanding in Buddhist psychology that no real or lasting happiness or satisfaction can occur within this paradigm. There is no equivalent here to Jung's individuation, and indeed the more one develops an autonomous being, the greater is one's delusion if one does not then use one's clarity of perspective to see through the whole system and then endeavour to reverse the process of experiencing the self as something real in itself.

However it is very rare for people to try autonomously to experience the transparency of the self. It is much more common to experience the tenth stage of *Becoming* (Tibetan: *srid·pa*), in which the processes and tendencies of this life build up such a powerful momentum that at the moment of death the consciousness is projected into another life still within this model of ignoring. Having ignored the opportunities afforded by the natural gaps in dualising consciousness occurring in sleep, orgasm and meditation, and being convinced that both self and other are real, there is no space to relax the powerful energies of craving for contact and feeling; for these indeed are seen as the very forces that give meaning to both life and self.

The final two stages are *Birth* (Tibetan: *sKye·ba*) and *Old Age and Death* (Tibetan: *rGas·shi*). These refer to the inevitability of another life within a cycle of ceaseless addiction to dualistic interaction.[5]

Karma

In the twelve stages we have just looked at, we have seen a gradual thickening of the psyche's arteries as layers of patterned responses deposit themselves on the open potential of being. One term which sums up this process is karma, and it might be helpful to look briefly at its dynamic. The Tibetan word for karma is *las·rGyu·'bras* – 'actions which are causes having consequences' – and the consequences are different from the immediate social and personal results of the action. For an action to be fully karmic, four stages are involved. The first is the *basis* (*gZhi*), the recognition of some entity, something or someone that is *there* in relation to my being *here*. Then comes *intention* (*bSam·pa*), when one responds to the object with the aim of acting towards it in some particular way. After this is the *activity itself* (*sByor*), in which one connects with the object and enacts one's intention. And finally there is *completion* (*mThar·thug*), when one sees what one has done and is happy and satisfied with the result. Thus one might see an enemy, plan to kill him, stab him to death and then be glad that one has done so. This would give rise to the full karmic consequence of murder through anger, and one would be reborn in the hells.

Now in any given incident, the karmic consequence can be stopped at any stage in the sequence. Thus, one can regret the action and so block the fourth stage, or hesitate and pull back from the act and so prevent the third. Or one can work at the second stage, and ensure that one's attitudes towards the world and other people are such that one's intentions are always positive. Working at any one of these stages is a way of coping with the world, of staying on top, but it has no power to free one from the ongoing dynamics of *samsara*, the Wheel of Becoming. That can only be accomplished by working at the first stage, and removing the *basis* for the perception of discrete entities. This stage therefore is the focus of all the Buddhist teachings on emptiness and tantric transformation.

Now it should be clear that one needs what might be described as a mature ego in order to take responsibility for the self, and start reversing the tide of karmic accumulation (see also Chapter 4). That 'mature ego' is itself a product of good karma, and in Buddhism there is a clear awareness that a lot of time and effort is required to bring about real change. The individual's capacity to make use of the teachings and meditation techniques is twofold. All beings have already within them the fully enlightened Buddha nature – that is given and is the true basis for all practice. But our relative situation is our own creation, the accumulated karmic patterns which determine our perceptions and responses.

Conclusion

This model of psychological development has many advantages. It lifts the burden of causality from childhood events and encourages a vaster perspective, giving a healthy sense of proportion to current events in adult life.[6] It also has a reversal procedure which shows how to turn the process of becoming back to and beyond the primary factor of ignoring. Unfortunately there is no space to discuss this here. The model we have examined stresses the negative aspects of dependence and relationships and certainly gives no support to theories of needs. The only real need is seen to be the need to know oneself deeply, not in terms of what one has done or is in the world, but in terms of what one is in oneself, as *being* rather than as being *this* or *that*. The model depicts the path of error, the straying into contingency where the illusion of a permanent self is maintained in the midst of constant change and adaptation.

It is an ideal system, not based on observation of case studies but on the observation by Buddha Shakyamuni of his own process. It is presented as a model which individuals can use to examine their own lives and understand the process of entrapment within which they live. It both explains how we have become what we are, and offers us the chance of realising our transpersonal, 'unborn' nature, which is permanent, autonomous and invulnerable.

Notes and References

1. The *Ārya Śālistamba Śutra* is a principle source for what follows. Tibetan and Sanskrit versions of it appear in Adyar Library Series, No. 76 (Theosophical Society, Adyar, India, 1950). I also rely on the *Mahāyāna Pratītyasamutpāda Śutra* found in volume *Cha* of the *mDo·sDe* section of the *bKha·'Gyur* (Kanjur).
2. For a further discussion see 'The Concept of Mind in Buddhist Tantrism', in H. V. Guenther, *Tibetan Buddhism in Western Perspective* (Dharma Publishing, Emeryville, USA, 1977), p. 53.
3. A. K. Chatterjee in his essay on Pratītyasamutpāda in Buddhist philosophy contained in volume CVII of the Calcutta Sanskrit College Research Series, Calcutta, 1975, gives an interesting discussion of causality from the Mādhyamika and Yogācarā points of view.
4. See chapter by Hartmann, Winnicott and Jakobson, 'The Crucial Issue: System-Ego or Person-Ego', in Harry Guntrip, *Psychoanalytic Theory, Therapy and the Self* (Hogarth Press, London, 1971). Their discussion highlights the difficulties that Western psychology has with accounting for the richness of infantile consciousness.
5. A more traditional presentation of these twelve stages can be found in Piyadassi Thera, *Dependent origination*, (Buddhist Publication Society, Kandy, 1959).
6. See Frank Johnson, 'The Western Concept of Self', in Marsella, De Vos and Hsu (eds.), *Culture and Self* (Tavistock Publications, New York, 1985). Johnson offers an interesting discussion of the self in current Western thinking and demonstrates its use as an interpersonal marker rather than as an existential experience.

CHAPTER 10

Self-Management Strategies in Early Buddhism: A Behavioural Perspective

PADMAL DE SILVA

Introduction

The religious goal advocated in Buddhism is the cessation of suffering – the attainment of nirvana. The Four Noble Truths, which encompass the main teachings of Buddhism, state that suffering (*dukkha*, also translated as unsatisfactoriness) is all-pervasive; that this suffering has a cause, which is desire or craving; that this suffering can be ended; and that there is a way in which this cessation can be brought about. Thus, striving for the eventual cessation of the cycle of suffering takes pride of place in Buddhism. As part of one's preparation for the task of achieving this ultimate goal, considerable behaviour changes – in the form of eliminating undesirable behaviours and developing desirable ones – are considered necessary; so are attitudinal changes (see Katz, 1982). The whole endeavour consists of the systematic and gradual transformation and development of the person, the culmination of which is the state of the *arahant* – that is, someone who has attained nirvana.

Yet the Buddha also recognised the need for, and the importance of, behaviour change in its own right. It was stressed that one should lead a life that was happy, contented, and did not harm others. Such a life, and the behaviours required for it, was considered important in its own right, irrespective of its relevance to the attainment of nirvana. For example, alcohol use was discouraged because it could lead to various demonstrable negative effects, such as quarrelsomeness, ill health, proneness to socially unacceptable behaviour, loss of wealth and eventual mental derangement (*Sigalovada Sutta, Digha Nikaya*; see de Silva, 1983).

This very clear socio-ethical standpoint provides the background to the matters discussed in this chapter. In so far as improvement in one's behaviour was considered an important goal, not only for the ultimate attainment of nirvana but also for socio-ethical reasons, it was natural that specific strategies for effecting the necessary changes were advocated and encouraged. In fact both the Buddha and his early disciples used and recommended specific strategies for behaviour change, when and where such change was deemed necessary (de Silva, 1984). The main aim of this chapter is to describe and examine a sub-class of these strategies, namely self-management techniques, and to highlight and comment on their behavioural nature.

Self-management and self-control are of particular significance in Buddhism. The Buddha repeatedly emphasised that one's emancipation lies in one's own hands. In the absence of the notion of God, Buddhism considers one's fate to be determined entirely by one's own actions. The Buddha, as teacher, can only show the way; one's task has to be accomplished by oneself. The Fourth Noble Truth, the way or path to the attainment of nirvana, is essentially a course of action to be followed, practised and cultivated by the individual. It consists of self-discipline in body, word and mind, of radical self-development. It has nothing to do with belief, devotion, prayer to a higher being, worship or ritual (cf. Rahula, 1967). The importance of managing one's own behaviour, and of self-control, is emphasised in numerous places in Buddhist texts. The following examples are from the *Dhammapada*:

> Irrigation engineers lead water where they want to. Fletchers make the arrow straight. Carpenters carve and shape the wood. Likewise, the wise ones control and discipline themselves.

> By endeavour, diligence, discipline and self-mastery, let the wise man make himself an island that no flood can overwhelm.

> One may conquer in battle a thousand men; yet the best of conquerors is the one who conquers himself.

The literature on which this discussion is based is that of early (Theravada) Buddhism. This consists of the original Canon (the three *Pitakas*, namely *Sutta*, *Vinaya* and *Abhidhamma*) in the Pali language, which was in its final written form by the first century

BC, and the early Pali commentaries on them, which were in their present form by AD 500 (Malalasekera, 1928; Webb, 1975). The later developments, including the Mahayana traditions and the various schools of Zen, are not surveyed here. It must be noted, however, that these other Buddhist traditions, especially Zen, also possess a rich and fascinating array of self-management strategies. Some of these have been commented on by other authors (see, for example, Shapiro, 1978).

Self-Management Strategies

In the following sections, a number of selected self-management strategies found in early Buddhist literature will be briefly discussed.

Self-Awareness Training

The main form of self-awareness training is mindfulness meditation (*satipatthana*), which is one of the main meditation techniques in the practice of Buddhism. In this, which is described in detail in the *Satipatthana Sutta* of the *Majjhima Nikaya* and the *Mahasatipatthana Sutta* of the *Digha Nikaya*, the disciple is trained, with the help of graded exercises, to become aware, or mindful, of his body, sensations and feelings, thoughts, and mental contents. The primary aim is to develop continuous and objective monitoring of one's actions and experiences. For example, one is trained to become aware of one's breathing, and of one's postures. This total awareness of one's own actions and experiences has a clear role in one's attempts at self-control and self-management. It is claimed to lead to physical and mental calm, and to an enhanced ability to control one's responses. In addition to its role in contributing to the self-development that is needed for the aim of achieving the *arahant* state, it is also recommended, in the texts, for many day-to-day purposes: for example, as a means of achieving peaceful and trouble-free sleep. It is also claimed that it helps one to develop objectivity in one's perceptions and clarity of comprehension, and to enable one to free oneself from dogmatic beliefs and theories (see Nyanaponika Thera, 1962; Sole-Leris, 1986).

Anger Control and the Development of Loving Kindness

The virtues of controlling aggressive feelings and, conversely, of developing loving kindness (*mettá*) are extolled in early Buddhism. In the *Visuddhimagga*, an early authoritative expository text by Buddhaghosa, one is advised on how best to set about developing loving kindness towards all. The meditative exercises recommended for this embody a hierarchical approach: one is advised to begin with oneself as the target, the easiest stimulus for this purpose, and then gradually progress outwards – cultivating, in succession, thoughts of loving kindness towards:

1. someone liked and admired;
2. a companion;
3. a person towards whom one's feelings are neutral;
4. a disliked person or enemy; and, finally,
5. all living beings.

Control of Pain

It is acknowledged in the early Buddhist texts that at least some pain control can be achieved by psychological techniques. There are instances, recorded in the *Samyutta Nikaya*, in which someone in considerable pain is advised to engage in mindfulness meditation as a means of alleviating it. For example, the venerable Ananda, the Buddha's personal assistant, once went to see a sick householder named Sirivaddha in the city of Rajagaha. Learning from the patient that he was in much pain, and that the pains were increasing, Ananda counselled him to engage in the meditation of mindfulness. A similar episode is recorded with reference to another householder, Manadinna; Ananda once again offered the same advice. Likewise, it is recorded that the Buddha himself visited two ailing monks, Moggallana and Kassapa, who were in pain, and advised each of them to engage in mindfulness meditation. Perhaps the most impressive, and most explicit in terms of the rationale for this use of meditation, is the account given of the venerable Anuruddha. He was sick, and was grievously afflicted. Many monks who visited him, finding him calm and relaxed, asked him how his 'painful sensations made no impact on his mind'. He replied, 'It is because I dwell with my mind well grounded in mindfulness. This is why the painful sensations that come upon me make no impression on my mind.'

The view embodied here is not an isolated or incidental one. It is clear from the *Samyutta Nikaya* that this is in fact the Buddhist view of pain. There is an important section of the text that gives a clear expository account which highlights this. It is worth quoting from this:

> The untrained layman, when touched by painful bodily feelings, weeps and grieves and laments . . . and is distraught . . . But the well-trained disciple, when touched by painful bodily feelings, will not weep, not grieve, nor lament . . . nor will he be distraught . . . The layman, when touched by painful bodily feelings, weeps, etc. He experiences two kinds of feeling: a bodily one and a mental one. It is as if a man is hit by one arrow, and then by a second arrow; he feels the pain of two arrows. So it is with the untrained layman; when touched by a painful bodily feeling, he experiences two kinds of feeling, a bodily one and a mental one. But the well-trained disciple, when touched by a painful bodily feeling, weeps not, etc. He feels only one kind of feeling: a bodily one, not a mental one. It is as if a man is hit by one arrow, but not by a second arrow; he feels the pain of one arrow only. So it is with the well-trained disciple; when touched by a painful bodily feeling, he . . . feels but one feeling, bodily pain only.

The view of pain contained in this expository account is clear: physical pain sensations are usually accompanied by psychological correlates, which is like a second pain. The disciple who is trained (in mindfulness meditation), however, sees the physical sensation as it is, and does not allow himself to be affected by psychological elaboration of pain. Thus his experience is limited to the perception of the physical sensation only. It is this account of pain that provides the rationale for the instances cited above, where those in pain are advised to engage in mindfulness meditation.

Stimulus Control

It is recognised that when a particular unwanted behaviour is dependent on the presence of an identifiable stimulus, that behaviour may be eliminated by getting rid of the stimulus in question. A case is cited, in the *Dhammapada Commentary*, of a monk by the name of Kuddala who kept returning to a lay life on account of his attachment to certain material belongings – a pint-pot of seed beans and a spade. In the end, after seven such returnings spanning a period of seven years, he was determined to break this attachment to lay life, so he threw away the items in question. He did not leave monkhood ever again. There are other similar cases in the texts.

Control of Unwanted, Intrusive Cognitions

Intrusive cognitions are regarded as a major problem, especially as they could interfere with and frustrate one's meditative efforts. Early Buddhist texts offer very specific techniques for the control and elimination of these. In one discourse, the *Vitakkasanthana Sutta* of the *Majjhima Nikaya*, which is addressed exclusively to this matter, a package of techniques is recommended, which is hierarchically organised. Five different techniques are suggested, each one to be tried if the preceding one fails to achieve the desired results. These are further elaborated in *Papancasudani*, the commentary to the *Majjhima Nikaya*. The techniques are:

1. switch to an incompatible and opposite thought;
2. ponder on harmful consequences;
3. ignore the cognition and distract oneself;
4. reflect on removal of causes; and,
5. control with forceful effort.

A different, sixth, method is suggested in the *Satipatthana Sutta*, in which one simply concentrates on the intrusive thought, with no effort to get rid of it. The thought is then said to lose its potency and even disappear (see Chapter 15).

A Behavioural Perspective

The self-control and self-management strategies outlined above may be seen as primarily behavioural in nature. The aim of each is a specific behavioural change, and the steps recommended or used are specific, well-defined behaviours. Even though the descriptions are at times given in mentalistic language, as is the case with some of the methods for the control of intrusive cognitions noted above, the required responses are essentially clearly defined behavioural ones. This is an important observation to make, as often Buddhism has been seen as similar to and comparable with insight-orientated and dynamic psychology, and as very different from the modern behavioural views of behaviour and behaviour change. In fact, there is a great deal in Early Buddhism that is akin to the behavioural position and, more specifically, to behaviour modification as practised today. This has been highlighted recently by both Mikulas (1978, 1981) and de Silva (1984, 1985). Given that the Buddha acknowledged the need for specific changes of behaviour when and where required, often in their own right, it is not surprising that specific and practicable techniques were used and advocated to achieve these changes. Some of the well-established modern behaviour-therapeutic techniques such as modelling, fear reduction by graded exposure, social skills training, including behavioural rehearsal, aversion and the systematic use of rewards, and some cognitive-behavioural methods, are reported in the early Buddhist literature to have been used over two millennia ago (for a fuller discussion, see de Silva, 1984). The self-management strategies discussed in this chapter likewise bear striking resemblance to some of the techniques in modern behaviour therapy.

For example, the value of self-monitoring is fully acknowledged in present-day behaviour modification as a way of achieving greater control over one's own behaviour, very much in the way that mindfulness training is claimed to achieve similar results (Mikulas, 1986; Thoresen and Mahoney, 1974). To quote Kazdin (1978, p. 333): 'Control over behaviour can be enhanced by observing one's own conduct.' Similarly, the hierarchical approach to the development of loving kindness closely resembles the graded-hierarchy approach of Wolpe's anxiety-reduction methods and their successors (Wolpe, 1958). The assumption is that this finely graded, step-by-step approach ensures the gradual establishment of the desired response, without it being disrupted by counter-responses of a high intensity at each point. One attempts each stage only after the previous, less difficult, one has been mastered. It is interesting to note that the anger control methods recently developed within behaviour therapy also include this approach.

The cognitive-behavioural techniques of pain-control in today's behavioural medicine may also be compared with the early Buddhist approach to pain noted above. Indeed a recently published research paper actually reports the use of mindfulness meditation for the self-regulation of chronic pain (Kabat-Zinn, Lipworth and Burney, 1985). The rationale given for the use of this meditative technique in this context is in fact not very different from that implied in the Buddhist texts. Kabat-Zinn (1982) states that training in mindfulness meditation can enable one to focus on sensations as they arise, rather than attempt to escape from them. It helps one to recognise the bare physical sensations, unembellished by psychological elaboration. These psychological aspects one learns to observe as separate events, and this 'uncoupling' of the physical from the psychological has the effect of changing one's overall experience of pain. To quote, 'The nociceptive signals (sensory) may be undiminished, but the emotional and cognitive component of the pain experience, the hurt, the suffering, are reduced' (Kabat-Zinn, 1982, p. 35). It should be clear how close this view is to the account of pain and its control by mindfulness meditation provided in the *Samyutta Nikaya*, noted above.

If this is a relatively new development, then stimulus control as a way of behaviour change has, by contrast, been fully recognised in modern behaviour therapy for some time and is very widely used (cf. Mikulas, 1983a). Finally, the Buddhist strategies for the control of unwanted, intrusive cognitions include most of the strategies that have been used by practitioners of behaviour modification for similar problems, especially obsessions. The Buddhist techniques noted above include ones clearly similar to the current techniques of thought-stopping, thought-switching, satiation/habituation training, and distraction (cf. Marks, 1981; Rachman and Hodgson, 1980; Wolpe, 1958). They also include techniques similar to other well-established behavioural strategies which are normally used for other behavioural problems. For example 'ponder on harmful consequences' resembles the covert sensitisation technique of Cautela (1967), and 'switch to an opposite and incompatible thought' is similar in some ways to the habit reversal of Azrin and Nunn (1973). A more detailed comparison of these early Buddhist strategies with developments in modern clinical practice is available in de Silva (1985).

Discussion

The main significance in the present context of these remarkable similarities between early Buddhist and modern behaviour-therapeutic strategies for self-management is not so much that Buddhism seems to have anticipated some aspects of behaviour therapy by over two thousand years, as the fact that they highlight the essentially behavioural nature of these Buddhist techniques. The techniques embody attempts to alter target behaviours directly – that is, at a behavioural level, as against indirectly via other avenues. Along with the specificity of the target response, and that of the steps to be taken, this directness of the approach makes them fall very much within the realm of behavioural methods (cf. Wolpe, 1958). This aspect of Buddhism has often been neglected, but needs to be given full recognition. It does not, of course, mean that early Buddhism relies solely on such methods for behaviour change. Indeed much change is, it is claimed, achieved by developing insight, which is mainly the product of prolonged self-training and insight-orientated meditation. For example, when one reaches the *arahant* state, fundamental behaviour changes follow naturally (see Katz, 1982). Yet at the level of many day-to-day behaviours, when and where changes were deemed necessary, the Buddha and his early disciples used and recommended direct behavioural methods. As noted above, the self-management strategies that have been the subject of this paper are only a part of a large repertoire of behaviour modification techniques found in early Buddhism. In the context of the overall empiricist/realist standpoint of early Buddhism, as expounded in the *Kalama Sutta* of the *Anguttara Nikaya* and several other discourses, the use and advocacy of such behavioural techniques is not surprising. What was needed, when a target behaviour had to be modified, was a technique that was well-defined, easy to use and demonstrably effective. The fact that Buddhism relies on other methods to bring about the more fundamental changes, such as the total elimination of lust and of all forms of aggression, should not detract from the considerable contribution that these behavioural self-management techniques were acknowledged to make.

Finally, a brief comment is in order on the relevance of the study of these Buddhist strategies to the practice of psychological therapy today. Apart from the obvious historical interest, it can be argued that there are several ways in which such study has clear practical relevance. Firstly, those self-management and other strategies found in Buddhism which have no modern counterparts so far can be clinically and experimentally tested; and, if shown to be useful for the purposes they are claimed to serve, may fruitfully be incorporated into the practice of therapy and counselling. Secondly, it can be assumed that the acceptance of, and compliance with, modern therapeutic strategies by Buddhist client groups will be enhanced if it is shown that they are similar to techniques found in Buddhism. In fact there is some evidence on this point already (cf. de Silva and Samarasinghe, 1985; Mikulas, 1983b). And thirdly, it is possible that some of the Buddhist techniques, geared as they are towards modification of one's response patterns and thus towards personal development, will prove useful as prophylactic measures aimed at reducing various forms of psychological dysfunction. This is very much in line with a recent move towards preventive psychology, one example of which is Meichenbaum's 'stress inoculation training' (Meichenbaum, 1985). If these strategies help to enhance one's equanimity and tolerance of stress, and thus reduce one's vulnerability to anxiety, depression and other stress reactions, then they have a positive contribution to make to the prevention of psychological disorders.

Acknowledgement

The author wishes to thank the Leverhulme Trust for a research award supporting his work on early Buddhist concepts and strategies of behaviour change.

CHAPTER 11

Tibetan Buddhist Mind-Training

MALCOLM WALLEY

Introduction

At the heart of the Tibetan Buddhist system of *lojong* or mind-training, which is aimed at developing the altruistic mind of enlightenment or *bodhicitta* (the motivation to strive for enlightenment for the benefit of all beings and the removal of all suffering), is the transformation of personal construct systems. Such transformations are radical to the extent that habitual patterns of construing the world are actually reversed, as when for example others take on greater significance than self, or when adverse experiences become welcome opportunities to practise patience or develop loving kindness. Through such reversals, the direct perception of self and of phenomena becomes radically transformed, and the removal of all psychological suffering becomes an attainable goal.

The Nature of Tibetan Buddhist Mind-Training

This emphasis upon cognitive reversals, together with the development of a sophisticated system of techniques designed to bring them about in sufficiently motivated individuals, gives Tibetan Buddhist mind-training its particular flavour. The experience of people past and present who have practised these reversals are indicators of our potential for personal change, and endorse the saying of the *Dhammapada* that:

> We are what we think.
> All that we are arises with our thoughts,
> With our thoughts we make the world.

The mind-training tradition can be distinguished from less conceptual forms of Buddhist psychological development such as vipassana or samatha meditation, and the account that follows is based primarily upon teachings received from Geshe Kelsang Gyatso and other eminent Tibetan lamas over a period of several years. Valuable firsthand accounts of these teachings are available, for example by Geshe Gyatso in his commentary upon Shantideva's ninth-century *Bodhisattvacharyvatera* ('A Guide to the Bodhisattva's Way of Life' – see Gyatso, 1986), and by Geshe Langri Thangpa (see Gyatso, 1984).

The historical origins of the Tibetan system lie within classical Indian Buddhism, and the theoretical basis of mind-training is the view that the root cause of human unhappiness and dissatisfaction is self-grasping, with personal well-being directly bound to the fluctuating fortunes of a strongly felt sense of 'self' or 'I'. In Buddhist psychology, self-grasping is essentially an ignorant view in that it derives from a completely mistaken perception of the actual nature of the self and of phenomena in general. From this mistaken belief in a solid and fixed self arises the attitude of self-cherishing which strives to protect and sustain this fictitious entity. The extent to which the individual becomes bound up in this impossible task renders him vulnerable to the negative and positive constructions imputed upon experience.

Western therapies, for example Beck's cognitive behaviour therapy, the rational emotive therapy of Ellis, and Kelly's personal construct therapy, seek to modify personal construing in order to improve psychological well-being to an acceptable level. Buddhist mind-training by contrast has as its central aim the complete removal of *all* suffering, irrespective of our present level of contentment.

Procedure in Mind-Training

The following 'Eight Verses of Mind-Training', given here in the translation used by H. H. the Dalai Lama during his 1981 tour of Europe and the USA, are by Geshe Langri Thangpa, and form an important and widely used traditional Tibetan work.

With the determination to attain the highest goal, for the benefit of all sentient being, which surpasses even the wish-fulfilling gem, may I hold these dear at all times.

Whenever I associate with others I will regard myself as the lowest among all, and hold others most dear, from the very depths of my heart.

In all actions may I search into my mind, and as soon as an afflicted emotion arises endangering myself and others – may I firmly face it and avert it.

When I see beings of unpleasant and unfortunate character, oppressed by very strong negativity and afflictions, may I hold them dear – as though chancing upon a precious treasure.

When others, out of envy, treat me badly with abuse, slander or scorn, may I take the defeat upon myself, and offer the victory to others.

When someone whom I have benefited hurts me unexpectedly and very badly, may I regard him as my very best teacher.

In short, may I offer benefit and happiness to all my mothers, both directly and indirectly. May I secretly take upon myself the misfortune and suffering of these mothers.

May all this remain undefiled by the stains of the Eight Worldly Concerns and may I, recognising all phenomena as illusory, without any attachment, be released from bondage.

Geshe Langri Thangpa's rendering of even earlier traditional advice, along with Shantideva's *Bodhisattvacharyvatara*, have formed the basis for the training of Tibetan monks, nuns and lay people (particularly those of the several schools of thought descended from the Khadampa tradition) for several hundred years. Experienced and accomplished teachers have always elucidated for their students the brief instructions contained in these texts through discourses and personal guidance, and this practice continues to the present day. During the mind-training, the practitioner (particularly within the Gelugpa tradition), engages in debate, analysis and meditation which together tackle personal attitudes and assumptions about the status and adequacy of his world view, again with the overriding motivation to obtain complete relief from psychological suffering.

'Debate' sometimes sounds to Westerners a rather abstract and theoretical exercise, but in practice, although it is a highly rigorous and ritualised activity requiring a thorough grounding in logic, the intention behind it is for the individual to gain an intuitive, heartfelt realisation of the issues being tackled rather than a simple conceptual understanding of them. This realisation is at all times supported by concentrated analytical meditation on such things as the benefits of weakening self-grasping. The novice also gains inspiration through interaction with experienced and accomplished practitioners, who demonstrate by their own lives that the goal is actually obtainable.

Debate and analysis lead to radical changes in the cognitions which the practitioner uses in relating to the world, and through the practice of meditation normal assumptions about the nature of self and of phenomena become overturned at a direct, experiential level. These themes are looked at in more detail in the two sections that follow.

Cognitive reversals in attitudes towards the self

Buddhist mind-training focuses upon two main issues, namely:

1. the attitude of self-cherishing; and
2. the existential status of the self.

Self-cherishing is held by *lojong* and *bodhisattvacharyvatara* training to be the principle root of human suffering. Kelsang Gyatso (1984, p. 268) states:

> From exalted kings down to the lowliest of insects, all beings
> are beset by their self-cherishing attitude . . . Fear, anxiety,
> dissatisfaction and suffering will arise continuously until this inner
> devil of self-cherishing is completely exorcised.

This presents a powerful diagnosis of the primary cause of mental disorder. The therapeutic strategy to be adopted is equally succinct:

> To summarise, whatever joy there is in this universe arises from
> cherishing and desiring the happiness of others.

Buddhist cognitive training has always devoted considerable attention to analysing the *consequences* of self-cherishing. Since in disputing the merits of self-cherishing Buddhist psychology stands the 'normal' mode of relating to the world on its head, a good deal of psychological resistance in this area may need to be overcome. Such resistance also has to be tackled when working with everyday neuroses, since Buddhism, as a kind of 'grand therapy', questions the effectiveness of *all* psychological modes of adaptation, irrespective of formal classification.

Specific Buddhist strategies for tackling self-cherishing are described fully in Hopkins (1983), in particular the practices of developing equanimity, exchanging self with others, and *tong len* (taking and giving). With the development of equanimity, a person discriminates less strongly between those who are positive and those who are neutral or negative towards him or her. Equanimity thus provides the ground out of which effective compassion and love can grow. Far from being a state of indifference, it allows for the full appreciation of those to whom we relate, and ensures that our reactions to everyday events become more balanced and smoother, allowing us greater psychological space within which to deal with situations.

Traditionally, the practices of equanimity, of exchanging self with others, and of *tong len* are accompanied by certain preliminary exercises aimed at wearing away distortions of reality by meditating on the nature of suffering, impermanence, causality, etc. Success is reflected in a firmer grounding in reality, together with an increasing realisation that self-cherishing and the attitudes that go with it are a waste of time, in that lasting well-being and fulfilment can never be gained by them. Buddhist theory sets no limit upon the extent to which constructs can be modified by these practices given the appropriate level of motivation and effort by the student.

The second main line of attack upon the perils of self-cherishing is thoroughly to challenge the status of the self-cherisher. This is discussed in the next section.

Cognitive Reversals in Attitudes towards Adversity

Procedures such as the above are interwoven with the second principle of construct change, namely the construing of suffering and of negative experience.

In Buddhist psychological training, the pervasiveness of suffering and adversity in the world provides the primary motivation for seeking liberation. Also, the adversity which others have to bear helps us develop compassion towards them combined with the intention to act for their welfare. It becomes possible, therefore, to nurture constructive attitudes towards negative events, with the result that commonplace responses of anxiety and aversion towards suffering are discouraged or gradually extinguished. These may then be replaced by cognitions involving an accepting or even welcoming attitude towards misfortune, since misfortune may be a way of expending negative karma, the unavoidable consequences of previous unskilful actions. As the meaning of suffering becomes transformed in this way, so the direct experience of adversity is modified, with suffering for example being perceived as light and soft in nature rather than dark and heavy.

The advice given in four, five and six of Geshe Langri Thangpa's verses quoted earlier focuses upon interpersonal relationships. In the context of the fourth verse, contact for example with others who are suffering psychologically (as for instance in a psychiatric hospital) can be seen as providing a wonderful opportunity for us to develop our skills and test out our mental training, while the prospect of meeting some really 'heavy' people can be savoured with the sort of relish an Olympic finalist has at the chance of winning a gold medal. What useful advice this is for those of us who have to work in socially demanding settings!

By contrast, verses five and six seem to contain less helpful advice, or rather advice which in the loftiness of its aspirations may be more relevant to a spiritual discipline than to a psychological one. It's useful to note this, because it helps us to see that in spite of the clear and constructive common ground between Buddhism and modern psychology, there yet remain some marked distinctions between the objectives and world views of the two. Verse eight also illustrates this point with the advice that the practitioner should 'remain undefiled by the eight worldly concerns' (gain and loss, pleasure and pain, praise and blame, fame and obscurity). Remaining 'undefiled' in this way is clearly a major undertaking for the modern Westerner, and one not typically emphasised in the Western literature on personality and psychotherapy!

However, in spite of the above, it is nevertheless helpful to nurture states of mind which are more resilient to the negative responses of others. Somewhat paradoxically, this can be accomplished by maintaining attitudes of warmth towards the people making these responses, and by maintaining the equanimity which provides one with the necessary psychological space and balance.

Verse seven develops this point further by referring to taking and giving (*tong len*). In *tong len*, cognitive reversal is effected by the practice of taking on the problems, difficulties and sufferings of others. Since this is what most of us normally avoid, having enough to cope with in our own lives, *tong len* serves to test the strength of our self-cherishing. We help achieve *tong len* by allowing in our meditation the sheer immensity of the suffering of others to envelop our self-cherishing. Such a meditation releases us from the domination of this self-cherishing, and allows us to contemplate the emptiness, space and freedom that such release produces. Arising from this freedom comes the energy and capacity to benefit others, which is then utilised and reinforced with a spirit of willingness and joyfulness. Full success in the cognitive reversal associated with *tong len* is achieved when an attitude of mastery is developed over what are normally regarded as unwelcome events and general adversity in our lives.

Cognitive Reversals in the Perception of Phenomena

Since Buddhist psychological training gears much of its effort towards questioning personal assumptions about the nature of self and of phenomena, it has generated a number of philosophical schools each of which represents a level of sophistication appropriate to the psychological development of the practitioner concerned (see, for example, Claxton, 1986). In general, all Tibetan Buddhist traditions recognise the Prasangika-Madhyamikan view of Nagarjuna as the highest and most refined development of Buddhist philosophical thought. In terms of this view, the worldly cognitions to be challenged and eventually reversed are that self and all phenomena exist validly *as they appear* – in other words, that they are self-existent. Geshe Langri Thangpa articulates this challenge in the last of his *Eight Verses of Mind-Training* when he says that all phenomena are to be regarded 'like illusions'.

Buddhist mind-training therefore often begins with an appreciation of the fundamental fact that all phenomena are changing, are in flux. Nothing is permanent or fixed. It thus emphasises that our lived reality does *not* consist of static and unyielding features, a realisation that is particularly relevant to the sense of helplessness over one's predicament that we encounter, say, in depression.

Buddhism regards this realisation of impermanence as a subtle and advanced form of perception. The gross perception of im-permanence may be appreciated fairly readily within a modern scientific discussion supported by natural observation, but the direct and personal realisation of subtle impermanence only comes after prolonged meditative practice at high levels of concentration.

The distinction made by Buddhism between gross and subtle perception reflects an important divergence from theory and practice as recognised by Western psychology and psychotherapy, and emphasises again the importance that Buddhism places upon intuitive realisation as opposed to mere intellectual understanding. Intuitive realisation represents a depth of understanding which radically alters an individual's world-view and changes the quality of his or her life. Such realisation (even though aided by the forms of debate mentioned above on the subtle aspects of reality) is achieved only after much effort, often over long periods of time. The stress placed upon it by Buddhist psychology is a function of the conviction that the mind is the principal organ of knowing and the direct source of information about the nature of reality. As there are no theoretical limits to the mind's capacity to know, advanced practitioners are considered able to perceive levels of subtlety about natural phenomenon which modern science can attain only by means of sophisticated scientific instruments.

The Buddhist world-view also places great emphasis upon the concept of 'interdependence'. As with impermanence, there are various degrees of subtlety and sophistication to this concept. Again at one level there is intellectual understanding, which appears to equate comfortably with several areas of modern science ranging from relativity theory to ecology (H. H. the Dalai Lama has suggested that 'relativity' could be the slogan of Buddhism!). Through intuitive understanding, however, one appreciates that everything is ultimately related to everything else, and therefore must in some way be interconnected. Individual actions can thus have wide-reaching consequences, which implies that one can never be completely and permanently isolated from others (a helpful realisation perhaps for those experiencing a sense of alienation through depression or extreme anxiety).

Another concept, that of interdependence, is also employed by Buddhist psychology as one of the main logical arguments behind a belief in the absence of inherent existence in phenomena. The argument states essentially that if all phenomena are inter-dependent, then nothing can exist independently. If nothing exists independently, then nothing can be self-existent. This conclusion that all phenomena, whether people or things, are completely empty of self-existence, means that nothing substantially exists 'out there', independently of the perceiver. This reasoning is part of the Madhyamikan-Prasangika view that no-thing can exist except via the process of conceptual imputation.

At another, more therapeutic level, the Madhyamikan perspective may be regarded as the ultimate development of the notion that we construct our own reality; indeed that in essence our constructs *are* our reality. This being the case, by changing our cognitions we can change the reality in which we live. Only the conceptual imputations which we make upon perceived interdependent conditions constitute our real phenomenal world. The therapeutic implications of this are that we have a tremendous capacity for psychological change.

Buddhist philosophical schools have been developed to serve the goal of gaining release from all forms of suffering. In so doing, they provide antidotes to the principal cause of suffering, namely 'ignorance'. Liberation (or Nirvana) is attainable through the gaining of knowledge. Therefore 'faith' in a particular philo-sophical school becomes a lived reality and not merely a satisfactory intellectual model which will ultimately be overturned as with models in modern Western science. The intention of Buddhist philosophy is not to try, out of arrogance or pride, to adopt the most sophisticated view, but rather to select internalise and integrate whatever view seems to us to be the most personally valid. Buddhist philosophical schools thus provide the necessary framework and support for nurturing cognitive change and psy-chological development, and the more refined and subtle the philosophical school, the greater the consequent potential for substantial cognitive shifts.

Comparisons with Some Western Psychotherapies

Increasingly, Western approaches to psychotherapy emphasise the importance of working with cognitions and perceptions in order to effect lasting and meaningful changes in behaviour. To the rational emotive therapy of Ellis (Ellis and Grieger, 1977) and to the cognitive therapy of Beck (Beck, 1976) we can add in this context Gestalt, Rogerian, and other similar therapies. Apter (for example, 1982) points out that a recurrent problem in mental disorder is the inability to 'reverse' or 'shift' from one metamotivational state to another. In the course of his discussion, Apter suggests that widely different forms of therapy are effective simply because they initiate and facilitate such reversals. In terms of Apter's *reversal theory*, reversals are primarily from the *telic* to the *paratelic* state, that is from a purposeful, goal-directed state to a non-purposeful, activity-orientated one. From the Buddhist view, an inability to reverse desirably between telic and paratelic or between any pair of contrasting states would seem to be symptomatic of the self-grasping associated with a rigid self-image.

Gestalt therapy advocates a reversal of perspective whereby one may take the role of the other through imaginal exploration. This recalls the Buddhist practice of exchanging self for others, and the practice of cherishing one's opponents. Some of these features are also to be found in Rogerian counselling, which values empathy, warmth and psychological acceptance.

Rational emotive therapy (RET) corresponds to Buddhist thought-training in a number of ways. Not only are the methods utilised similar, but the Buddhist intention to effect cognitive shifts seems also to be part of Ellis' strategy. The degree of reversal implied by RET is illustrated in Ellis' claim that 'profound philosophical change' may result from his therapy in that old beliefs may be replaced with new, and habitual emotional states may be redefined in new and more positive ways (for example, 'anxiety' may be redefined as 'stimulation'). Another similarity with Buddhism is that RET also encourages debating and disputing the effectiveness of tightly grasped cognitive modes and behavioural adaptations, thus bringing into focus the consequences of self-grasping and self-cherishing.

Similar correspondences are apparent in Beck's cognitive therapy, which emphasises the important influence of 'automatic thought' at the sub-vocal level upon psychological functioning. In cognitive therapy, observation and transformation of this automatic thought via introspection looks very like the close observation of mental processes followed as part of the meditation practices adopted in mind-training.

Certain aspects of behaviour therapy also find counterparts in Buddhist mind-training. For example role models, in the form of accomplished practitioners and teachers, are important in mind-training, as is the use of behavioural rehearsal. Desensitisation training, too, is found in Buddhism, and is often carried out during visualisation meditations, while operant conditioning incorporating self-reward strategies is also used.

Finally, the operant techniques of thought-stopping resemble in vigour Shantideva's metaphor of the guard standing at the door of the mind with a sword, ready to decapitate unwelcome intruders (delusions). The Tantric technique whereby the teacher suddenly and unexpectedly lets out a fierce shout during sitting meditation in order to deepen pupil's awareness has similar vigour. Such strategies help to keep the mind clear and free from interference, while practices involving the development of forbearance and the sustaining of love and compassion in the face of antagonisms (and which help dispel the Eight Worldly Concerns mentioned earlier) might be regarded as some ultimate form of stress inoculation, or anxiety management training.

Conclusion

This chapter has focused upon the methods used by Buddhist mind-training to effect substantial changes in personal cognitions in relation specifically to perception of self, attitudes to adversity, and perception of phenomena. The mind-training tradition developed within Tibetan Buddhism provides workers in Western psychotherapy and other helping professions with a valuable resource. Through an appreciation of these traditions – which are based upon a wealth of experience in working with psychological difficulties – psychologists may be encouraged to examine their own assumptions as to the potential which exists for modifying individual construct systems in the direction of greater psychological well-being.

CHAPTER 12

Scepticism, Zen and Eastern Psychotherapy

PAUL THOMAS SAGAL

There are major differences in outlook between West and East (together with some important similarities, as I shall attempt to show). The assumption for example that ego strength and greater rationality will lead to happiness figures strongly in the Western intellectual tradition, but in the East, under the influence of the great religious traditions of Hinduism, Buddhism and Taoism, things are seen very differently. Happiness is considered to involve peace of mind, and peace of mind is to be attained not through the ego and its rationality, but through egolessness and the cessation of thinking. With their emphasis upon peace of mind, Eastern traditions are in fact more fruitfully classified in some ways as psychotherapies than as religions, or at least as psychotherapeutic philosophies, and it is in this way that I intend to treat them in the present chapter.

Psychotherapy Western Style

Western psychotherapies differ in many important respects amongst themselves, and in order to draw my parallels and contrast between West and East I am going to concentrate not upon the Freudian view of man as driven by dark instinctual forces, but upon the more client-centred approach which sees man as rational, social, and open to appeals for co-operation (as for example in Rational Emotive Therapy, or RET (see Chapter 11)). In this form of therapy, the therapist attempts to initiate clients into becoming their own therapists, to be more rational and thus to dispute their own irrational ideas more effectively. When the therapist can put himself out of business, the client is cured. The therapy is thus both directive and argumentative, requires the client to do homework, and is an especially clear case of the therapist as educator (see, for example, Ellis, 1962).

This emphasis upon rationality means that, within this form of psychotherapy, we need not only a theory of the emotions, such as that produced by writers like Ellis, but also a theory of rationality. To date, this need has been largely sidestepped, and even if we trace back through history to the Stoic philosophers, whom I regard as the philosophical predecessors of rational therapy, we find a tendency to follow common sense and intuition, and to be dogmatic about what was rational and what was not. Epicetus, one of the founding fathers of Stoicism, clearly saw the primary task of philosophy as that of making people more rational rather than that of defining what was and was not rational.

Though the Greek Sceptics were able to show just how dogmatic and hence vulnerable Stoicism was in this area, they themselves did little better and despaired of ever finding a criterion which would neatly distinguish the rational from the irrational. Indeed, they were driven to argue that such a criterion did not exist, leaving us to grapple with the problem that if they were correct, our search for a definition of rationality to underpin our psychotherapy is doomed to failure.

If there is no criterion for distinguishing the rational from the irrational, this means we must take the word 'rational' out of such terms as Rational Emotive Therapy, and see where this leaves us. At first sight, it leaves us with Irrational Emotive Therapy, but if we can have no sure criterion for distinguishing what is rational we can have no sole criterion for distinguishing what is irrational either. So I prefer to use the term Sceptical Emotive Therapy (SET), and as I shall attempt to show in this chapter, this helps us get closer to the parallels between Western and Eastern psychotherapies, because scepticism was viewed, both among Greek Sceptics of the West and the Buddhists of the East, as constituting in itself a form of therapy.

This absence of a sure criterion for distinguishing rational from irrational thoughts or beliefs has of course profound implications for therapy, because if we can't say that it is *irrational* thoughts or beliefs that get us into trouble, what can we say? The answer is that we can say it is not the thoughts or the beliefs that get us into trouble so much as our response to these thoughts and beliefs. And we can say that in consequence we must take every one of them with the proverbial pinch of salt. We need to suspend our beliefs (*epokhe*). This suspension of belief is itself a form of cure for emotional upsets, because what prevents peace of mind (*atarakia*) is attachment to beliefs. When we are attached to our beliefs we are required to defend them, and when we have to defend them we become anxious. If we were to believe nothing, we would be invulnerable.

In Buddhism, the key belief that must be rejected is the belief in the existence of our own selves or egos. This belief and our attachment to it is the source of most of our pain and suffering. The psychologically healthy way to go through life is with egolessness, and many of the meditative and dialectical techniques in Buddhism are designed to destroy belief in the self (see Chapters 4 and 6).

This is true not only of Buddhism of course, but also of other Eastern thinkers. Krishnamurti (1973) for example teaches that the way to liberation is by abandoning thinking and believing, especially with respect to the self. Life, for Krishnamurti, should be lived with as little thinking as possible, because thinking is only useful to solve technological and practical problems. Other kinds of thinking, especially theoretical and philosophical thinking, get us into trouble since they breed attachment, and attachment breeds pain and suffering. For Krishnamurti, we should go through life in a meditative state in which we respond to the present moment, and in which we give up images, thoughts, beliefs and theories.

Sceptical Emotive Therapy of the kind advocated by Krishnamurti has proved to be the dominant psychotherapeutic approach in the East, whereas in the West the main historical link has come through Plato, Aristotle and the Stoics, and has emphasised what we have already seen is at best a very contentious distinction between rationality and irrationality (this is even true of Freud's ego psychology). The question now arises, how do we choose between a rational emotive and a sceptical emotive therapy? The question places us squarely in the lap of epistemology, the philosophical discipline which explores the nature and extent of human knowledge. The relevance of epistemology to psychotherapy was something well-known both to the Greek Sceptics and to Hindu and Buddhist thinkers, but unfortunately in the

West we seem to have either lost or forgotten the ability to take it seriously today.

Scepticism in the West

We seem also to have lost or forgotten the ability to take scepticism seriously. In the centuries since the Greek Sceptics, there has been no real attempt to apply it as a guide to life in the form either of ethics or of psychotherapy. Saint Augustine, for example, only entertained scepticism for the purposes of attempting a refutation of it, and in medieval times the dominant philosophies of Platonism and of Aristotelianism persisted in the same tradition. The latter in fact went even further and refused to entertain scepticism at all, and due to the influence of Aristotle upon Christianity, it became in consequence a heresy even to utter sceptical ideas. In particular, no one was allowed to express scepticism towards religious faith or revelation, and those who doubted human reason and experience were forced for their own safety to disguise their doubts under the cloak of an appeal to a higher certainty.

Thus Nicholas of Autrecourt, who has been called the medieval Hume and who was the closest thing to a full-blown sceptic in the Middle Ages, got into numerous difficulties with the authorities. His works were burned, and he was prevented from holding a teaching position simply for putting forward arguments along the lines that if God can do anything not logically impossible, then the future can always be different from the way we expect it to be, since God Himself can make it different. Hence there can be no knowledge with respect to the future. Causal connections cannot be known because causation involves the expectation of future connections between two events, and in the light of God's power to make things different these connections cannot be relied upon. So fiery furnaces which have always in the past caused things to burn up may not do so in the future!

Scepticism in the East

Far from acting as a barrier towards scepticism as in the West, Eastern religions have tended at least to tolerate its expression and at most (as in the case of Buddhism) actively to encourage it. The subtle consequences can be seen for example in the respective approaches in the West and the East to the problem of human anxiety. Whereas in the West anxiety is seen to be an unavoidable feature of the human condition, in the East it is seen as omnipresent but avoidable, and to be the direct consequence of ignorance. Buddhism in particular offers an explicit way towards overcoming this ignorance both at theoretical and practical levels. It does this by, to return to my earlier terminology, offering us a Sceptical Emotive Therapy, a therapy which argues that ignorance is basically the experience of thinking we know things that in reality we do not know at all.

We think we know that the world is composed of innumerable distinct individual substances, things which persist in space and time, and that among these substances the one with which we are most intimately acquainted is the individual self or ego. It is our commitment to this ego that is the cause of anxiety, pain and suffering, and we need to be persuaded to give up this commitment and the false belief which sustains it, and the way to do this is through argument and psychological disciplines (meditation, for example) which allow us actively to live the absence of the ego, not simply to accept its absence at the intellectual level.

People sometimes ask – What is Buddhism? Is it a philosophy, a religion or a psychotherapy? Earlier, I called it a 'psychotherapeutic philosophy', but in a way this is an oversimplification, because historically in the East distinctions between philosophy, religion and psychotherapy simply were not made. There are no words in Sanskrit for 'philosophy' or for 'religion' in the Western sense of these terms, and the psychotherapeutic emphasis almost always present in Eastern philosophy has tended to be soteriological (that is, concerned with the curing and saving of man's soul). Thus, in a way, all Eastern thought at this level is ethical, in the broad sense of being concerned with how human beings ought to live their lives.

Like the existentialist, the Buddhist begins with a diagnosis of the human condition. The first noble truth of Buddhism is that life is painful. The meaning of the Sanskrit work *dukkha* is not far removed from existential anxiety. For one thing, death or rebirth constantly loom before us, and neither of them is attractive. Furthermore, we seem never to be satisfied with what we get out of life. We always want something more, or at least something different. No matter how well things go one day, there is always tomorrow to worry about; there is no security, no peace of mind.

For the Buddhist, this pain and suffering can be avoided. The illness can be cured. To cure the illness, we have first to identify the cause, and the second noble truth of Buddhism is that the cause is desire, or attachment (*tanha*). The only way the world can get us down is by our letting it. This reminds us, of course, of Stoicism. The world can get us down because we are attached to things in the world, especially to our own egos. Attachment to the ego is the root of pain and suffering. The ego is our most precious 'possession', and we will suffer anything to protect it. Unfortunately, the ego is never safe. Threats to it are constantly arising and need to be dealt with. Anxiety is ever present.

The third noble truth tells us that the malady of attachment can be cured. The fourth noble truth provides us with an eightfold path which, if followed, will lead us from attachment, and hence provide a cure for the pain, the suffering, the anxiety. Key steps on the path are right opinion (right view) and right meditation. Right opinion means that we have to overcome our ignorance, our dogmatism. Substances do not truly exist, or at least if they do we have no knowledge of this existence. Thus there really is no world of *things*, at least in the way in which we conceive of this world, and in consequence no world of things to which to become attached. This being the case, attachment itself becomes an illusion. As already intimated, this lack of substance applies equally to the ego, leaving nothing either to which we can become attached or with which we can do the attaching. There is neither object nor subject.

This absence of object or subject is not something to take on trust. Buddhism teaches that we must realise it for ourselves, and that the way to do this is through meditation. Meditation is the experimental, practical component of Buddhism and of most Eastern psychological and spiritual disciplines. In the meditative state, which ideally is the state in which we should go through all of life, we are without ideas and beliefs. And it is ideas and beliefs, products of thought, which produce attachment and its consequent pain and anxiety. The meditative state is a state of openness and emptiness. Thoughts may enter during it, but they are permitted gently to exit without being attended to.

Buddhist Meditation

There are many different meditation techniques in Buddhism, but most have to do with emptying the mind or releasing the ego. Breathing exercises and mantra (sound) meditation are two examples. There is nothing magical about meditation. It is not a vehicle for the exercise of secret powers. Recently the West has discovered (or rather rediscovered) the practice, and is putting it to use in medical treatment (see, for example, Benson 1976). But it cannot be stressed too strongly that meditation is a vital part (perhaps *the* most vital part) of Buddhism, since it is argued that intellectual grasp of its teachings is insufficient in itself to turn lives around. We need something to do and to experience if we are to change our lives. From the practice of thoughtless awareness in meditation, everything else seems to follow.

But meditation is not just sitting on one's cushion and concentrating on the breathing or on a mantra. As the practice of meditation develops, one comes to see that meditation permeates the experience of each part of our lives. In fact, meditation *is* our lives. Put another way, meditation is the straightforward business of daily existence. You eat when you are hungry, drink when you are thirsty, and sleep when you are sleepy. This experience of the 'suchness' of things is particularly emphasised in Zen and Tibetan schools, where it is maintained at all times that the spiritual or enlightened life is simply the everyday life. Samsara, the world of change pain and suffering, and Nirvana the world of release from these things, are one and the same. Small wonder that such a truth must be understood experientially and not merely intellectually if it is to be fully grasped!

This realisation that meditation is ultimately the practice of everyday life answers those critics who argue that meditation is a selfish activity, involving withdrawal from the world and its concerns. Another answer comes with the further realisation that when we give up our egos in the meditative state we are freed to act morally towards each other, since in the Buddhist view selfless and moral behaviour are one and the same thing. Moral behaviour thus does not arise from following rules, but rather as a spontaneous product of the meditative state. There is no room for emotions like envy and greed, no room either to feel insecure with others since there is no ego to feel insecure.

Buddhism and Dogma

I have classified Buddhism as a sceptical approach, and it has always claimed for itself a particular kind of freedom from dogma, and to differ from other organised religions in this respect. But aren't the Four Noble Truths, after all, examples of dogma? One answer to this is that they are simply empirical or experimental truths, and as such not really subject to question. But this answer seems weak, because it assumes an absolute empirical knowledge which, if the world is open to question in the sceptical sense, theoretically should not exist. A stronger answer therefore is to advance the notion of a ladder, which you climb and then toss away. Once you are where you want to be, you don't need the ladder any more (unless of coure you need to come down!). The Noble Truths get us on the Buddhist path, they motivate us, and as such serve principally a persuasive or rhetorical function. Once we are on the path and living a meditative life we no longer have need of them. They are an effective means of getting us on the path because they meet the needs of human beings in the human predicament of pain and suffering. We recognise the picture they conjure up.

And of course our attitude to the ladder is greatly helped if we are sensitive to what might be termed the paradoxes (apparent contradictions) of scepticism. For example, if we can know nothing, how can we know that scepticism is a characteristic of a number of important Buddhist thinkers such as Nagarjuna, the founder of the Buddhist sceptical dialectic, and maybe the greatest theoretician of scepticism in all intellectual history? To help with an 'answer' to this, it is useful to remember that the twentieth-century Austrian philosopher Ludwig Wittgenstein also used the analogy of the ladder, and in the *Tractatus Logico Philosophicus* said of his own writings that the reader who truly understands them will see that they are nonsense. In other words, Wittgenstein needed the 'nonsense' to get where he wanted to be.

Freedom from Conditioning

Another way of looking at Buddhism and related Eastern disciplines is to see them as attempts to help us break out of our personal histories of conditioning. Our personal history is what causes each of us our suffering. In the West, the behavioural therapist believes that suffering can only be reduced by reconditioning, using a process such as behaviour therapy. Buddhism offers a quicker (and perhaps surer) way out. Through meditation we can become 'thoughtless', and hence escape from our history of conditioning which largely manifests itself in our patterns of thought.

Take for example the fundamental philosophical question 'What should I do with my life?'. Buddhism tackles this by first rejecting the 'I'. The question is one which is raised from the point-of-view of the self, and so long as we accept the question without reinterpretation, 'I' will never escape pain and suffering. This is fully explained in the various writings of D. T. Suzuki (for example 1953), the outstanding interpreter of Zen to the West. Suzuki shows us we have to be careful not to be taken in by questions, even by our original most important question about our own lives. If 'What shall I do with my life?' means something like 'What can I hope to get out of my life?', we are already lost. The 'What can I get out of it' perspective cannot be separated from attachment to the ego.

This point makes Buddhism an especially radical kind of psychotherapy, since it rejects original questions and assumptions. We need to give up even the very wording of our questions. Thus, in a sense, Buddhism cannot be said to offer *us* happiness, since there is really no *us* to be happy. Buddhism offers a short-cut to enlightenment, but 'it is a hard way, not centered around bliss or power, but based upon awareness, which links it with modern psychotherapeutic group work emphasising the here and now approach' (Dhiravamsa, 1974, p. 62).

Zen Buddhism

My argument is now intentionally taking me somewhat away from Buddhism in general and towards Zen Buddhism in particular, for there are some interesting and distinctive features of Zen that merit our special attention and that of all the Buddhist schools link it most closely to scepticism. Zen is often characterised as a combination of Indian Buddhism and Chinese Taoism. From Taoism it gets its love of nature and appreciation of simplicity, and also perhaps its feeling for humour. Taoism is in fact one of the few philosophies with a sense of humour. It doesn't even take itself seriously. It is suspicious of words. The Tao that can be spoken is not the real Tao. Those who know do not say, and those who say do not know. The way is beyond language, for in it there is no yesterday, no tomorrow and no today.

The aim of Zen, like other forms of Buddhism, is of course enlightenment. But Zen argues that enlightenment (*satori* in Japanese) can be obtained quickly. It offers a simple, direct, yet steep path, relying almost completely on meditative and argumentative technique rather than upon the study of scripture or philosophy. In general, Zen is against traditional authority and almost totally iconoclastic. There is no more reason to bow down to the statue of the Buddha than to spit upon it. If your house is cold and you are out of firewood, burn the wooden statue of the Buddha. In Zen, you must stop talking and thinking. Talking and thinking make for preferences, biases and attachments. When you make even the smallest distinction 'heaven and earth are set infinitely apart'. If you wish to see the truth, then hold no opinion for or against anything. To set up what you like against what you dislike is the disease of the mind.

In Japan, two main schools of Zen developed, Soto and Rinzai. The Soto school stresses sitting meditation, with mantra and breathing, as a means to enlightenment, but Rinzai is more complex, making use of *koans* (literally 'court-cases' but really more like riddles) to break down rational thinking and empty the mind. The koan method is ultimately rhetorical or persuasive, and forms a practice where reason ends up killing itself. You sit in a *zendo*, a large meditation hall, and meditate on the koan your teacher, mentor, guru, therapist, has given you. Just as in mantra meditation where the teacher knows just the right sound for you, the Zen master knows just what koan you should work on. You take up your meditation posture, and meditate on your koan (for example 'What is the sound of one hand clapping?'). No matter how rationally you work at it, you fail to come up with an answer, and eventually come to realise that the question cannot be answered rationally at all. Your master will help you see this when he responds, usually unsympathetically, to your doomed efforts at rational treatment.

And so you keep at it until at last you make an appropriate response. The response must come spontaneously, and an experienced Zen master is able to recognise whether the spontaneity is there or not. When you pass your first koan test you are given another on which to work (for example 'does a dog have Buddha-nature?'). And when you have gone through the necessary sequence of koans, your mind will be changed. The pointlessness of talking and thinking will be evident to you, and you will have obtained satori. This method doesn't sound easy, and it isn't. The master in Rinzai Zen acts as a directive therapist not by giving you the right answer, but by exhibiting little patience with wrong ones. No attempt is made to build up a rapport between the master and yourself (though admittedly this rapport does sometimes develop), and everything is focused upon satori. Why focus on anything else when satori is the ultimate and universal cure? Koan meditation involves what could be termed the hari-kari of reason. Reason grapples with the koan and ultimately commits suicide. The absurdity of using reason is exhibited directly to you whenever you're tempted to try to employ it.

Zen has in some ways proved the most popular form of Buddhism in the West. This is probably because its message is so simple and direct. It is perhaps also because of its intriguing nature: a religion which has little in common with other religions, a philosophy which is at the same time an anti-philosophy, a psychotherapy with a clear-cut technique and a clear-cut goal, satori. Yet in fact Zen is perhaps the most difficult form of Buddhism to practise. It is uncompromising. The pain of sitting, the frustrations of koan meditation, the absence of objects to worship, of authoritative scriptures to study, often even of a community to support you, make this apparently simple path a very hard one to follow. Nevertheless, the attraction of its promise is a powerful motivator. The promise not merely to cure you of this or that affliction, but to make you super-healthy. At a single stroke, to free you in fact from all aspects of your bondage.

Conclusion

Returning to the Kiplingesque words with which I started this chapter, I have tried to show that East and West can meet within the context of sceptical philosophy. I have also tried to show, however, that differences between East and West remain, in particular in the context of respective attitudes towards the self or ego. The question so vital to the West, 'what shall I do with my life?', commits the Westerner to the identification and separation of 'I' from the world outside ('I' from the 'not-I' if you prefer). To the Easterner, the question is stopped in its tracks by an interrupting question 'who is this "I"?', a question which ultimately leads to the realisation that it is this 'I' that causes all the trouble.

In the West, our inherited world-view of self–other–object usually remains unquestioned, in spite of the fact that the philosophy that underpins it then has to wrestle with such problems as 'How can the subject *know* other and object?'. In the East, this world-view is seen simply as a dangerous way of strengthening the ego, of making it more 'rational'. The East proposes an alternative view which sees life not as a matter of selves and their achievements, and which sees sanity in fact as residing in a divorce from this very self and from the subject–object distinctions to which it gives rise and which in turn help to sustain it. True human nature is seen as ego-less, and it is in this ego-less state that humans should go through their lives.

This is why the Eastern sage so often looks to us like a fool, an idiot or even worse. Take, for example, the Taoist glorification of the useless man. The sage is as 'useless' as an ugly tree which manages to live and thrive. Everybody leaves it alone. It bears no fruit, its trunk and branches are unusable, and its leaves inedible. The more we ponder on this image, the more we realise that what we are up against is a fundamental value barrier between East and West, a barrier which makes us ask, 'How serious is our disease? And how radical a cure for it are we prepared to accept?'.

CHAPTER 13

Meditation and Personal Disclosure: The Western Zen Retreat

JOHN CROOK

Supreme accomplishment is to realize immanence without hope.
Tilopa[1]

Introduction

The Vietnamese Buddhist writer Thich Nhat Hanh (1974) has had this to say about Zen in the West:

> Zen does not yet exist in the West as a living tradition. Many monks are teaching the practice of Zen there, but this practice remains oriental; foreign to western culture. The fact is that Zen has not yet been able to find roots in this soil. Cultural economic and psychological conditions are different . . . One cannot become a practitioner of Zen by imitating the way of eating, sitting or dressing of the Chinese or Japanese practitioners. Zen is life; Zen does not imitate. If Zen one day becomes a reality in the West, it will acquire a Western form, considerably different from Oriental Zen.

The possibility of a Western Zen also poses the problem of a lay Zen for, although there are Zen monasteries in America and Europe following ancient traditions, the majority of those attempting to practise Zen remain lay men and women. For these practitioners, instead of the protection given by the walls of the convent and the mutual endeavours of fellow trainees, there is the constant encounter with the many forms of egotistic energy with which most people relate to their everyday worlds. Tough as the monastic environment may also be, the often overwhelming effect of engagement in worldly relationships is commonly the one difficulty that can be reduced there. While strict training in the monastery can and should lead to a return to the market-place, those who try to train without the walls are often especially heroic in their endeavours. But many fall aside in confusion.

Several authors have already addressed this and related questions; some from an intellectual and academic viewpoint (see Merrell-Wolf, 1973; Humphries, 1949; Pirsig, 1974; Suzuki, 1953; Watts, 1957), some with personal accounts of their own struggles (see Kennett, 1977/78; van Wetering, 1972, 1984; Amphoux, 1986) and some with a close examination of Zen in the context of attempting to teach and practise it in the modern world (see Brandon, 1976; Kapleau, 1965, 1980; Kennett, 1978). In most cases, however, it is with the transmission of oriental modes of practice that these writings are concerned. Little attempt has been made to see what happens if the Western mind, using its own energies and contradictions, can realise Zen practically with minimum direction but accurate facilitation based on a clear comprehension of the goal of training. One particular effort in this direction has revealed startling insights and possibilities (Harding, 1974).

For ten years now I have been running several specially constructed five-day Zen sesshins (retreats) yearly for lay people at a remote farmhouse in mid-Wales. Recently I have felt the need to put together some ideas about the nature of the process of change I have observed in participants during the retreat, and that which some participants have described to me in letters months or years after their participation in a sesshin. This chapter begins to explore this issue on which I am continuing to work (see also Chapter 8).

The Participants

The retreat is designed for lay people who may or may not have prior experience of meditation or Buddhist teachings, or consider themselves Buddhists. People come almost entirely because they hear of the retreat from friends who are former participants. Advertising produces only a very small minority of enquirers. Although in the early days retreat numbers were sometimes as low as 6–8 persons, I cannot recall having had to cancel a retreat for lack of interest. Today we accommodate around 16–17 people under harsh winter conditions, and up to 25 people, some under canvas, in summer. Participants are usually 'middle-class' but with a variety of class origins and social affiliations, and a wide range of incomes. Many are university-educated and a considerable proportion are in the helping professions. The proportion of counsellors, doctors, psychotherapists and psychiatrists has risen annually over the last few years – some individuals being prominent in their fields. The age-range is great, from about 19 to 75, and individuals may profess inclinations loosely discernible as atheist, agnostic, Humanist, Christian, Marxist or Buddhist. Many have received some training in the sciences, and professional scientists and university teachers are often in evidence – perhaps influenced by my own academic qualifications (which, however, have nothing to do with the process in hand!). There are usually rather more men than women, but the ratio varies considerably from retreat to retreat.

People come primarily not because of an interest in Buddhism or Zen, but out of a feeling that the retreat may be helpful in relation to a personal problem. Basically participants are seeking to alleviate their suffering. Some participants have strong counter-cultural or feminist orientations, or may have embarked on a vigorous search for new or different ways of living. Only a few have read anything significant about Zen or Buddhism, and not many participants are actually Buddhists. For Buddhists there are, of course, 'safer' and more orthodox establishments available. In summary, participants are *not*:

1. necessarily committed to a particular path;
2. especially convinced that Zen offers a solution;
3. experienced in religious retreats;
4. monks or nuns; or
5. practitioners of any sustained training schedule.

These facts are important in trying to understand the process. In particular the retreats can only be compared with caution to actual monastic Zen sesshins of the Ch'an, Soto or Rinzai traditions, conducted by monks either for other monks in training or for especially committed Zen Buddhists who may have been in training already for some years. It follows that descriptions of experiences by Western Zen Retreat participants cannot therefore automatically be equated with experiences reported by monks in the classical literature. I shall not therefore be assuming that reported experiences are necessarily *kensho*, *satori* or enlightenments. It can be said, however, that reports by WZR participants, and events occurring in interviews (*dokusan*) during the retreats, are sometimes very close in form and content to those described, for example, in Kapleau's 1965 transcripts of trainee interviews with a Japanese master and the retreat reports in Master Sheng-Yen's book *Getting the Buddha Mind* (1982). It thus follows that some of the underlying psychological processes may be the same. Furthermore, my personal experiences in a variety of forms of Buddhist training point to an underlying unity.

The Practice

The retreat is built out of a considered blending of three elements: zazen practice, the communication exercise of Charles Berner (see Love, 1976), and physical activity. These are combined into a daily schedule which changes slightly as the days progress. On the first two days emphasis is on sustained zazen, on the third and fourth day on questioning in the communication exercise. On the last day zazen is emphasised once more. Interludes of physical exercise may include a run up the hill behind the house before dawn, manual work, and a one-hour hill-walk. Sessions of physical exercise are derived from hatha yoga or Mahamudra training, and often there is an evening session of one of the action yogas of Bhagwan Shree Rajneesh. These can be especially powerful in helping participants break through emotional blocks.

Zazen

The traditional sitting posture is adopted (see for example the Zazen Rules in Kennett, 1972) and a meditation method employed. There is a range of methods available: counting the breath; watching the breath; observing thoughts on an inhalation, letting them go on the exhalation and observing what is there when they have gone; repeating the Buddha's name; repeating a name of the Buddha, suddenly stopping it and looking into the gap so caused; searching the heart (see below); examining a *hua t'ou* or mental device that evokes a witnessing of the mind before it is stirred by a thought (that is, an ante-thought – see Lu, 1964, p. 47); or seeking a response to a paradoxical question based upon a case history from old Zen records (*koan*).

In the WZR it is 'Searching the heart' or *shik-an-taza* which is the main method employed in zazen. Here the practitioner endeavours to discover what 'just sitting' is; every thought that arises is allowed to do so until it is recognised as what it is (– a worry over a child, a loss, a social blunder, a moment of sexual bliss, a theoretical inspiration) and then it is released, let go of entirely. The mind returns to the state before thought (the *hua t'ou*). The practice is summarised as 'let thru – let be – let go' – there is to be no encouragement of thoughts, but rather a repeated letting go of all states that arise. Searching the heart can be a long, exhausting process; with low energy states it is painful indeed, with high energy there is the occurrence of scattering. Eventually after many hours the mind seems to quieten down, the hassle reduces of its own accord. This is *samatha*, or stillness meditation. With persistence, the method leads towards deep inward trance. In zazen one is encouraged to look directly into this quietening mind to perceive its very nature. Penetrative insight can reveal a mind that is empty of thought and notional content – there is simply a reflecting process, like that of a mirror.

In the WZR, Zazen is used at first primarily to allow the participant to 'arrive'; to let the diffuse energies which he has brought with him settle, and moments of tranquillity appear.

The Communication Exercise

The onset of the communication exercise breaks up all this gentling, and sets the mind going again in vigorous pursuit of a question. But the initial practice of zazen has begun to clarify the enquiring mind so that penetration may now go deep. Zazen may also have loosened emotional feelings usually repressed or hidden behind layers of rationalisation or social pretence, and which are now clamouring for release. In Charles Berner's system, two participants sit opposite one another, each taking turns of five minutes to respond to a question from the partner who remains open and alert, receiving whatever comes with acceptance but absolutely no comment. This alternation continues for 30–50 minutes, after which there is a break before the process is resumed – each participant now, however, paired with a different member of the group but persisting with his original question. The questions are in fact root koans shorn of all traditional background. In the WZR the following questions are given and usually in the following order: (1) Who am I? (= Tell me who you are); (2) What am I? (= Tell me what you are); (3) What is life? (= Tell me what life is) and (4) What is another? (= Tell me what another is). A useful question that is commonly used after 'Who am I?' is 'How is life fulfilled?', for which (3) may or may not be a necessary preliminary depending on the depth of the earlier answers. Other questions used in the WZR include 'What is love?' 'From where does love (truth, life, it, etc.) come?' 'What am I like if completely alone?' 'What is meaning?' 'What is Death?' or the more advanced. 'Tell me what the Cross is?' or 'What is working with karma?' These supplementary koans are given within contexts which arise in the interviews between practitioner and facilitator. The skill of the facilitator is needed to select a koan which has direct relevance at a heartful level for the practitioner – for example 'From where does love come?' given to someone recently deserted by a spouse or love or proposing to desert.

As Berner saw, the value of these misleadingly simple questions, lacking entirely the trappings and verbal paradoxes of traditional koans ('What is the sound of one-hand-clapping?'), lies in their direct pointing to the state of the practitioner here and now. 'Who am I?' or 'How is life fulfilled?' have no enticing frills – they point straight to the basic dilemma. Like the Kamakura warrior koans (Legett, 1985), they can arise on the spot in the relationship between practitioner and facilitator, and their choice is a matter of 'skilful means'.

In traditional Rinzai Zen, the practitioner sits and meditates on his koan seeking to break through the barrier it represents. In the Enlightenment Intensive (as Berner called his system) and in the WZR the communication between two persons allows direct personal disclosure in which participants face the fear of risking to share their guilty, shameful or agonising thoughts and feelings with another. It may take several hours before a participant can trust partners sufficiently to disclose an emotional barrier which must be stated and released before further work on 'Who am I?' can continue. Such issues of disclosure, fear, risk and trust are

162   *Space in Mind*

present in traditional settings when the monk faces the master. In the WZR they are constantly present as the participants work with one another in the communication exercises.

Intense work in the communication exercise arouses strong emotions. Once a participant has shared emotion it is rare for the partner not to be deeply affected. The sharing can move to a very profound level of mutual understanding and compassion. Very deep suffering, undisclosed for years, can be released in this way with powerful effects. Sometimes states of great intensity and confusion are aroused and the facilitator's experience of humanistic therapies such as neo-Reichian bioenergetics, gestalt or psychosynthesis is needed in the interview room where body-work as well as heart-to-heart confrontation may be used.

Action Yoga

The use of Bhagwan Shree Rajneesh's action yoga involves the whole group in vigorous exercises which help literally to shake out (the 'Kundalini' exercise) or blow out (the 'Dynamic') energies suppressed, cathected to unshareable ideas or simply too far below the surface to appear in verbal presentation. The permission to shout, rage, scream, dance, roll about and laugh is a shared act of trust with the facilitator, whose role as an authority-figure is thereby softened, allowing his care for the group to be more easily perceived. In addition, for some, it constitutes a previously inconceivable performance of fantasy themes involving experiences of regression to childhood. The personal meaning of these emotional events is subsequently explored when the communication exercises are resumed.

The Schedule

These main practices are combined in a timetable that begins at between 5 am and 6.30 am (depending on the season) and ends around 10.30 pm. The day opens with chanting, using orthodox texts from the various Buddhist traditions as well as hymns written specially for the purpose. The day divides into either Zazen sessions (2 × 30 minutes with a cycle of slow or fast walking between) or Communication Exercises (usually 2 × 30 – 50 minutes, with a five-minute break between) with walks, meals, work periods, and action yoga cropping up as appropriate.

Discipline and leadership

The retreat is strictly disciplined in the manner of a traditional Zen sesshin. A set of vows – of silence, gratitude, compassion and diligent practice – is taken at the start of the retreat, and to break any of these persistently is taken to indicate an unwillingness to work and is followed by a request to leave (this has occurred only twice in ten years). The prime rule is that of silence – which means a total absence of conversation rather than a prohibition of all remarks such as simple requests for information. Conviviality when it develops is not suppressed, but rather contained and reflected upon as a result of the silence rule and reminders to 'Hold your Questions!'

Of necessity, the facilitator tends to have a high profile role, especially at the start of the retreat. This is in order to generate an outer discipline vital for the success of the inner work. Furthermore, an assertive expression of the role may be important in helping participants to feel secure. The facilitator must have confidence in the process, and complete openness towards anything a participant may produce. Once the pattern of the retreat is well established and the koans have taken hold, the facilitator can increasingly allow the group process to unfold naturally. He (or she) will be spending more time in giving interviews, and will ask assistants or senior participants to organise the time-keeping and other administrative tasks.

The two permanent figures around which the retreat unfolds are the facilitator and the cook. The role of maintaining discipline, and a willingness to exert authority in the interests of the group as a whole, may fall from time to time on either or both of them, and needs to melt naturally into a nurturing role as time goes along. Both facilitator and cook may in some ways be seen as occupying parental roles to the family of participants, and indeed oedipal expressions of feeling may sometimes make themselves felt. The facilitator needs to be able to use such responses creatively in the

164 Space in Mind

interests of the participant, and not to react with an authoritarian or overly 'parental' stance.

Anyone attempting to facilitate a process such as this will need to have completed periods of intensive Zen training including orthodox sesshins with a skilled master, training in counselling or therapeutic work with clients and some personal work in psychotherapy. He or she will also require a 'supervisor' with whom to share the events and experiences of running a retreat. Untrained individuals should not attempt work with this degree of interpersonal involvement.

The Retreat Process

The evening on which people arrive is spent in organising bed spaces, getting to know the layout of the building and meeting fellow participants. Around 9.30 pm an assembly is held, and people asked why they have come and what their hopes and fears may be. This plenary sharing helps the facilitator to get a preliminary impression of individuals' attitudes – especially important where newcomers are concerned and to make sure that no one has come with severely aberrant or misinformed expectations. It also allows individuals to get to know one another a little socially before the discipline of the retreat is imposed, and to experience each other's seriousness in the endeavour. The sesshin begins with a short opening ceremony before lights out, after which silence begins.

The first day is usually a hard one. Zazen is difficult, the mind chatters incessantly, the early start and a poor night's rest rapidly induce sleepiness and the struggle to resist leads to low energy states, even depression. Some may find all this overwhelming. The collective energy and focus of the group is poor, and even the facilitator will feel drawn down by the prevailing atmosphere. Occasionally individuals want to leave at this point. Interviews with each participant begin in the afternoon, and this establishing of contacts between facilitator and participant helps lighten the atmosphere. Chanting and the use of the Kundalini exercise raise energy and help concentration. The evening meditations are more satisfactory.

On Day 2 most participants experience an improvement in

zazen, and some experienced individuals may make rapid progress towards meditative absorption. In the afternoon, the communication exercises begin with a burst of energy and often enthusiasm. By the evening, however, the toughness of confronting the koan hour after hour, and the onset of difficult disclosure frequently bring about a return of low energy states. Again these may be alleviated by physical exercise and chant. People become deeply involved with their questions. Most answers to 'Who am I?' begin by references to roles and experiences, but gradually move to the sort of statement 'I am the kind of person who . . .' with verbal descriptions of feelings. Personal problems and situational dilemmas begin to be shared.

Day 3 calls for great personal application. Considerable emotional expression may occur, so that the sounds of weeping, rage, grief and distress often ring through the building. But these are helpful signs as individuals are freeing themselves to express their life dilemmas as they are actually felt in here/now experiencing. It is more difficult for those who cannot feel free to express emotion, cannot find emotions to express, or who feel imposed upon by the emotions of others. Rationalisers may get very angry, and this anger may be aimed directly or indirectly at the facilitator, who may sometimes feel he is riding a bucking horse. The expression of great emotion is, however, not always a necessary or even desirable activity. Those who have a clear perception of themselves, and those who get emotional blocks out of the way early, begin to look very directly at their moment-to-moment experience and try to see its form and source. Whether by reason of a highly focused intentionality or because of catharsis, some individuals may have breakthroughs into moments of serenity or joy – which, however, dissolve again into other hassling mental diversions as new thoughts come up for attention.

During Day 4 a subtle change comes over the group. Participants now tend to come forward for interviews (*dokusan*) either because of persistent perplexity, pain or distress or because insights seem to be arising. For those caught in circular or spiralling systems of thought which like repeated traverses of a cul-de-sac seem to iterate endlessly without release, these interviews are often of great importance. The facilitator endeavours to mirror the individual process of the meditator, and by precise questions and other skilled responses, to bring the individual to insight into his own mental attachments and personal myths and the need for their acceptance.

Individuals now have the appearance of emptying themselves of self-expression. To an outsider they might appear drained or exhausted, but in fact they are entering a highly concentrated state with an increasing level of a type of energy that allows high attentiveness. Such a state may last for hours while the individual 'crosses the desert'. The level of focused energy in the room may seem almost palpable – the atmosphere is intense but no longer tense – highly creative and insightful communication exercises occur. It is now possible for some individuals in their quest for themselves in 'Who am I?' to go beyond words and experience the living moment non-discursively with a clarity of apprehensive immediacy in which the subject – object dichotomy may dissolve. Such experiences may be accompanied by moments of profound inner stillness, a rising sense of physical and mental bliss, and an awareness seemingly unlimited by previous imputations of self-regarding thought. This extraordinarily acute awareness may be associated with feelings of profound gratitude, openness to others and compassion. Only a few experience this state in depth, but many discover a radically quietened mind in which self-acceptance leads to a loss of personal anguish, together with the emergence of a new view of life in which openness and optimism are characteristic. There is in particular a remarkable feeling of having shed a burden, and a consequent feeling of freed energy.

Day 5 sees a reduction in questioning, with the koan now used more as a simple focusing device than as a question to be answered. Many have realised that in any case there is no answer – rather the paradox inherent in the koan may be resolved through a change in perception. This is like observing those illusory figures in psychology textbooks – seen from one mental stance an old woman stands upon the page – a second later there is a beautiful girl. The cognitive reorganisation now has an opportunity for stabilisation into a changed attitude, but whether this can be maintained following the retreat depends upon many factors in an individual's life. Usually the experience fades quite quickly and much now depends on how an individual's philosophy of life and attitude to living have been affected.

A koan is 'dropped' when an individual experiences a certainty that he or she is quite clear about 'Who I am' (say). This certainty may be associated with the experiences described above, and usually crystallises into a form of words given to the facilitator in a manner which indicates resolution. The participant is now energetic, clear in mind, peaceful, resolved, self-accepting and certain, and this shows in marked changes in posture, breathing, eye energy and facial expression; so that the form of words used is of relatively less importance. When a koan is 'dropped' in this way, the participant is usually asked to savour the result and to continue sharing it with others. This may go on until the end of the retreat, or occasionally a further koan may be given.

Generally, about a quarter of a group's membership has an experience approaching the above description, another half have reached a degree of self-acceptance that frees them deeply to face life's problems, while most of the remainder have experienced and learnt a great deal about themselves and the human condition. A limited number may be profoundly disappointed or leave as puzzled as they came – but even here very few of this number actually regret attempting the retreat. They rightly feel that to have come through it at all is something which, on a wider scale, is exceptional and which may have hidden benefits.

What is the long-term effect of participating in Zen sesshins? This is a difficult question to answer since over a period of years individuals grow in many ways, simply as a result of further life-experience and of joining in social activities. In the late 1970s, I distributed over a hundred questionnaires to past participants from which the above assessment of the actual experience of a sesshin was drawn, but apart from a general authentication of the value of the retreat specific detail was difficult to obtain. Personal letters, sometimes of great length, have, however, indicated the considerable influence of these retreats on the life course of at least some individuals.

Very rarely an individual may be adversely affected by the retreat. There is a condition known to the Japanese as 'stinking of Zen'. After a WZR it is possible for the release of energy to produce excessive exhilaration, amounting to a manic euphoria which the subject projects in wildly ambitious expectations of others. Only two cases have occurred in ten years, both young women, and a spell in hospital care was required before the condition subsided.

It is likely that those subject to schizoid breaks are more at risk than others, but the rarity of these occurrences suggests that the proportion of people at risk at the WZR is no larger than that in the general population.

A Psychological View of Changes Experienced during a Retreat

The solving of a koan in a Western Zen Retreat has a strongly self-affirmative character, but one that appears in a curiously apophatic mode. Instead of assertions about identity and personal history, one finds a frequent use of process words – 'I am peace', 'Life is living', 'Another is an adventure', accompanied by a clarity of awareness which lacks easily attributed boundaries in either time or space. What is being affirmed is the quality of the living moment rather than the personhood of the experiencer – yet there is no self-doubt about who it is that manifests that quality. The conventional attributions of parts and processes to oneself as descriptive categorisations in social discourse are replaced by expressions springing with direct immediacy from a realm of insight and feeling, which lacks the necessity of being named.

A way to explain this is by means of the concept of *dis-identification*. The human individual is a self-conceiving mammal whose concepts of self function to maintain individual distinctiveness, both introspectively and socially, in a world of inter-personal relations. Infants come to impute to their body–mind experience the properties of agency in interaction with others – especially mother. The discovery of agency is followed by the imputation to the self so realised of properties or qualities which arise in social interaction (Lewis and Brooks, 1977; Horrocks and Jackson, 1972).

A powerful view of the way in which identification with such conceptual realisation occurs has developed in Western thought in the writings of G. H. Mead (1934), Homans (1961) and Tajfel (1978) (see also Chapter 3). Social acts are seen as events through which individuals learn the perspectives of others about themselves, and incorporate them into 'identity constructs' which constitute their cognitive being. A person only becomes such through a progressively elaborated process of role-taking in relation to another. People not only conceive of themselves largely as others see them, but tend to act in accordance with the expectations that others may hold. More recent views, based both on observational evidence and sociobiological theory, affirm that, apart from needs for social approval, infants are from the beginning also strategists. They pursue nutritional, affectional and self-expressive goals that form the eventual basis for autonomous action in the world, the creation of economic well-being and the rearing of a family (see Crook, 1980, Chapter 9).

Erikson (1950) and Sullivan (1955) showed how the development of identity constructs was severely affected by the emotional content of the child–parent relationship. Whenever a child's need for support and explanation is met in an open, caring manner, its development can proceed in a constructive, positively self-evaluative way that leads to the learning of self-affirmative skills and expression, combined with tolerance for others. Where, however, the child is subject to loss (Bowlby, 1969, 1973), to repeated bad temper and punishment, to denigration or abuse, these threats to the emergence of a positive self-evaluation produce habitual anxiety which, when projected onto other figures, becomes the basis for the complex affect-laden habits in adulthood by which actual relations with others are distorted by fantasy.

Masking operations, suppression, schizoid denial and excessive egotism are devices to protect the self from largely imagined threats derived from fears of the parent. Such devices become deeply ingrained in the character of the individual – basically as attempts to support a negatively valued but necessary sense of personal identity. Naturally, interactional styles based on such patterns in adult life tend to evoke similarly distorted patterns in others leading to the whole range of 'games people play' (Berne, 1966).

At the onset of a retreat, some participants are presenting themselves to one another through the screen of such self-protective social attitudes based on their guarded suspicions of others. Their shaky identity constructs, often based upon years of hurt, determine an often highly defensive or over-assertive stance. Other individuals may have varying degrees of self and other understanding based on life experiences or work in therapy or 'growth' groups. In either case, to come to the Zen Retreat has required an act of trust or courage, because participants know that these restricting habits of personal closure are precisely those they will confront in the course of the retreat. In the communication exercise it is precisely these attitudes that are disclosed to another.

Jourard (1971) has described the therapeutic value of self-disclosure of this kind. As trust develops and deeper topics are broached, the individual experiences relief from the tightly bound defensive positions of self-constriction with which he or she tends to face the world. Self-disclosure is an important aspect of co-counselling, a system of mutual therapy which Charles Berner used as a model for the Enlightenment Intensive process, and which has a close resemblance to the communication exercise. As the disclosure moves from the merely conceptual to the direct expression of hurt through weeping, rage or distress, so the whole body–mind process is activated and the 'armour' (as Reich termed it) can literally relax – muscular, endocrinal, sympathetic nervous and mental tensions all move towards release or relaxation. Every authentic statement or presentation becomes literally a letting go of 'stuff', and a thorough release of a theme allows a disidentification from it so that, for the time being at least, it does not recur. There is thus a progressive abandonment of restrictive identity constructs, together with the forms of their physical incarnation.

The motivation for self-disclosure seems to lie in an awareness of the need to share. This sharing can, however, only occur with another felt to be positively regarding; a person not necessarily warm but certainly capable of non-judgemental sympathetic listening. There may be also an element of confession present, as thoughts of shame and guilt are spoken often with profound expressions of remorse, longing for clarification or atonement. Participants have to learn that they can trust one another's common humanity.

Disidentification leads to an abandonment of conceptual constrictions, and the mind is free to look into the emptiness so created – a consciousness increasingly freed from self-regard and even from the dichotomy between subject and object itself. It is the nature of this consciousness that is the focus of Buddhist self-examination and about which Western psychology has had little so far to say (see Chapter 13).

Conclusions: Perplexity and Preceptual Truth

Whether one is an Eastern monk or a Western lay person, the root of the motivation for Zen training lies in perplexity. Perplexity arises within the unsatisfactory character of life itself with its inherent difficulties in self-evaluation, in personal goal-satisfaction and its termination in death. Buddhism itself seems to have arisen in response to an increasingly complex life resulting from the emergence of an urban, class-based hierarchical society in ancient India with its consequent problems of identity, self-esteem and meaning for individual lives (Ling, 1973). Contemporary Western life, with its rapidly changing social norms, breakdowns of social and familial structures and secular value system, raises similar issues in florid form.

The Buddhist response may seem a strange one to anyone who has not undertaken training – for the uncovering of a characterless 'unborn' mind 'empty' of itself seems an unlikely basis for life in a highly fragmented and competitive social world. To understand the purport here, it becomes necessary to penetrate to the depth of meaning attributable to such definitions of Zen as 'the self making the self into the self'. Fortunately, there is an ancient Japanese story which helpfully illustrates the meaning and value of Zen training.

Once upon a time there was a bed of squashes ripening in the corner of a field. One day they began quarrelling. The squashes split up into factions and made a lot of noise shouting at one another. The head priest of a nearby temple, hearing the sound, rushed out to see what was wrong. He scolded the wrangling squashes saying 'What ever are you doing. Fighting among yourselves is useless. Every one do zazen!'

The priest taught them all how to sit properly in zazen and gradually their anger died away. Then the priest said, 'Put your hands on top of your heads.' The squashes did so and discovered a peculiar thing. Each one had a stem growing from its head which connected them all one to another and back to a common root. 'What a mistake we have made!' they said, 'We are all joined to one another, based on the same root and living one life only. In spite of that we quarrel. How foolish our ignorance has been.' After that this reader hopes they all lived happily ever after. (Taken from Kosho Uchiyami Roshi, 1973.)

The story illustrates the experiential fact that as a result of
Zen training the habit of discrimination in producing dualistic
distinctions between self and others diminishes, and may even
disappear altogether for a time. In this freedom from self-concern
there is a sense of participation not only in a social but also in a
universal process. 'Emptiness' of self-nature means awareness of
the interdependence of all the phenomena of experienced life. This
is the stem of the vine. Unthreatened by the processes of others in
a sense of community, compassion arises, anger dies down, love
in its broadest sense appears.

A training such as this recalibrates the meaning attributable
to a person's model of the real – dualistic functioning remains
appropriate in contexts where action is needed and planning done,
but action itself is now perceived within the wider context of a
pervasive non-dual base. The Zen task is to develop the skilful
means to apprehend this wider, psychologically validated, view
of reality and then to discover how to move creatively within it.
This is the self making the self into the self.

Given the current norms of society – the practitioner of Zen
will almost inevitably find himself to be the possessor of an
outsider's vision. Faced continuously with the problem of value
in contemporary society, life becomes a permanent koan – how
to live according to preceptual truth within contemporary society.
Since training leads to the Bodhisattva's concern for the welfare
of others, it seems inevitable that a Zen trainee, whatever the
details of his personal strategy, will adopt values of a generally
altruistic nature – focused more on the common good than on
personal advancement. Yet, as skilful means to this end, action in
pursuit of an appropriate career, economic livelihood and family
life are not to be seen as inappropriate. In holding the koan ever
in mind the appropriate way becomes plain. In this there is no
magic solution – the effects of karma, personal conditioning, are
very strong and need endless review, witnessing the failures, the
errors and the disappointments. Life is making life into life and
there are no short-cuts – only the emergence of an understanding.
As Philip Glass the composer recently remarked, the meaning of a
work of art is today always completed by the hearer. In the view
of Zen that too is true of the work of life.

Note

1. See Chang, G.C.C., *Six Yogas of Naropa*, New York, Snow Lion, 1963, p. 29.

CHAPTER 14

Why Be a Buddhist Monk?

LYN GOSWELL

Introduction

In 1977 four Western-born Buddhist monks arrived in Hampstead, London, from their training monastery in Thailand. They came at the invitation of a group of English lay Buddhists to establish a Sangha, or monastic community in Britain (Sumedho, 1983).

Over the last ten years, these four have been joined by more than seventy Western men and women, mostly university graduates in their late twenties and thirties, who are choosing to exchange the secular benefits of education, career, personal and financial independence, and sexual and family relationships for the monastic life of poverty, chastity and obedience.

This raises a number of very interesting questions about the individuals, about the community, and about the relationship of both to the Western world, some of which I have attempted to answer using the methods of modern research. In this chapter I will attempt to describe these methods (in particular the interviewing procedure), and the results obtained by them, thus identifying some of the psychological factors that appear to be associated with being a Buddhist monk in the Western world.

In particular, my research was designed to find:

1. the factors that motivate Westerners to become interested in meditation and in Buddhism, and to adopt a monastic life-style and continue in it; and
2. the changes, emotional social and spiritual, that take place in their lives as a result of monasticism, and the way in

which meditation, the monastic rule and the monastic routine interrelate to produce these changes.

Research Methods

By the time the monastic community was established in 1977 I had already been interested in Buddhism and in the practice of meditation for some fifteen years, and I was therefore interested in the venture from the start. I paid a visit to the community, and was encouraged by the monks and nuns to undertake a formal research project as a way of finding the answers to some of my questions.

It was clear to me that the main source of my research information must be the monks and nuns (and the associated laypeople) themselves, and that I must involve them from the start in the actual planning of my project, using the method known as 'participatory inquiry' (see, for example, Reason and Rowan, 1981). This method means that the individuals being studied are involved as full participants in the research, not just as subjects under investigation. They take part in every aspect of the research, from the initial planning and the data collection through to the examination of results and the generation of any theories arising from them. Participatory inquiry thus aims to enable both the processes taking place in a community and the interrelationships between these processes to emerge fully. The goal of the inquiry is therefore not just to collect some interesting facts, but to produce the kind of facts which allow the formulation of what is called a 'grounded theory' (Glaser and Strauss, 1975), a theory which can accurately account for the patterns of behaviour observed.

Research Procedure

After obtaining their consent for the general research design, the Abbot and Sangha were invited to reflect on their monastic experience and on how it might be explored, and to suggest areas within this experience which they felt should be included in the study. They were also invited to suggest specific questions that might be asked, to name the people whose views should be particularly sampled, and to offer any other suggestions that might be relevant.

From this work there arose three main research strategies, namely that I should:

1. visit the monastery frequently and observe for myself;
2. interview a fair sample of the Sangha in depth; and
3. live in the monastery for a block of time as much like a member of the community as possible.

I pursued each of these strategies, but for the purposes of this chapter I intend to focus primarily upon strategy 2, the information yielded by the in-depth interviews with members of the Sangha.

Interviews with the Sangha

At the Abbot's suggestion, each of the interviews was tape-recorded, and a transcript was sent to each participant for reading and correcting before it was used as part of the research data. Initial discussions with the Sangha yielded a core of open-ended questions which were used as a stimulus to start people talking.

Most interviews took about one and a half hours, but a few were as short as one hour or as long as three. Variation was also observed amongst interviewees as to which area of questioning produced the most material. But the aim of the interviews was to encourage participants to open up on topics important to them. For example the effect Christianity had had on their coming to Buddhism, the sense of bereavement in themselves and in their families at the time of ordination, and the way in which they had learned to deal with hindrances to practice such as greed, sexual desire or anger.

What follows below is the essence of the replies to these questions. Extracting the essence in this way necessarily means that some of the richness and variation of individual responses is lost, but the material has been checked by two large groups from within the Sangha. These groups were drawn primarily from individuals who did not contribute to the original collection of data, and who were thus able objectively to assess (and confirm) that it constituted an accurate reflection of common monastic experience.

Responses to Interview Questions

Question One

The responses to the first question, *How did you first become interested in meditation and in Buddhism?*, were the most varied obtained. Some individuals had developed this interest only after a long and active personal search. By contrast, others had experienced it almost by accident, seeking ordination only a matter of weeks later. For yet others, the interest had come about as a result of reading, or of drug-taking, or of travel to the East, or of meeting some very impressive person. For others, it had been largely an inner process. It is therefore extremely difficult to generalise an answer to this first question. However, it does seem that individuals within the Sangha have come to meditation and to Buddhism as a result of experiences which fall into three main categories:

1. an encounter with suffering and unhappiness from which they search for an escape;
2. a realisation of the ultimately unsatisfactory nature of the search for pleasure, and a desire for some intense ecstasy, mystical experience or meditational high;
3. a strong sense of curiosity about the nature of the self and of existence, a confusion and puzzlement, a desire to sort out ideas, a *not-knowing*.

Of course, these three categories are not mutually exclusive, and many individuals acknowledged being influenced by more than one of them.

When I reported these three categories to the Sangha they pointed out to me that the classical Buddhist psychology of the *Visuddhimagga* (see Buddhaghosa, 1976) divides human motivation into three main types: that which comes from *aversion*, that which comes from *greed*, and that which comes from *ignorance*.

So the data uncovered in the West during the twentieth century provides empirical confirmation of observations made in the East 2,500 years ago!

Question Two

The second question was *What factors made you decide to become ordained?* Broadly speaking, responses included a closely intertwined mixture of rational, intuitive, unconscious and emotional factors, and showed in most cases a clear developmental pattern as follows. Not everyone followed each step in this pattern (as revealed in the three categories reported above for example, some individuals laid more stress upon step 2 and others more stress upon step 3), but the sequence it contains nevertheless remained remarkably constant.

1. First, there was often a deep religious or mystical sense as a child, with a fascination with questions about God and the meaning and purpose of life, together with an attraction to prayer.
2. Later, there came an increasing awareness of the physical and mental suffering in life, both of self and of others. Many individuals reported contact with illness or death in those close to them.
3. The next step often involved a realisation that the achievement of the worldly goals of money, fame, success and comfort do not remove this suffering. Several of the monks who had been rich young men described lying naked on some tropical beach, eating pineapples and dallying with the girls, smoking dope and splashing in the warm blue sea, only to find themselves appalled gradually to discover that an earthly paradise with every material need satisfied still does not guarantee happiness or real fulfilment.
4. Next there often came an emotional sense of desperation or depression, a need 'like a drowning man needs air', a very powerful motivation to find the answer to this lack of fulfilment.
5. For several individuals, there came at this time a sense of deep disappointment that the Christian Church did not seem able to meet this need at either intellectual or emotional levels, nor by example through the lives of its clergy.
6. Thus when they discovered Buddhist teaching, there was often a sense of instant recognition of its truth, and very often a feeling of déjà vu. Some reported rather tentatively that they

felt they may have been monks in previous incarnations, or certainly Buddhists, such was the strength of the emotional thrill and feeling of recognition. Several also described having, at about the same time, a mystical experience of seeing 'how it is', which confirmed this recognition for them.

7. Thereafter there came a gradually growing intellectual understanding of the Buddha's teaching on suffering and the way to its removal (see also Rahula, 1962), and a realisation that this was a way of life that was possible and worth following. It made sense and appealed to their reason (see Green, 1978), and they developed a strong conviction that it would work for them and lead to liberation if followed totally.

8. Attempts to follow the teachings closely in the ordinary world in which they were then living brought the realisation that they needed more structure and discipline, more guidance and form, and the presence of supportive companions.

9. At about this time they typically visited a monastery, and watching and listening to monks and nuns in action they were impressed by their peace and wisdom. They could thus see that the path does work in practice, at least for some people. They also reported an emotional attraction to the presence of the Sangha. Not only did the members of the Sangha exhibit peace, they also facilitated this quality in those they were with. The monastic life thus seemed infectious at a 'gut level'.

10. Eventually each recognised that the monastic life-style was, for them, the ideal form in which to continue their practice.

11. Then came the experience of living in the monastery as a lay person for a short time, with an opportunity thus to sample the monastic life at close quarters.

12. The final step was deciding to stay and be ordained for a year as a novice.

In discussing this final step, many people stressed that it was not exclusively a rational decision. They described it in a number of different ways.

For those who had spent some time in the monastery as lay persons, staying on just seemed the natural thing to do. It seemed obvious, gradual, and no big deal. 'What else are you going to do?'

For those who had simply visited, there was a sense of in-evitability, of growing commitment, of a strong urge to give themselves to the life. Recognising the impending decision often brought a sense of panic though. Like standing on top of a cliff, ready to jump into the unknown. 'Beyond me was a black hole.' 'I knew I had to jump into death.' 'It was a challenge I knew I had to take, although I don't like challenges.' There was a clear awareness that the mind was being carried along by powerful unconscious processes. There were strong emotional needs, but even deeper there was the feeling that 'This is something I have to do', almost a sense of inevitability or even of predestination. 'I knew I had to do something difficult in this life.' Looking back, many individuals could even see how the events of their lives had been leading up to the moment of decision, however unapparent it may have been at the time.

Question Three

The third question was *What changes have you experienced within yourself during your years in the robe, in your meditation, in living by the rule and as a member of the community?* No one person described their whole history from first taking the robe up until the present, but after talking to people at all stages, from postulants of a few months to people with eight or ten years of ordained experience, I was nevertheless able to put the various accounts into the form of a continuum. I have confidence in the validity of this continuum, as it was submitted for approval to the two groups, mentioned earlier, drawn from those members of the Sangha who did not take an active part in the research. The continuum consisted of the following stages.

1. In the beginning of the monastic life, there is characteristically much inspiration, much eagerness to get into 'my' practice under ideal conditions, and to become enlightened as soon as possible. Meditation during this stage is often an attempt to escape into peace from the austere realities of monastic life, and to attain some high mystical state.
2. Subsequently, in marked contract to this early hope and expectation, there comes a period of much restlessness,

boredom and physical pain. Doubts creep in about the practice, about the chosen way of life, and about personal vocation. As time goes on, individuals begin to touch the fear and sorrow inherent in having a human body. Often many previously repressed feelings of frustration, anger, hatred and depression come to the surface, and many, especially among the younger monks, experience an unexpectedly sharp and potentially overwhelming increase in sexual feelings. One young postulant confessed, 'I'm supposed to be so pure and here I am so sullied. I was never such a sex-maniac in lay life.' This in turn leads to feelings of fear and self-hatred, and to doubts as to whether it is going to prove possible to stay in the robe. Further, living in close proximity to people whose company one has not chosen often brings up intense feelings of dislike. One monk said, 'I realised I felt like killing my room-mate.' Being hemmed about on every side by the limitations to personal freedom inherent in keeping to the rules can also produce great tensions ('a pressure-cooker effect' one individual called it). and everyone seemed to have personal monsters with which to struggle.

3. At this point, depression and despair occasionally prompt some people into leaving the monastery. In Buddhism one is, of course, free to be ordained as a postulant for a year, either to try the life as an aid to one's own practice or as a service to the community, and there is no shame attached to subsequent decisions to leave.

4. For the majority who remain, however, there now follows a period during which the essential lessons are gradually being learned as a result of letting go the desire to be and to experience something special or something different from what is actually present. This letting go is accomplished by being aware of one's greed, lust and anger, rather than trying to be rid of them; by accepting and enduring physical and emotional pain, and by developing a 'welcoming mind'. Individuals thus come to recognise the importance of practising compassion towards themselves, towards others afflicted by the same tyrannical mind, and indeed towards the very mind states themselves. They learn also to see doubt as a condition of mind which arises and passes away.

5. The next stage is a plateau where the urge to 'get somewhere'

begins to dry up, and the practice is simply 'being here now', and attempting to stay open and welcoming to each experience. One monk told me that the Abbot likened this time to the Israelites' forty years in the wilderness. It contains a sense of the self being gradually ground down, bringing frequent feelings of despair followed by resignation followed by reluctance followed by surrender and at long last by real acceptance and the welcoming mind.

6. As the years pass, there is a change in one's understanding of the purpose of the community's rules, and a gradual assimilation and grasp of the heart of the teachings. This understanding is now a personal, direct and intuitive 'knowing', rather than just an intellectual grasp. A personal experience of such things as the truth of the three signs of being, namely impermanence, unsatisfactoriness and the absence of independent existence.

7. More patience and compassion then develop, and it becomes easier to let go of things, of feelings and of opinions. In the words of monks and nuns 'You begin to taste the peace of letting go, and feel more relaxed.' 'The mind becomes unburdened, and there is a sense of lightness, spaciousness and ease, much more sense of awareness, of calm and peace, and an ability to be more in the moment.' 'The distinction between the mind and its contents also becomes much clearer, and a sense of detachment develops.' 'Somewhere along the line the fear of death goes. Death becomes nothing special, just a part of life, and this is a great relief as you recognise the power the underlying fear of death has for most people.'

8. More experienced monks and nuns take the mindfulness, clarity, calm and peace of mind almost for granted – *of course* these things develop. But what they become aware of over and above these is the opening of the heart. There is more interest in and time for other people, and less concern for the self. In fact the self has begun to wear away through a process of attrition, as the likes and dislikes which kept it going lose their power. As one nun put it, however, the self 'takes a long time to die'! Another had it that 'Really it's just a gradual process of becoming nobody and nothing. You begin to experience the joy and freedom which come from renunciation.'

Conclusion

One senior monk summed up the whole experience of the monastic life in the following words:

> In meditation and in life the process remains the same, just being aware moment by moment of what is arising and passing away, and being at peace with it, accepting it and letting it go. It's just that gradually it gets easier; clearer and easier, more spacious and more fun.

SECTION 4

Counselling and
Therapeutic Practice

INTRODUCTION TO SECTION 4

Amongst those students of Eastern spirituality who adopt what we might call a fundamentalist approach, there is a degree of opposition to the idea that Eastern spiritual techniques, in particular Buddhist techniques, can on occasions be classed and used as therapy. This is seen for example in such statements as 'Dharma is not therapy.' Those who take this line argue that spiritual techniques are powerful things and must only be practised for spiritual purposes and under the guidance of a truly enlightened master (assuming you're lucky enough to find one!). There are of course certain strengths to this argument. In the West, the current mania for identifying the 'active ingredient' in any process or substance, and then abstracting and marketing if for instant results, can work to the detriment not only of the results themselves but also of a proper recognition of the wider benefits that might be gained from the holistic use of the process concerned. The craving for instant results can also encourage the emergence of instant experts, men and women who imperfectly understand the full potential and implications of the material they are using, and yet who claim the competence to guide and influence others.

Nevertheless, there are also weaknesses to this argument. Principal amongst them is that it divorces the spiritual aspects of human life from the psychological in a way which is unjustified by the teachings of the spiritual masters who gave us the techniques in question, and limits spirituality to one special corner of human inner experience. It thus ignores the lesson implicit in such diversely expressed statements as 'Nirvana and Samsara are the same', and 'Zen is your ordinary everyday life', and presupposes that working on one's spiritual health does nothing for one's psychological health and vice versa. It ignores the fact that the East has had no need to develop separate disciplines respectively of spiritual development and psychotherapy, since in the East the former has always contained the latter. It ignores the fact that the very statement 'Dharma isn't therapy' reveals that the speaker has fallen into the Western dualistic notion of parcelling out into fragments what is in fact the integral process of inner development.

In addition, the insistence of this fundamentalist argument that only those in perfect spiritual health should have the temerity to use spiritual techniques to help others smacks of an élitism the dangers of which are too obvious to need elaboration, and which in spirit goes contrary to the compassionate intention of the Buddha and other key figures in Eastern spirituality to alleviate all human suffering.

On a less exalted level, this insistence also denies the experience of those of us who, without any special claims to enlightenment, have consistently found Eastern spiritual techniques to blend helpfully with Western insights in therapeutic work (therapeutic work in our own lives we hasten to say, not just in the lives of our clients). By therapeutic work we mean work which facilitates life changes orientated away from the behaviours that give life its unsatisfactory nature. Sometimes the level at which these changes take place is a relatively minor one, as when an individual sees that stress in a place of work can be reduced by being more analytical and mindful about the minutiae of everyday life. Sometimes the level is more profound, as when an individual learns to sever an attachment to negative states of mind. And sometimes it is profounder still, as when he or she is able to identify negative emotional states as they arise, refrain from identifying with them, and ultimately trace them back to their source in attachment, aversion and erroneous conceptions of self.

In the chapters that follow, therapy is examined from a number of different angles, each designed to show how Eastern practices can prove of increasing value in Western therapy. Ngakpa Chögyam, a Westerner and ordained yogin who has spent many years in India studying under Nyingma and Dzogchen masters, shows how Tibetan tantric practices, for all their apparent complexity, yield simple and highly effective strategies for working with and transforming even the most negative emotions. Richard Jones focuses specifically upon the problems associated with the family and upon the work that can be done in family therapy. Finally, David Fontana attempts to reconcile apparent anomalies between Eastern and Western therapeutic approaches to the self, and looks at the place of Buddhist techniques in Western psychological counselling.

JOHN CROOK
DAVID FONTANA

CHAPTER 15

The Intrinsic Spaciousness of Being: Working with Colours and Elements In Tantric Psychology

VEN. NGAKPA CHOGYAM OGYEN TONGDEN

Introduction: The View

Only through experience do we begin to perceive our world differently. Any philosophical speculation or intellectual thought that is not experienced cannot be integrated at the level of our fundamental perception of the world, and will remain only an idea at best. It follows that the experience of meditation practice is essential as a means of realising the Buddhist view, for it is only within the development of the meditational experience that we may become transparent to ourselves through witnessing the mechanics of our stylised perceptual modes.

According to the Tibetan Tantric view there are three spheres of being: the outer world of our surroundings, the inner world of our perceptions, and a spatial continuum that underlines and interpenetrates both. This spatial continuum displays itself as five fields of primary energy which make up the elemental basis of both external and internal phenomena. These fields are: Solidity or Earth, Fluidity or Water, Combustion (heat) or Fire, Mobility or Air, and Emptiness or Space. The prime purpose of Tantric psychology is transmutation, which, rather than trying to 'get rid of our problems', works with liberating the energy bound up in them. The pattern and individual character of our psychological and emotional framework is 'symbolic' in the sense that we symbolise our being in ways that take the form of one or other of the fields. Our expressed make-up is derived from an encyclopaedia of all the symbols of our free nature. As such it offers a key to discovering that nature.

Every state of mind, however distressed, is linked dynamically to an aspect of the intrinsic freedom of the spatial continuum. The Tibetan Tantric methods reveal that mind is intrinsically free (unconstrained by symbols), and that this complete openness of mind needs to be personally disclosed rather than created. There is no idea here that one has to structure and adhere to some healthy philosophical outlook artificially, for all intellectual formulations, however positive, are based on wishful thinking and some sort of idealism rather than on direct experience. Indeed, although the view of our distorted emotional patterning which we are now about to explore may be attractively illuminating, if it remains in the realm of theory it won't actually be of any help to us.

As soon as we are able to witness our stylised perception directly we will become aware as to whether what we are exploring is heartfelt or intellectually fabricated. When we are able to see ourselves in operation, then other people also become increasingly transparent to us, and this may enable us to help them. In healing ourselves, we may develop the clarity and insight essential if we are to facilitate the healing of others.

The Background to Practice

To discover how to use Tantric psychology in working with our emotions, we need some understanding of the Tantric perspective, in which human beings are seen as lacking psychological health and freedom. In Tibetan medicine, the first premise which prospective doctors have to acknowledge is that they themselves are ill. The doctor/therapist – patient relationship is considerably influenced by the fact that Tibetan doctors see themselves as having specific knowledge to help others suffering from more severe and externally manifested variants of their own illness – the illness of duality. This duality is the mind–constructed division of experience into a perceiving subject and a field of perception. This polarisation of *perception* and *field of perception* occurs when we react inappropriately to the intrinsic spaciousness of being. Such maladaptive reaction appears to be our 'characteristic human predilection', and seems to evolve in five recognisable patterns of distorted experience. The five patterns take their character from the Elements (Earth, Water Fire, Air and Space) as they manifest in terms of our emotional/psychological energies.

These maladaptive behavioural patterns are all designs or scenarios which have been personally evolved by us, their performers, to create the sensation of well-being or security. We all have these 'perceptual philosophies' and ultimately, although we may consider ourselves to be well-balanced, emotionally stable people – we are all subject to the continual irritating prickle of 'life', which is never quite what we want or need it to be. The people whom we may describe as being emotionally/psychologically unstable or unbalanced have merely complicated these 'perceptual philosophies' and act out highly convoluted 'sub-plots' that can be farcical or tragic. If we or our clients have such problems, it is because our life circumstances have 'conspired' to facilitate our integration of increasingly distorted 'perceptual philosophies'. In order to unlearn these unhelpful 'skills', we first need to examine the apparent benefits we derive from implementing them.

These peculiar benefits take their characteristics from our distorted reactions to the 'Intrinsic Spaciousness of Being', each characterised by the qualities of the five elements. Exploring the nature of each maladaptive habit pattern requires that we examine the nature and functioning of the natural elements. From a merely intellectual point of view, the psychology of Tantra is delightfully picturesque and poetic in the way that it draws 'analogies' between the elements and the states of mind to which they are linked. To the practitioner of Tantra, however, these are not analogies, but *dynamically linked* configurations of lived experience.

The system of elements and their subtle psychological/emotional counterparts enables Tantric practitioners to see the phenomenal world as a psychological teaching aid. I have explored these ideas more fully and in less condensed language elsewhere, (Chogyam, 1986).

Distorted Reaction Patterns

Let us take a look at these five distorted reaction patterns. The reaction of the distorted Earth element to the intrinsic spaciousness of being is one of insignificance and insubstantiality, and the tangent we take leads us to cultivate solidity and power. The need to surround ourselves with overt displays of wealth and dominion grows out of our deep-rooted sense of poverty and worthlessness. To compensate for this hollowness, we become builders of empires – we hoard wealth and accumulate seemingly cogent definitions of who we are in terms of status, ownership, control, fame, worship and dominance. Excessive pride and arrogance feed the rigidity of our frames of reference – obduracy and wilfulness lead us further into antisocial interpersonal behaviour.

The distorted Water element's reaction to the intrinsic spaciousness of being is one of fear and lack of power, and the tangent that we take is one in which we feel justified in lashing out. Justification feeds our anger and sense of resentment and we see the world as a field of combat. We come to regard 'emotional-overkill' as an effective means of keeping our fear at bay, and have the unfortunate tendency to shoot first and ask questions later. If we feel ourselves to be powerless, we necessarily feel compelled to arm ourselves to the teeth. We magnify the 'strike-potential' of others out of all proportion, because we identify them with the spaciousness we fear. We rapidly 'learn' that attack is the best form of defence. But when we feel ourselves to be naturally empowered and confident, we can afford to be gentle and tolerant.

The distorted Fire element reaction to the Intrinsic Spaciousness of Being is one that gives rise to the feeling of isolation and loneliness, and the tangent we take is one in which we generate the compulsion to cling to the comforting proximity of people, places, things and ideas. We find our world to be an emotional desert and attempt to crowd out our loneliness by indiscriminately grabbing at the experience of union with any focus of our fleeting attention. In some ways, this pattern is similar to the distorted Earth-style reaction – but whereas the distorted Earth style finds only the sensation of emptiness and insubstantiality in the process of hoarding and scanning, the distorted Fire style finds only the emptiness of isolation and separation in the process of consummation. In the Earth style we misinterpret the discovery of insubstantiality as the need to consolidate further; we need to scan mightier ramparts and bastions of personal reality. In the Fire style, we misinterpret the discovery of isolation/separation as the need to unify as quickly as possible with further and yet further focuses of seductive proximity.

The distorted Air element reaction to the Intrinsic Spaciousness of Being is one of anxious vulnerability and the tangent we take involves us in self-generated accelerating suspicion. We suspect that complex contrivances are in motion, born out of the sinister unknown, whose designs are to undermine us in ways that are not immediately apparent. We lack any sense of stability – we feel that whatever sense of somethingness which we are manipulating to counter the threat of oblivion exists ridiculously precariously in comparison to the lurking threat of that worrying 'nothingness'. We become tense, agitated and hyperactive as we keep our concentration continually moving – trying to keep everything under surveillance at once. We never know in which moment we could be tricked or treacherously betrayed if we falter in our vigilance. Our feelings range from envy through jealousy and suspicion to paranoia.

In some ways, this pattern has similarities to the distorted Water element reaction, but whereas in this style, we fear direct, coherent and obvious assault, the Air style is one in which fear in the form of uncertainty and nervousness arises out of not knowing how and when suspected assault will manifest. So, rather than lashing out at 'obvious' but mistaken threats, we engage in high-tension speculation.

The Water-style defence mechanisms are fairly direct and brutal – we could compare them to jet-fighter planes or battleships. But the Air style defences are far more complex, intricate and indirect; there is absolutely no trust involved in anything – we wouldn't even get our fighter planes off the ground because we become involved with interminable double-checking. We become obsessed with grotesquely convoluted analyses of the range of hidden plots against us – we could compare the Air-style maladaptive pattern to counter-counter-counter-espionage against double/triple/quadruple agents.

The distorted Space reaction is fundamental, it underlies the other four because it is the initial misapprehension giving rise to the other four and into which they subsequently collapse. This fundamental distorted pattern is one in which we are quite simply and utterly overawed/overwhelmed by the sheer vastness of Space. The tangent that we take is maybe better described as one in which we feel completely unable to take any kind of tangent – we become incapacitated and depressed. We cut off from the outside world and become introverted, locked inside ourselves – we play blind, deaf and dumb to experience and seek shelter in oblivion.

Transformation

These five distorted reaction patterns exist within each other and most 'healthy' people have a balance of these patterns in their less tortuous manifestations. Some 'healthy' people have imbalances of one or more Element patterns but their energy generates qualities, abilities and talents as well as destructive habits and tendencies. Some people have great elemental imbalances that become fuelled by circumstances to such an extent that we designate them as emotionally unbalanced or psychologically disturbed. But whatever the imbalance, the essence of Tantric psychology is that our distorted element reactions to space are dynamically linked to our liberated potentialities.

The arrogance/obduracy of the distorted Earth element reaction can be transmuted into *equanimity/equality*.

The anger/aggression of the distorted Water element reaction can be transmuted into *clarity/insight*.

The indiscriminate and obsessive consuming nature of the distorted Fire element can be transmuted into *discriminating awareness/- compassion*.

The paranoia of the distorted Air element reaction can be

Table 15.1 Relations between responses to Intrinsic Spaciousness of Being and the effects of their transmutation

Element	Response to Intrinsic Spaciousness	Reactions to the response	Effect of transmutation
Earth element	Feeling of insignificance	Cultivation of solidity and power	Equanimity
Water element	Fear, feeling powerless	Lashing out, recklessness	Clarity
Fire element	Isolation, loneliness	Clinging to comforts	Compassion
Air element	Anxiety, vulnerability paranoia	Excessive analysis	Confidence
Space element	Sense of being overwhelmed	Incapacitation, depression	Pervasive intelligence

transmuted into *confidence/ability and self-accomplishing method/-activity*.

The deliberate torpor and depression of the distorted Space element reaction can be transmuted into *ubiquitous intelligence and pervasive awareness*.

With this model of perverted perceptual philosophies and emotional habit patterns (as distortions of the liberated energy of our emotions) we are able to see ourselves and our clients in a different light. Our/their personality problems, obsessions, neuroses or whatever are also doorways to our/their liberated potentialities. Experiential familiarity with the Tantric view of the emotions enables us to recognise in ourselves, and help clients to recognise, positive qualities within what have come to be devalued as merely 'treatable complaints'.

If we look carefully at anger for instance, we can see many of the qualities of clarity, as distorted yet recognisable reflections. Anger is hyper-intelligent – often in a state of anger we release heightened capacities of wit and memory. Sarcasm is delivered with speed and unusual accuracy – we know just where the exposed emotional nerves are in others and we make rapier thrusts at them with the surgical sharpness of our hatred.

In this view of our emotions as 'reflections' of fields of liberated energy, our method of freeing ourselves is one of making direct contact with our emotional energies rather than one of becoming involved at the level of reactions which involve ourselves either in expression, repression or dissipation.

These three familiar methods of working with emotions are linked to the three *distracted tendencies* of *attraction, aversion* and *indifference*, which are the ways in which we react to everything that presents itself as long as we 'hide' from the spaciousness of being. Attraction, aversion and indifference underpin the fabric of our motivation as long as we equate the Intrinsic Spaciousness of Being with annihilation, and as long as we have this conception we can only react in these three ways. We continually scan our perceptual horizon in order to establish reference points to prove to ourselves that the Intrinsic Spaciousness of Being is just a bad dream. And so we are attracted to whatever makes us feel solid, separate, permanent, continuous and defined. We are averse to anything that suggests the opposite and indifferent to whatever we are unable to manipulate. It is this dense web of motivation and patterned perception that almost entirely restricts the *natural 'sparkle'* of our being. We cannot get rid of the cause of our bad feeling by repressing it, nor by expressing it, nor by dissipating it.

Many people have found that through being helped to express their anger (for example) they have overcome such problems as depression (which can be caused by repressing feelings of anger), but this has led to the mistaken view that it is healthy to express anger. In Tantric terms, to express anger is only to *intensify the distorted reflection* and to create further illusory distance from the liberated energy of that emotion.

To express anger is only to condition ourselves with a pattern of perception that triggers angry responses more readily in more varied situations. Simply speaking, if we regard our anger as a healthy release, we're just training ourselves to be angry people. We avoid the side-effects of repression, but we acquire the side-effects of expression.

Dissipation is the least injurious activity in terms of side-effects whether dealing with anger or with any emotion, but it doesn't deal with the root of our dilemma, and until that is directly confronted, an emotion will always re-emerge when our circumstances trigger one of our five distorted responses.

The practice of meditation in the context of working with emotions gives us another option, one in which we neither repress, express or dissipate our emotional energy, but one in which we let go of the conceptual scaffolding and wordlessly gaze into the physical sensation of the emotion. This is what I describe as 'staring into the face of arising emotions in order to realise their Empty Nature'.

Staring Meditation

Meditation (according to the system known as *Dzogchen Trek-chod*) involves finding the presence of awareness in the sensation of the emotion we are experiencing. Simply speaking we locate the physical 'seat' of the emotion within the body (it may be localised or pervasive). This is where we feel the emotion as a physical sensation. We then allow that sensation to expand and pervade us – we become the emotion. We cease to be observers; we stare into the face of the arising emotion with such completeness that all sense of division between 'experience' and 'experiencer' dissolve into the Intrinsic Spaciousness of Being. In this way we open ourselves to glimpses of what we actually are – we start to become transparent to ourselves. Through this *staring*, the distorted energy of our emotions liberates 'of itself', and enters into its own condition – that of fundamental freedom. In order to use meditation in this way, we need to have developed the experience of letting go of obsessive attachment to the intellectual/conceptual process as the crucial reference point on which our sense of Being relies. In short, we need to be able to dwell peacefully in our own experiential space, which is free of conceptual activity and yet in which there is pure and total presence.

Through the practice of meditation, we discover that we can make direct contact with the unconditioned essence of our spectrum of liberated potentiality; we can begin to work with our emotions. We begin to see through our own patterns of perception. Working with emotions in this way enables us to empathise accurately with others. In a counselling context, we become able to see through the complex of pain and problems with which we're presented.

To present Tibetan Tantric psychology in such a contracted way inevitably makes the language in which it is expressed rather dense and difficult – I have had to cover a lot of ground in a very short space. Essentially Tantra is not a matter for academic intellectual research but for personal experience. Explanations of this kind are based on *realised reasoning* rather than on conventional logic, so assimilation requires the development of the meditative experience. If material of this kind is not personally verified its primary value is lost – it becomes inapplicable; an unworkable theoretical construct. A considerable number of great Tantric Masters have been completely illiterate and often not at all given to elegant expression or the elucidation of complex logical analyses. In order only to answer questions their *method* was often to introduce pupils directly to practice, rather than to present explanations. None the less, explanations may often spark our *intrinsic enlightened nature* and inspire us to practise. I hope that the words of this inconsequential yogi will be of some use to that end.

CHAPTER 16

Family Therapy and Dependent Origination

RICHARD JONES

Introduction

A system has been defined as:

> an assembly of parts where:
> 1. the parts or components are connected together in an organised way,
> 2. the parts or components are affected by being in the system (and are changed by leaving it),
> 3. the assembly does something,
> 4. the assembly has been identified by a person as being of special interest.

Compare this with the Buddhist principle of dependent-arising, as expressed for example by Chang (1972, p. 12):

> . . . no thing, whether concrete or abstract, mundane or transcendental, has an independent or isolated existence, but all things depend upon one another for their existence and functions.

The respective thinking behind these two attempts at definition appears very similar. However, it is arguable that there are still traces in the first attempt of a linear perspective containing the notion that it is possible to separate a whole into parts which then exist in isolation from each other. The second attempt therefore describes more adequately the reality which I propose to discuss, a reality in which the therapist (for my purposes the family therapist) attempts to empty his or her mind of any traces of conceptualisation, and meets the members of the client family just as they are. By conceptualisation I mean speculation arising from conventional descriptions of people, including diagnostic descriptions such as social roles, or attributions by other family members or by referring agencies.

My purpose is not to deny that these descriptions can be useful, but to make a conscious choice to understand families and their members in a way which differs from them. A quote from Govinda (1969, p. 265) helps illustrate my point:

> The Buddha's teaching does not attempt to deny the importance
> of differentiation in favour of absolute oneness, or to proclaim the
> undifferentiated equality of all things. It does not strive after the
> destruction of contrasts, but after the recognition of their relativity
> within a unity existing simultaneously with them, within them
> and beyond them.

The Systems Approach to Family Therapy

Two natural systems, the human being and the human family, interest me here. Conventional wisdom in individual psychology constrains the therapist to examine what it is that is wrong with the individual *as an individual*. The individually orientated psychologist does of course acknowledge the importance of context, and indeed accepts that what is worked on in the consulting room must in some way be generalised to other and more natural settings. He may indeed even assist this generalisation by attempting during therapy to prepare the individual for return to these natural settings. But as an effort towards the understanding and amelioration of the individual's total predicament this does not, in my view, go nearly far enough. There remains implicit in it an assumption that somehow something must be done to make the person 'fit in' better. The trap for the psychologist who approaches problems in this way is essentially that they are seen *as problems*: they are given the status of things or entities to be altered. He is beguiled by the request to 'do something about' a reported problem, and misses an opportunity to reframe the situation so that the problem ceases to have its reified existence. The way to avoid this trap is to eschew what Selvini-Palozzoli *et al.* (1978) describe as 'cultural and linguistic conditioning', or what might be called linear/Cartesian/dualistic epistemology.

Cultural and linguistic conditioning, together with the problem-centred therapeutic approach associated with it, constrain the family therapist to examine a single entity, be it the client or the client's symptom, and attempt to change it. By contrast, what I shall call a *systems* understanding of family therapy (as exemplified by what is known as the Milan Approach), stresses the neutrality of the therapist. A useful metaphor for this neutrality can be drawn from the Buddhist teaching that all is in a state of flux and change. There is thus no need to try to change (any)thing, because there is (no)thing to change. Instead of a static entity to be changed, there is only a pattern re-emerging from moment to moment, and in the context of attitudes which are congruent with its appearance. It is not that my client is for example anxious, but rather that under certain conditions and in certain viewing frames he or she may *appear* to be anxious. Anxiety is not a thing in itself but a process, and any attempt to treat it as a thing becomes one of the conditions for its appearance and reappearance.

Entity and Process

The systems family therapist is therefore less concerned with entity than with process. As implied in the quotation from Govinda above, this doesn't mean that entity is never a useful concept. In certain domains (for instance when dealing with solid objects), it remains a necessary concept for survival. But in others – and particularly in the domain of human relationships – it is a major hindrance. This can perhaps be illustrated by referring to Chang (1972) again. Chang lists some of the contrasting qualities of the entity (*svabhava*) way and of the process (*nihsvabhava*) way as follows:

Svabhava Way	*Nihsvabhava Way*
independent	interdependent
unitary	structural
entity and substance	events and actions
static	dynamic
fixed	fluid
bound	free
definitively restricted	infinite possibilities

clinging and attachment   release and detachment
being   non-being
thatness   whatness

It is with the *nihsvabhava* way that I identify systems thinking and the Milan Approach, and indeed the 'mind only' stance of Buddhism in some of its forms (See also Chapter 1).

In terms of the Milan Approach, the family that comes to the family therapist for help can be described as having a linear understanding, in that they behave 'as if' they have a *svabhava* way of understanding their problem. Some or all of the family members act 'as if' one member is to blame for what is happening, 'as if' his or her behaviour is fixed and static and a permanent part of an identifiable personality. There is little or no verbal acknowledgement of the interrelationships between family members, and of how behaviour by one family member is related to behaviour by the others. There may be no real recognition of relationships, or at best a recognition only of a naive one-to-one correspondence between one person's behaviour and that of another. Behaviours may be seen always to be linked in a simplistic causal fashion, and the relationships between any sequence of behaviours and its wider context may go unnoticed. (This idea that events, or ideas, are always linked together in this simplistic causal fashion is described in the Milan Approach as *circular causality*.)

So how can such families be led to acknowledge the fact that the behaviour of their individual members is contextually bound – and led to acknowledge it moreover in a way that yet allows to these individuals reasonable autonomy of action? To answer this question, it is useful to introduce at this point the Buddhist terms *shih* and *li*, or content and form. *Shih* is defined by Chang (1972) as understanding events in the realm of phenomena in terms of their distinctive and differentiated nature. For example, the river flows, the tree grows. By contrast, *li* is understanding them in terms of their underlying principle, the immanent reality beyond sense perception. For example the principle of gravity and the principle of inertia. In Hwa Yen Buddhist thought, the ultimate *li* is the universal one mind, or *tathata* or suchness or emptiness. 'It is through the merging of the distinct matter (*shih*) into the non-differentiated principle (*li*) that the truth of mutual identity is revealed.' (Chang, 1972 p. 136)

Experience and Reality in Family Therapy

In family therapy this merging is helped if the therapist refrains from trying to understand family members in terms of an intellectual model, because the act of observing them within the framework provided by the model constricts the therapist's direct experience. The reality of family therapy is that the therapist is both context and actor in the very experience which he may be trying to frame and alter. Therefore in observing the family the therapist is in a sense observing himself. The implication is that if he or she is to function from within the context of direct experience, the therapist must therefore confront the question, 'What is it that I'm looking for?'. To borrow for a moment from the metaphors of modern physics as applied to two interacting sub-atomic systems: '. . . before any measurement is made, neither system possesses a unique attribute.' (Wolf 1985, p. 49)

The question, 'What is it that I'm looking for?' therefore also implies the question, 'What unique attributes am I, the therapist, bringing to the interaction between myself and my clients?', and prompts the further question 'What will be the consequences of my having interacted with them?'. For example, attempting to *do* something for my clients suggests a different intent from attempting to *learn* something from them, the main difference being that the former implies subject acting upon object (the imposition of authority), and the latter subject learning with object (a process of sharing). The latter is much more akin to the Tibetan doctor's strategy of using the illness of the patient to remind himself of his own illness.

The notion of subject learning from object contains the view that the family and individuals within the family are complete in themselves, and need not justify their behaviour because they are already perfectly co-evolving (cf. Bateson, 1973). Just as each individual already expresses the Buddha mind, with nothing needing to be added or taken away, so it is with the family. There is a sense in which the family already operates perfectly. In the metaphors of Buddhism, the family pattern (*li*) pervades the family as a collection of individuals (*shih*), as indeed does the pattern of each individual within the family (*li*).

The idea I'm trying to communicate is of the simultaneity of experience and reality in therapy. The therapist's task is to interact with the family in as total a way as possible, to strive for an understanding that acknowledges the function of the therapist's belief systems, and acknowledges that they are ultimately always speculative because they cannot be known as the truth. The therapist therefore does not work with a concept of what is 'right' for the individual or the family, because to hold such a concept is to cling to one's own preconceptions. The family is responding to the situation in which it finds itself at that time in the only way it can, and to have an idea of how best to restructure it is to lose sight of this fact.

How Change Occurs

When faced with this approach, people are prompted to ask how, therefore, does change occur within the family? In a sense, this question is superfluous because, as already pointed out, change is already occurring by the very nature of the ever-changing state of things. However, the therapist can join the family in a way which potentiates what is already happening – by expanding the awareness of the family members through asking questions and making statements which help demonstrate the connectedness between individual family members. The family members have come to therapy with a *svabhava* thinking, and by working with them in a *nihsvabhava* way they can be exposed to a different reality. By the exploration of what Wilden (1972) calls the 'relations between relations', the family members begin to experience this reality.

Another way of expressing this is by saying that in terms of the Buddhist principles of flux and of dependent-arising, the family in reality has no fixed behaviour pattern, however much the family members may imagine they have. These family members may therefore choose to adopt an understanding of their own predicament which allows them to abandon the *svabhava* perspective upon their lives. As Govinda (1969, page 270) puts it: 'While in the past everything is final, rigid, unalterable law, causality – the present is living relationship, which is alterable, fluid and nowhere final. Thus the present is the liberation from causality.'

What does all this mean in practical terms for the family

therapist? It means that he or she realises there is no fixed family history, although realising at the same time that individual family members have internal representations of this history based on previous and current relationships, and that these representations are usefully thought of as 'living history'. These realisations can be brought home to the family by including as many of the actual historical family figures as possible in the family interview, so demonstrating to family members the importance of a continual updating of the representations of reality which we operate in the course of our understanding of the world. The contradiction between what individuals think is true on the strength of their previous observations, and what emerges in other contexts where these self-fulfilling prophecies do not operate unchallenged, can then become apparent to family members.

By working as a team, and routinely being reminded that there is no one explanation of what is happening, an opportunity is created for therapist and for family members not only to enrich the complexity of their personal understanding, but to learn the flexibility of negotiating shared realities in the knowledge that these realities are provisional and may be more or less useful. This therapeutic approach fits the scientific metaphor in that it tests hypotheses and demonstrates that, by the nature of things, no hypothesis can be held over a long period of time. The continual updating of hypotheses reminds therapist and clients of the essential uncertainty of their lives, and is reminiscent of Korzybski's statement that the map is not the territory (see Bateson, 1973).

It also reminds the therapist that the pattern (*li*) which he discovers is related to the pattern which he predicts will be discovered. Thus in a sense it is the creation of his or her initial hypothesis, while at the same time also being the creation of the events (*shih*) prompted by the interaction between individual family members themselves.

In identifying *li* as an explanatory principle (in terms of the one universal mind) I may be in danger of identifying 'God's hand' in everything, the immanent God of medieval times (Wilden, 1980). However, I choose to take this risk because of the complex nature of human behaviour. When we examine others (and hence ultimately ourselves) we are nature looking at nature, and therefore cannot help but face unifying principles. *Li* can stand for many different levels of explanation, and it is at the deepest level that I am suggesting we should attempt this explanation. To build on my previous metaphor, if I search for the universe in the people I meet, I allow the emergence of the infinite possibility that lies within. If I attempt to control or judge, I rediscover a subject/object split, and create the possibility of rigidity and blame, and return to the *svabhava* way of understanding.

Conclusion

The connectedness and complexity of human relationships emerges in a systems approach to change. There are thought-provoking links between this approach and the philosopy of Hwa Yen and of Zen Buddhism. The interplay between the individual and the family can be viewed in the light of the concepts of *li* and of *shih*, which stress the interpenetrating nature of form and content in a way which sheds some light on the complexitites of these human relationships, and which helps our understanding of the cosmic dance of which we are all a part.

CHAPTER 17

Self and Mind in Psychological Counselling

DAVID FONTANA

Introduction

If I had to name the single most important causal factor underlying the problems which clients present in psychological counselling, it would be the inability to value oneself. Explore deeply enough, and whatever the immediate cause of distress, there sure enough, acting as source and instigator, are feelings of personal worthlessness and shame. The client reveals a hopelessness about himself, a despair that often borders on self-disgust and hatred, and which effectively robs him of any chance of experiencing his own being in a positive and life-enhancing way.

The reasons for this self-rejection, suffice it to say, are deeply embedded in the individual's temperamentally mediated responses to earlier experiences. The child is born with no clear picture of himself. As he (or she) grows towards independence and autonomy in the first years of life, he builds up this picture on the strength of what others tell him (by word and deed) about himself, and on the strength of the consequent emotions experienced by him. So effective are these early lessons, and so firmly rooted are they in the unconscious, that they resist the influence of later experiences, however much at variance with them these later experiences may be. Thus the child who is early filled with guilt and self-doubt, and with a gnawing sense of 'wickedness' and of failure to reach other people's expectations, tends to carry these burdens with him through life, regardless of how outwardly successful that life may be. The picture of himself, accepted in ignorance and innocence from others, becomes part of the very fabric of his existence.

Without any real awareness of its origins, he accepts it as true, and interprets his life events very much in the light of it.

So the task of the counsellor becomes to help the client break free from this early conditioning, and start to experience himself as he really is. And in and through this personal liberation, to begin to experience others as they really are as well. For the inability to value oneself leads inevitably to the inability to value others. Self-rejection leads almost always to a morbid over-preoccupation with the self and its problems, and to a rooted tendency to see others in terms only of their relationship to this self. Thus they are either impossibly overrated or unfairly underrated, either hero-worshipped as the client imagines he sees in them what he would like to see in himself, or done down as he imagines through their inferiority he can boost his own self-esteem. Whichever way it goes, other people are simply used as a means towards salving his own existential misery, rather than appreciated and understood for themselves.

How does Eastern psychology, or for the purposes of this chapter more specifically Buddhist psychology, help the counsellor in this task? How does Buddhist psychology help the client find value and therefore meaning in his own life, and by extension value and meaning in the lives of others? How does it, to paraphrase Christ's words, help him love both himself and his neighbour, and love them with the same kind of love? In an attempt to condense the answer into one short chapter, let me focus on three specific aspects of Buddhist psychology, namely the teachings on *self*, on *attachment/aversion*, and on *mindfulness*. Each of these teachings gives rise to specific methods for thinking about and practising one's life, and thus for changing at a profound level the way in which one experiences reality. Let me take each of the three in turn.

The Self

I don't propose to become involved in a deep discussion on the meaning of the Buddhist doctrine of *annata* , or no-self. I've tried to do this elsewhere (Chapter 4). Perhaps of all readily accessible Buddhist doctrines it has caused most confusion and misunderstanding in the West, prompting many people to interpret it as a nihilistic teaching designed to make them doubt their own experience (the alacrity with which some accept this interpretation can smack at times of a morbid desire for self-punishment and self-extinction). At a practical level, the doctrine of annata is designed simply to present the self as a dynamic, fluid *process* rather than as a rigid, static *structure* (See Chapter 6). As such, the doctrine has much in common with state-based as opposed to trait-based theories of personality in the West. It sees the self as subject always to change, modified and re-shaped, however subtly, by each moment of experience, with each experience, thought and action influencing whatever follows.

This dynamic model of the self gives the individual a much more appropriate construct with which to work in order to effect personal change. If the self is changing anyway, then why not take the direction of this change into one's own hands? The 'self' which one has been rejecting, which one feels unable to value, is simply a habit of thinking. A fiction within which one has become imprisoned, and around which there are no bars beyond those created by one's own imaginings. Often the simple realisation of this fact is enough to bring the individual a sense, if not of liberation, then at least of what liberation must be like. A sense of the infinite potential of his own being, infinite in the sense that there are no boundaries upon the activity of his own fundamental awareness. And since the self is a process and not a structure, this glimpse of freedom inevitably affects the individual's subsequent experience. His problems don't drop from him overnight, but he cannot behave in future as if he has never had an insight into the illusory nature of these problems. He has seen the origin of these problems in his reactions to the events of his earlier life, and he has seen their continuation in his subsequent habits of thinking. The illusion was created by, and is being sustained by, the actions of his own mind.

Attachment and Aversion

The next step suggested by Buddhist psychology is to help the client examine the nature of these actions. Since the self is a dynamic process, these actions must be equally dynamic. That is, unlike repetitious movements within a closed system,

predetermined by the nature of the system itself, they are open
and fluid. If they have become repetitious, this is due not to their
essential nature but to the chosen behaviour patterns of the client
himself. Buddhist psychology explains these patterns primarily in
terms of *attachment* and *aversion*. The individual characteristically
responds to his experiences either by attaching (clinging) to them
and wanting them to continue, or by averting (withdrawing) from
them and wanting them to cease. Pleasant experiences usually
evoke attachment, and unpleasant experiences aversion (though
as we shall see in a moment, 'pleasant' and 'unpleasant' are not
always what they seem).

This predilection for attachment and aversion brings with
it a range of consequences. It limits our freedom, since we
are constantly craving after our attachments and seeking to
escape from our aversions. It keeps us from the realisation
that external reality, just like the internal reality of the self, is
changing (impermanent). It promotes suffering, since inevitably
the things to which we are attached – even our very ownership of
them – change and pass away, leaving us to mourn for what once
was. And in terms of the self, it means we become locked into
our destructive habits of self-rejection. This last requires a little
explanation, particularly as I spoke a moment ago of attachment
and aversion as the *chosen behaviour patterns of the client himself.*
Not surprisingly, the client objects strenuously to the notion that
he *chooses*, through attachment and aversion, to become locked
into destructive psychological habits. Since these habits cause him
nothing but suffering, he can't accept that they're anything to do
with his own choice. He can accept the more abstract idea that his
own habits of thinking play a part in sustaining his misguided view
of himself, but the idea that he chooses these habits carries with
it the suggestion that there's something desirable, even enjoyable
about them. Naturally he baulks at this.

Nevertheless, this suggestion isn't far from the truth. Because
once caught up in the idea of the self as a permanent, ever-present
structure, the individual is forced to give that structure some
identity. If he exists only as that structure, then he must strive
to develop some picture of what that structure looks like. If
he loses this picture, then the structure literally ceases to exist.
He's faced with the existential dread of his own dissolution, the
kind of dread seen in many neurotics and psychotics as they

desperately try to hold pieces of their personality together and pretend to be whole. Almost anything is better than this dread. Thus the client will go on relating to the bruised and damaged self-image built up for him in childhood, rather than face its dissolution and his own (imagined) destruction. Paradoxical as it may seem, he becomes fiercely and tenaciously attached to his own wounds, because to him these wounds confer identity. He recognises them as himself, and at a deep level the thought of abandoning them is far more painful than the thought of living with them.

Thus in a very real sense he chooses to continue with his misguided habits of thought about his own reality. He insists to the counsellor that he wants to change, yet change is one of his deepest terrors. To the confident, secure person change presents no threat. His confidence is based upon the knowledge that change is the reality within which he exists. To the fearful, insecure person, change is the reality within which he ceases to exist. Change takes from him even that little he has. So when he speaks to the counsellor of his desire to be different, to break free from his suffering, what he is really saying is that he wants to remain the person he is, with the single difference that he wants that person to be happy.

Not only is this attachment to his wounds apparent in the client's general approach to himself, it's evident in his response to his specific problems. Waking depressed each morning for example, he becomes immediately attached to his depression. He identifies with it: 'I am depressed' (notice how the use of the verb 'to be' emphasises this identification!). Feeling fear, or anger, or guilt, he quickly becomes these things. He recognises himself in them. 'That's me', 'That's the way I am', 'That's me all over'. Should he experience a moment of joy he mistrusts it. His mind immediately hunts around for some reason why he shouldn't be joyful. Unable to recognise himself in the joy, his mind searches for an anxiety to make himself feel himself again. It's exemplified for me by the case of a girl recently brought to my attention who reported waking up one morning feeling happy until she remembered who she was!

Since much of this attachment takes place at the subconscious level, it takes time for the counsellor to help the client recognise it. And it takes time for the client to recognise that far from giving him the security of identity, this attachment is actually getting in the way. We are already secure, because we are a process and remain a process. Nothing can alter that. Insecurity only comes from trying to congeal that process and then hang on to this congealment, like a river that tries to turn itself into one of the rocks which it flows so easily past. Or like a flame trying to turn itself into one of the cinders around which it dances and plays.

Mindfulness

Which brings me to the third of the three aspects of Buddhist psychology that I want to discuss, namely mindfulness. The way to help bring one's attachments, whether to false aspects of the self or to the world around one, into consciousness, is to become more mindful of the moment-by-moment experience that goes to make up our lives. Most of the time we go through life so locked into our own thinking, so encapsulated by the internal dialogue chattering away in our heads, that we're aware neither of what is going on around us nor of what is actually happening in our own minds. The more nervous and anxious the client, the more self-rejecting and guilty, the more preoccupied will he be by this dialogue. Listening to precious little else, he goes through life without noticing he's alive. Not for nothing does the command 'awake' ring through the teachings of all the great spiritual masters, Christian, Buddhist, Sufi and Hindu. Unless he awakes to himself, to reality, the individual cannot hope to be free.

In practical terms, this awakening demands the operation of mindfulness. We see mindfulness in one form in sitting meditation, and it is doubtful if true mindfulness can develop without this practice. But we also see mindfulness in the training of our awareness towards the world of everyday objects and everyday experience, and towards our own reactions to these things. Asked to practise this kind of mindfulness, a clear, thought-free awareness of what is happening around and within one, most people admit they can't do it for more than a few seconds together. A few seconds, and thoughts rise up once more and the mind goes wool-gathering. A few seconds, and emotions arise from nowhere and aren't noticed until they've taken over full control. If nothing else, this experience brings home to the individual the full extent of his need to practice. It brings home to him the precise degree to which he has lost command of his own being, and the steps he must take to regain this command.

I haven't space to go into the various techniques of sitting meditation to which the client can be introduced at this point, and most of them will be familiar to readers anyway. But let me just touch on two other techniques of mindfulness which I consider valuable. The first of them, mindfulness directed outwards, takes up no extra time and can be practised for a few minutes on odd occasions during the day. It involves carrying out a simple running commentary, quietly or aloud, on each of one's actions as one goes about a routine task. Without this commentary, it is difficult even for the practised meditator to keep the mind focused for any length of time on the task in hand. With this practice, even the beginner can make progress. The results, in terms of sharpening up the concentration and establishing a proper relationship to the world around one, are incalculable.

The second technique, mindfulness directed inwards, involves watching the ebb and flow of one's reactions to events. Often these reactions are in the form of thoughts. Often they are in the form of emotions. As one watches them, so one becomes aware of cravings, of selfishness, of the first stirrings of fear or anger, of the tremors of joy or happiness. As one watches the play of these internal happenings, so one can see their origins, the reasons for one's cravings, the reasons for one's selfishness, the exact feather that has been ruffled to produce the anger. By identifying these reasons, one becomes with practice just that little bit better, day by day, at switching off the negative thoughts and emotions before they take control. This is very different from repression. The thoughts and emotions aren't bottled up or pushed back from whence they came. They're seen simply for what they are, and in that moment of recognition they begin to lose their power. One sees the absence of real *need* for the selfishness or the anger. And one realises – crucially – that these things are not caused by other people ('you make me so angry!') but by we ourselves. There are no magic buttons for other people to come up and press. It is our own mind that is at once the button and the finger that presses the button, and it is our own mind that can inactivate both button and finger.

Conclusion

Buddhist psychology is no more able than any other psychology to provide ready-made solutions for a client's problems. But more than any other psychology it can help make people transparent to themselves. It can help the individual see both the possibility of change and the real meaning of change. It can help him identify what he is doing to sustain his present condition. And crucially it can arm him with practices that he can go out and use. None of these practices are particularly easy. No practices for effecting personal change ever are. Nor will they work for the individual who lacks the motivation to make them work. But for the person who really wants to know who is acting as his gaoler, and for the person who really wants to be rid of that gaoler and take the keys to freedom into his own hands, Buddhist psychology offers more promise than the better publicised psychological therapies currently on offer in the West. Rarely in conflict with these therapies, at either the theoretical or practical level, Buddhist psychology is a way towards health. A sure way and a gentle way. Particularly if the therapist has first followed that way himself!

Conclusion

JOHN CROOK AND DAVID FONTANA

In this book we have attempted to show a number of ways in which Western psychology and Western-educated people can benefit from Eastern psychological theory and practice. We don't pretend to have been exhaustive in our coverage, since the possibilities that stretch before us appear almost infinite in their scope and implications. But we hope the reader will have been helped to appreciate something of the way in which an infusion of Eastern concepts into our Western thinking can broaden our view both of the meaning that underlies human experience and of the techniques which can be used to modify and enrich it.

It is often argued that Western and Eastern psychologies are irreconcilably separated from each other by the respective cultural contexts in which they have been spawned. There is some basis for this view. Just as languages show vast differences from each other in vocabulary and syntax when the various groups to which they belong are isolated from each other, so do social beliefs and practices and the view of humanity which they express. The variations between these beliefs and practices are often so extreme in fact that any attempt to effect a reconciliation between them can appear as at best an uneasy compromise, much indeed as an attempt to effect a reconciliation between different languages would produce an artificial construction of little living value.

Cultural growth, like language growth, is a long slow process which can only occur in response to genuine human need. So a true meeting of Western and Eastern ideas should be less like the uneasy amalgam that results from abruptly rolling two different coloured pieces of plasticine together, and more like the harmonious composition that comes from gradually adding varied shades of colour to a painted landscape. A true meeting is effected by taking the universal phenomenon of Man as a starting-point, and allowing different cultures to provide different perspectives upon it. Each of these perspectives helps build up a rounded picture, much as a series of different impressions of the same image go to produce a hologram. None of the perspectives is false in itself, but none tells the whole story. Only when they are put together does the story emerge, allowing us to marvel at the fact that we were once so easily satisfied with a flat, single-dimensional viewpoint.

Now what of the future? The tragic circumstances surrounding the occupation of Tibet have led to an unprecedented exodus to the West of specialist teachers of Buddhist psychology. The impact of the lamas has been remarkable: great personalities such as H.H. The Dalai Lama or Lama Thubten Yeshe have impressed not only by the force and relevance of their teachings but above all by the inviolability of their moral stature. In some ways the holocaust in Tibet may have similar effects on Western culture to the fall of Byzantium, in both cases an exodus of remarkable scholars bringing benefits to the lands of their adoption. Ever-improving systems of communication and of travel from East to West have also added to the flow of ideas across cultural borders. But the traffic isn't only one-way. Western ideas, particularly in the form of Western consumerism and mass entertainment, are busily flowing East, and threatening to submerge the very cultures that have produced (and been produced by) Eastern spirituality and Eastern psychology. We are thus faced by the paradox that while Eastern ideas are finding a home in the West, they may be under increasing threat on their own territory. As a consequence, their very survival may depend in the future as much upon the West as upon the East, and if they actually have anything of value to contribute to our understanding of man, their accommodation by the West becomes increasingly vital.

Japan, the home of Zen, is of course unique. Having adopted Western industrialism and modern technology it has outcompeted the West in almost every major enterprise. Yet to what extent Japan represents an emerging balance of East–West ideas remains uncertain. The extraordinary success of Japanese materialism remains balanced, for example, by the creative school of philosophy at Kyoto which follows in the tradition established by the great D. T. Suzuki (see Abe, 1985). Certainly the business success of South-East Asia generally means that East and West are beginning to share rather than to differ in cultural and social problems.

Even so, if Western mainstream psychology and Western religious institutions show themselves hostile to traditional Eastern ideas, an accommodation is unlikely to take place, with the result that such themes will remain, to the detriment of all, on the fringe of what is deemed academically and theologically respectable. This hostility stems, in the case of mainstream psychology, primarily from a belief that Eastern ideas are 'unscientific' (in the sense that they can't be put to experimental test). In the case of religious institutions it stems from a belief that Eastern ideas threaten Western spirituality.

Neither of these beliefs has much to support it. The first is negated by the fact that Eastern psychology is in many ways more, not less, scientific than Western, in that it asks each person to take nothing on trust but to apply the practices it teaches in his or her own life, and then like a scientist assess the results to see if they're worthwhile or not. True this is a more subjective, existential approach to science than is common in the West; none the less it can be reconciled to Western methodology. In fact, with the growing respectability in the West of self-report as a scientific procedure, this reconciliation is already well on the way towards realisation. And the second is negated by the fact that, far from threatening Western spirituality, both Buddhist and Hindu traditions are much less exclusive in their approach than many Christian sects, and freely acknowledge that all the major religions lead, albeit by different pathways, to the same mountain-top.

A prerequisite for a continuing rapprochement between Western and Eastern psychologies is the presence of individuals who are willing to develop a thorough understanding of both approaches and thus put themselves in a position to identify the key points at which they complement each other. Essential to this task is a study of the terminology used by both approaches, in order to establish whether the apparent conflicts between the two are the result of semantics or of genuine differences. At present, of course, the incentives for such individuals to emerge are more personal than professional. Eastern psychology receives little academic attention from psychology departments in European universities and colleges, and there are few research and travel grants to be won by studying it. The academic world sometimes seems oblivious to the profound benefits to be gained from enhanced understanding between East and West, not only in the development of exciting ways of interpreting and modifying individual behaviour, but also in terms of co-operation and tolerance between different cultures.

The position is little better in departments of religious studies. Here some teaching of world religions goes on, but more from a comparative viewpoint than from any real wish to produce a new synthesis of ideas which will help revitalise spiritual or psychological thinking. Yet although, from a professional angle, there is still little incentive for academics or for their students to specialise in Eastern thought, a growing awareness of the interest taken in the East by society at large is at last attracting attention at departmental tea-tables and a few departments are sitting up to take notice.

In spite of this general lack of institutional support, the spread of interest in Eastern ideas continues. The extent of this interest can be witnessed in any bookshop. The quality of books published on Eastern ideas has improved immensely in the last decade, as has their number. Translations of high quality are available at accessible prices, and modern commentarial literature of insightful relevance to contemporary problems is steadily appearing.

In the United States of course there is greater interest, as witnessed by the development of wealthy private institutions such as the teaching centre of the late Chogyam Trungpa Rimpoche at Boulder, Colorado, and Shasta Abbey (Soto Zen) of Roshi Jiyu Kennett in California. These and many similar institutions sustain the production of a literature often of high quality and of considerable academic interest.

In this book we have done our best to show that the bringing together of Eastern and Western psychological ideas is not a mere esoteric exercise. We have tried to show that, on the contrary, it is an exercise of real theoretical and practical value, and one which we neglect to the impoverishment of our concepts of what it means to be human.

We have pointed particularly to the Eastern concern with space, silence, no-mind and the relativity of all conceptualisation. Most of our authors have circled about this theme and used it as a mirror within which to reflect Western themes that in one way or another probe in a similar direction. As Guy Claxton has pointed out in the concluding chapter of *Beyond Therapy*, the Eastern mirror has a depth to it unmatched by Western therapies. Speaking of the contrast between a therapist and a spiritual guide he writes '– they differ in the breadth and depth of their serenity. The therapist's is like a river, still pools interspersed with white water. The spiritual guides, who know that nothing can threaten them, not even death, because who they truly are is not bounded in either space or time, have a presence like a vast, flat lake'.

Claxton goes on to say that while a therapist's belief in self allows only a sporadic self-acceptance that can still be shaken by buried or unprecedented fear, an enlightened master cannot be disturbed for there is no longer any vestige of a distinction between self and experience. Masters are polished mirrors on which no reflection leaves a mark.

Spiritual guides of such quality are doubtless rare and some may lose their gifts with changes in circumstance, for they are, after all, only human and remain subject to karma; yet we believe the contrast is a valid one. Eastern psychophilosophy has a wider reach – going beyond the rational, the wordy, the conceptual, into the realms of wholeness. Western therapists are thereby offered the opportunity to let go of preoccupations with technique, with analysis, with patients as objects, and to expand their quality of being.

Ultimately, the issue for the Westerner is to come to terms with 'pervasion'. Beyond our rational distinctions lies the ineffable of which we are, and in which we move. To allow the conceptual and non-conceptual experiencing of pervasion to develop and instruct us is a way forward. It reduces individual and collective egotism – allows us to focus on global problems in a more holistic way. This looks like a path into a future of which Mahatma Gandhi would approve.

To conclude: listen to Krishnamurti:

> We do not know what love is, for in the space made by thought
> . . . love is the conflict of the me and the not-me. This conflict,
> this torture, is not love. Thought is the very denial of love . . . it
> cannot enter into that space where the me is not. In that space is
> the benediction that man seeks and cannot find. He seeks it within
> the frontiers of thought and thought destroys the ecstasy of such
> benediction.

It may take at least two generations for such a view to gain a wide assent in Western circles: the orthodox viewlessness is well entrenched. The Eastern position is both utterly radical and ruthless in its confrontation. Not everyone can attempt to run up the mountain full pelt; most prefer a gentle spiralling with long rests in pavilions for chats over tea overlooking the gradually expanding view. Yet so radical is this perspective that there is just a chance that the hectic Western rush to exploit this planet for personal and institituional gain, a process that is ultimately not sustainable, could be slowed down from within. The realisation that the ego and its ways are ultimately of little significance is after all the beginning of enlightenment. It may be that the Eastern wordless view will lead to that *perestroika* of our global comprehension essential for our survival.

References

Introduction

Blakemore, C. and Greenfield S., (eds.) 1987. *Mindwaves*. Oxford: Blackwell.

Claxton, G. (ed.). 1986 *Beyond therapy: The Impact of Eastern Religions on Psychological Thinking and Practice*. London: Wisdom.

Crook, J. H. and Rabgyas, T. 1988. The essential insight: a central theme in the philosophical training of Mahayanist monks. In Peranjpe A. C. *et al. loc. cit.*

Cupitt, D. 1987 *The Long-Legged Fly: A Theology of Language and Desire*. London: SCM.

Gudmunsen, C. 1977. *Wittgenstein and Buddhism*. London: MacMillan.

Hopkins, J. 1983. *Meditation on Emptiness*. London: Wisdom.

Katz, N. (ed.). 1983. *Buddhist and Western Psychology*. Boulder, Colorado: Prajna Press.

Komito, D. R. 1987. *Nagarjuna's 'Seventy Stanzas' – A Buddhist Psychology of Emptyness*. New York: Snow Lion.

Murti, T. R. V. 1955. *The Central Philosophy of Buddhism*. London: Allen & Unwin.

Ramanan, K. V. 1978. *Nagarjuna's Philosophy*. New Delhi: Motilal Banarsidass.

Peranjpe, A. C., Ho, D. Y. F. and Rieber, R. W. (eds.) 1988 *Asian Contributions to Psychology*. New York: Praeger.

Welwood, J. (ed.). 1983. *Awakening the Heart: East/West Approaches to Psychotherapy and the Healing Relationship*. Boulder, Colorado: Shambhala.

West, M. (ed.). 1987. *The Psychology of Meditation*. Oxford: Oxford University Press.

Chapter 1

Bailey, W. 1986. Consciousness and Action/Motion theories of Communication. *Western Journal of Speech Communication*, 59.1: 74–86.

Berger, P. L. 1973. *The Social Reality of Religion*. London: Penguin.

Birdwhistle, R. L. 1959. Contribution of linguistic-Kinesic studies to the understanding of schizophrenia. In A. Averbach (ed.), *Schizophrenia: An Integrated Approach*. New York: Ronald.

Bohm, D. 1980. *Wholeness and the Implicate Order*. London: Routledge & Kegan Paul.

Capra, F. 1975. *The Tao of Physics*. Berkeley: Shambala.

Cranach, M. von. and Harre, R. 1982. *The Analysis of Action*. Cambridge: Cambridge University Press.

Crook, J. H. 1980. *The Evolution of Human Consciousness*. Oxford: Oxford University Press.

Crook, J. H. 1988. The experiential context of intellect. In R. W. Byrne and A. Whiten (eds.), *Machiavellian Intelligence: Social Expertise and the Evolution of Intellect*. Oxford: Oxford University Press.

Crook, J. H. In press. Consciousness and the ecology of meaning: new findings and old philosophies. In M. Robinson and L. Tifen (eds.), *Man and Beast II*. Washington DC: Smithsonian Institute.

Cupitt, D. 1987. *The Long-Legged Fly: A Theology of Language and Desire*. London: SCM.

Duval, S. and Wicklund, R. A. 1972. *A Theory of Objective Self Awareness*. New York: Academic.

Glover, D. and Strawbridge, S. 1985. *The Sociology of Knowledge*. Ormskirk: Causeway.

Humphries, C. 1951. *Buddhism*. London: Penguin.

Krishnamurti. 1954. *The First and Last Freedom*. London: Gollancz.

Markova, I. 1982. *Paradigms, Thoughts and Language*. New York: Wiley.

Northrop, F. 1946. *The Meeting of East and West: An Inquiry Concerning World Understanding*. New York: MacMillan.

Radhakrishnan, S. 1953. *The Principal Upanishads*. York: Harper.

Suzuki, D. T. 1962. *The Essentials of Zen Buddhism*. New York: Dutton.

Taylor, C. 1975. *Hegel*. Cambridge: Cambridge University Press.

Taylor, C. 1979. *Hegel and Modern Society*. Cambridge: Cambridge University Press.

Thorpe, W. H. 1978. *Purpose in a World of Chance*. Oxford: Oxford University Press.

Watzlawick, P., Beavin, J., and Jackson, D. 1967. *Pragmatics of Human Communication: A Study of Interaction Patterns, Pathologies and Paradoxes*. New York: Norton.

Whitehead, A. N. 1929. *Process and Reality: An Essay in Cosmology*. Cambridge: Cambridge University Press.

Zukav, G. 1979. *The Dancing Wu Li Masters*. New York: Morrow.

Chapter 3

Berger, P., and Luckmann, T. 1967. *The Social Construction of Reality*. Harmondsworth: Penguin.

Blumer, H. 1969. *Symbolic Interactionism: Perspective and Method*. Englewood Cliffs, N. J.: Prentice-Hall.

Fromm, E. 1978 *To Have or to Be*. London: Jonathan Cape.

Harré, R. 1987. The social construction of selves. In K. Yardley and T. Honess (eds.) *Self and Identity: Psychosocial Perspectives*. Chichester: J. Wiley.

James, W. 1890 *Principles of Psychology*. New York: Henry Holt.

Morris, C. W. 1939. *Mind, Self and Society from the Standpoint of a Social Behavourist*. Chicago: University of Chicago Press.

Shotter, J. and Gergen, K. J. 1989. *Texts of Identity*. London: Sage.

White, L. 1959. Four stages in the evolution of minding. In S. Tax (ed.) *The Evolution of Man*, vol. 2, *Evolution after Darwin*. Chicago: University of Chicago Press.

Chapter 4

Ayer, A. J. 1973. *The Central Questions of Philosophy*. Harmondsworth, England: Penguin.
Bruner, J. S. 1966. *Towards a Theory of Instruction*. New York: Norton.
Capra, F. 1975. *The Tao of Physics*. Berkeley, CA: Shambhala.
Capra, F. 1982. *The Turning Point*. London: Wildwood House.
Govinda, Lama A. 1969. *The Psychological Attitude of Early Buddhist Philosophy*. London: Rider.
Govinda, Lama A. 1977. *Creative Meditation and Multidimensional Consciousness*. London: Allen & Unwin.
Herrigel, E. 1953. *Zen in the Art of Archery*. London: Routledge & Kegan Paul.
Jung, C. G. 1962. *The Secret of the Golden Flower*. London: Routledge & Kegan Paul.
Jung, C. G. 1978. *Psychology and the East*. Princeton, NJ: Bollingen Series.
Kennett, J. 1972. *Selling Water by the River: A Manual of Zen Training*. New York: Vintage.
Lu K'uan Yu. 1971. *Practical Buddhism*. London: Rider.
Maslow, A. H. 1968. *Towards a Psychology of Being* (2nd ed). Princeton, NJ: Van Nostrand.
Osborne, A. (ed.). 1971. *The Teachings of Bhagavan Sri Ramana Maharshi* (3rd ed). London: Rider.
Ranganathananda, Swami. 1978. *Science and Religion*. Calcutta, India: Advaita Ashrama.
Sogyal, Lama Rinpoche. 1979. *View, Meditation and Action*. London: Orgyen Cho Ling.
Suzuki, D. T. 1969. *Introduction to Zen Buddhism*. London: Rider.
Suzuki, D. T. 1970. *Essays in Zen Buddhism* (3 vols.). London: Rider.
Suzuki, D. T. 1971. *What is Zen?* London: Buddhist Society.
Suzuki, D. T. 1980. *The Field of Zen*. London: Buddhist Society.
Toyne, M. 1983. *Involved in Mankind: The Life and Message of Vivekananda*. Bourne End, England: Ramakrishna Vedanta Centre.
Wilber, K. 1982a. Odyssey: A personal inquiry into the humanistic and transpersonal psychology. *Journal of Humanistic Psychology*, 22(1): 57–90.
Wilber, K. 1982b. The pre/trans fallacy. *Journal of Humanistic Psychology*, 22(2): 5–43.
Wilber, K. 1983. *Up from Eden: A Transpersonal View of Human Evolution*. London: Routledge & Kegan Paul.
Zukav, G. 1979. *The Dancing Wu Li Masters: An Overview of the New Physics*. London: Rider.

Chapter 5

Blackmore, S. J. 1984. A psychological theory of the out-of-body experience. *Journal of Parapsychology*, 48: 201–18.
Blackmore, S. J. 1986. Who am I? Changing Models of Reality in Meditation. In *Beyond Therapy*, ed. G. Claxton London: Wisdom.
Blackmore, S. J. 1987. A theory of Lucid Dreams and OBEs. In J. Gackenbach and S. LaBerge (eds.) *Lucid Dreaming: New Research on Consciousness During Sleep*. New York: Plenum.

Chapter 6

Dennett, D. 1984. *Elbow Room: The Varieties of Free Will Worth Wanting*. Oxford: Clarendon Press.
Lifton, R. J. 1970. *Boundaries: Psychological Man in Revolution*. New York: Random House.
Molesworth, Sir W. 1841. *The Questions Concerning Liberty, Necessity and Chance in The English Works of Thomas Hobbes, Vol. V*. London: John Bohn.
Needleman, J. 1983. Psychiatry and the sacred. In J. Welwood (ed.), *Awakening the Heart: East/West Approaches to Psychotherapy*. Boulder, Colorado: Shambhala.
Nyanaponika Thera. 1986. *The Vision of Dhamma*. London: Rider.
Rabten, Geshe. 1983 *Echoes of Voidness*. London: Wisdom.
Welwood, J. (ed.). (1979). *The Meeting of the Ways: Explorations in East/West Psychology*. New York: Schocken Books.
Wilber, K. (1979). Psychologia perennis: The spectrum of consciousness. In J. Welwood (ed.), *The Meeting of the Ways: Explorations in East/West Psychology*. New York: Schocken Books.

Chapter 7

Ledi Sayaday. (1981). *The Manuals of Buddhism*. Rangoon: Department of Religious Affairs.

Chapter 8

Abe. M. 1985. *Zen and Western Thought*. London: MacMillan.
Baars, B. J. 1983. Conscious contexts provide the nervous system with coherent global information. In Davidson, R. J., Schwartz, G. E. and Shapiro, D. (eds.), *Consciousness and Self Regulation: Advance in Research*. New York: Plenum.
Berger, C. R. and Kellerman, K. A. 1983. To ask or not to ask: Is that a question? In R. N. Bostrom (ed.), *Communication Year Book*. Beverly Hills: Sage.
Berger, P. L. 1967. *The Social Reality of Religion*. London: Penguin.
Blackmore, S. J. 1982. *Beyond the Body*. London: Heinemann.
Blackmore, S. J. 1984. A psychological theory of the out-of-body experience. *Journal of Parapsychology*, 48: 201–18.

Blakemore, C. and Greenfield, S. (eds.), 1987. *Mindwaves*. Oxford.

Bohm, D. 1980. *Wholeness and the implicate order*. London: Routledge & Kegan Paul.

Brauen, M. 1980. *Feste in Ladakh*. Graz: Adademische Druck u. Verlagsanstalt.

Buck, R. 1984. *The Communication of Emotion*. New York: Guildford.

Chagnon, N. and Irons, W. 1979. *Evolutionary Biology and Human Social Behaviour: An Anthropological Perspective*. Mass.: Duxbury.

Craik, K. J. W. 1952. *The Nature of Explanation*. Cambridge: Cambridge University Press.

Cranach, M. von. 1982. The psychological study of goal directed action. In M. von Cranach and R. Harre (eds.). *The Analysis of Action*. Cambridge: Cambridge University Press.

Cranach, M. von., Kalbermatten, U., Indermuhle, K., and Gugler, B. 1982. *Goal Directed Action*. London: Academic Press.

Crook, J. H. 1980. *The evolution of Human Consciousness*. Oxford: Oxford University Press.

Crook, J. H. 1983. On attributing consciousness to animals. *Nature*, 303: 11–14.

Crook, J. H. 1987a. The nature of conscious awareness. In C. Blakemore and S. Greenfield (eds.), *Mindwaves*. Oxford: Blackwell.

Crook, J. H. 1987b. The experiential context of intellect. In R. W. Byrne and A. Whiten (eds.), *Social Expertise and the Evolution of Intellect*. Oxford: Oxford University Press.

Crook, J. H. 1989. Socio-ecological paradigms, evolution and history. In V. Standen and R. A. Foley (eds.), 1989 *Comparative Socio-ecology: the Behavioural Ecology of Humans and Other Mammals*. Oxford: Blackwell.

Crook, J. H. and Crook, S. J. 1987. Tibetan polyandry: problems of adaptation and fitness. In Betzig *et al.* (eds.), *Human Reproductive Behaviour*. Cambridge: Cambridge University Press.

Csikzentmihalyi, M. 1975. *Beyond Boredom and Anxiety: The Experience of Play in Work and Games*. San Francisco: Jossey–Bass.

Dennett, D.C. 1978. *Brainstorming: Philosophical Essays on Mind and Psychology*. San Francisco: Bradford.

Dickemann, M. 1979. Female infanticide, reproductive strategies and social stratification. In N. Chagnon and W. Irons (eds.), op. cit.

Duval, S. and Wicklund, R. A. 1972. *A Theory of Objective Self-Awareness*. New York: Academic Press.

Griffin, D. (ed.) 1980. *Animal Mind – Human Mind*. Berlin: Dahlem.

Hample, D. 1986. Logic, conscious and unconscious. *Western Journal of Speech and Communication*. 50.1: 24–40.

Harding, D. E. 1974. *The Science of the 1st Person*. Ipswich: Sholland Publications.

Harré, R. and Secord, P. F. 1972. *The Explanation of Social Behaviour*. Oxford: Blackwell.

Humphrey, N. K. 1975 The social function of intellect. In P. P. G. Bateson and R. A. Hinde (eds.), *Growing Points in Ethology*. Cambridge: Cambridge University Press.

Humphrey, N. K. 1983 *Consciousness Regained*. Oxford: Oxford University Press.

224   Space in Mind

Jaynes. J. 1976. *The Origin of Consciousness in the Breakdown of the Bicameral Mind.* New York: Houghton Mifflin.

Joshu Sasaki Roshi. 1983. Where is the Self? In J. Welwood, *Awakening the Heart.* Boston: New Science Library.

Kasulis, T. P. 1981. *Zen Action Zen Person.* Honolulu: University Press of Hawaii.

Langer, E. 1978. Rethinking the role of thought in social interaction. In J. H. Harvey, W. Ickes and R. Kidd (eds.), *New Directions in Attribution Theory and Research.* Hillsdale: Erlbaum.

McFarland, D. J. and Houston. 1981. *Quantitative Ethology.* London: Pittman.

Namkhai Norbu. 1986. *The Crystal and the Way of Light.* London: Routledge & Kegan Paul.

Nisbett, R. E. and Wilson, T. O. 1977. Telling more than we know. Verbal reports on mental processes. *Psychological Review.* 84: 231–59.

Parfit, D. 1984. *Reasons and Persons.* Oxford: Oxford University Press.

Sheng-Yen, Master. 1982. *Getting the Buddha Mind.* New York: Dharma Drum Publications. (Corona Avenue, Elmhurst).

Suzuki, D. 1932. *The Lankavatara Sutra.* London: Routledge & Kegan Paul.

Suzuki, D. 1953. *Essays in Zen Buddhism.* London: Rider.

Tajfel H. (ed.) 1978. *Differentiation between social groups.* European Monographs in Social Psychology, 14. London: Academic Press.

Vine, I. 1986. The ethology of consciousness: some implications of the sociobiological analysis of the human self-system. MSS. Pers. Comm.

Watzlawack, P. 1978. *The Language of Chance.* New York: Basic Books.

Wei Tat. 1976. *Ch'eng Wei-Shih Lun. The Doctrine of Mere-Consciousness by Hsuan Tsang.* (Translation with Commentary). The Cheng Wei shih Lun Publication Committee. 22 Fontana Gardens, F. 18. Causeway Hill, Hong Kong.

West, M. 1979. Physiological effects of meditation: a longitudinal study. *Br. J. Soc. Clin. Psych.* 18: 219–26.

West, M. 1987. *The Psychology of Meditation.* Oxford: Clarendon Press.

Chapter 10

Anguttara Nikaya (5 vols.). Ed. R. Morris and G. Hardy, 1900–1985. London: Pali Text Society.

Azrin, N.H. & Nunn, R.G. 1973. Habit-reversal: A method of eliminating nervous habits and tics. *Behaviour Research and Therapy*, 11; 619–28.

Cautela, J.R. 1967. Covert sensitization. *Psychological Reports*, 74; 459–68.

Dhammapada. Ed. S. Sumangala, 1914. London: Pali Text Society.

Dhammapada Commentary (5 vols.). Ed. H.C. Norman, 1906–1915. London: Pali Text Society.

Digha Nikaya (3 vols.). Ed. T.W. Rhys Davids and J. E. Carpenter, 1889–1910. London: Pali Text Society.

Kabat-Zinn, J. 1982. An outpatient program in behavioral medicine for chronic pain patients based on the practice of mindfulness meditation: theoretical considerations and preliminary results. *General Hospital Psychiatry*, 4: 33–47.

Kabat-Zinn, J., Lipworth, L. and Burney, R. 1985. The clinical use of mindfulness meditation for the self-regulation of chronic pain. *Journal of Behavioral Medicine*, 8: 163–90.

Katz, N. 1982. *Buddhist Images of Human Perfection*. Delhi: Motilal Banarsidas.

Kazdin, A.E. 1978. *History of Behavior Modification: Experimental Foundations and Contemporary Research*. Baltimore, Md.: University Park Press.

Majjhima Nikaya (3 vols.). Ed. V. Trechner and A. Chalmers, 1888–1902. London: Pali Text Society.

Malalasekera, G.P. 1928. *The Pali Literature of Ceylon*. Colombo: R.A.S.

Marks, I.M. 1981. *Cure and Care of Neuroses*. New York: Wiley.

Miechenbaum, D. 1985. *Stress Inoculation Training*. New York: Pergamon.

Mikulas, W.L. 1978. Four Noble Truths of Buddhism related to behavior therapy. *The Psychological Record*, 28: 59–67.

Mikulas, W.L. 1981. Buddhism and behavior modification. *The Psychological Record*, 32: 331–42.

Mikulas, W.L. 1983a. *Skills of Living*. Lanham, Md.: University Press of America.

Mikulas, W.L. 1983b. Thailand and behavior modification. *Journal of Behavior Therapy and Experimental Psychiatry*, 14: 93–7.

Mikulas, W.L. 1986. Self-control: Essence and development. *The Psychological Record*, 36: 297–308.

Nyanaponika Thera 1962. *The Heart of Buddhist Meditation*. London: Rider.

Papancasudani (Commentary on *Majjhima Nikaya*). Ed. J.H. Woods and D. Kosambi, 1928. London: Pali Text Society.

Rachman, S.J. & Hodgson, R.J. 1980. *Obsessions and Compulsions*. Englewood Cliffs. NJ: Prentice-Hall.

Rahula, W. 1967. *What the Buddha Taught*. London: Gordon Fraser.

Samyutta Nikaya (5 vols.). Ed. L. Feer, 1886–1898. London: Pali Text Society.

Shapiro, D.H. 1978. *Precision Nirvana*. Englewood Cliffs, NJ: Prentice-Hall.

Silva, P. de 1983. The Buddhist attitude to alcoholism. In G. Edwards, A. Ariff and J. Jaffe (eds.) *Drug Use and Misuse: Cultural Perspectives*. London: Croom Helm.

Silva, P. de 1984. Buddhism and behaviour modification. *Behaviour Research and Therapy*, 22: 661–78.

Silva, P. de 1985. Early Buddhist and modern behavioral strategies for the control of unwanted intrusive cognitions. *The Psychological Record*, 35: 437–63.

Silva, P. de and Samarasinghe, D. 1985. Behavior therapy in Sri Lanka. *Journal of Behavior Therapy and Experimental Psychiatry*, 16: 95–100.

Solè-Leris, A. 1986. *Tranquillity and Insight*. London: Rider.

Thoresen, C.E. and Mahoney, M.J. 1974. *Behavioral Self-Control*. New York: Holt, Rinehart, & Winston.

Visuddhimagga (2 vols.). Ed. C. Rhys Davids, 1920–1921. London: Pali Text Society.

Webb, R. 1975. *An Analysis of the Pali Canon*. Kandy: Buddhist Publication Society.

Wolpe, J. 1958. *Psychotherapy by Reciprocal Inhibition*. Stanford, Ca.: Stanford University Press.

Chapter 11

Apter, M. J. 1982. *The Experience of Motivation*. London: Academic Press.

Beck, A. 1976. *Cognitive Therapy and the Emotional Disorders*. New York: Academic Press.

Claxton, G. (ed.) 1986. *Beyond Therapy*. London: Wisdom.

Ellis, A. and Grieger, R. (eds.) 1977. *Handbook of Rational Emotive Therapy*. New York: Springer.

Gyatso, T. G. 1984. *Kindness, Clarity and Insight*. New York: Snow Lion.

Gyatso, T. G. 1986. *Meaningful to Behold*. London: Tharpa (rev. edn).

Hopkins J. 1983. *Meditation on Emptiness*. London: Wisdom.

Chapter 12

Benson, H. 1976. *The Relaxation Response*. London: Collins.

Dhiravamsa 1974. *A New Approach to Buddhism*. Lower Lake, Ca.: Dawn Horse Press.

Ellis, A. 1962. *Reason and Emotion in Psychotherapy*. New York: Citadel Press.

Krishnamurti, J. 1973. *The Second Penguin Krishnamurti Reader*. Harmondsworth: Penguin.

Suzuki, D. T. 1953. *Essays in Zen Buddhism*. London: Rider (3 vols.).

Chapter 13

Amphoux, N. 1986. *Diary of a Zen Nun*. London: Rider.

Berne, E. 1966. *The Games People Play: The Psychology of Human Relationships*. New York: Deutsch.

Bowlby, J. 1969/73. *Attachment and Loss*. Vols. 1.2. London: Hogarth.

Brandon, D. 1976. *Zen in the Art of Helping*. London: Routledge & Kegan Paul.

Crook, J.H. 1980. *The Evolution of Human Consciousness*. Oxford: Oxford University Press.

Erikson, E. 1950. *Childhood and Society*. London: Pelican.

Harding, D.E. 1974. *The Science of the 1st Person*. Ipswich: Sholland Publications.

Homans, G.C. 1961. *Social Behaviour: its Elementary Form*. New York: Harcourt, Brace.

Horrocks, J.E. and Jackson, D.W. 1972. *Self and Role: A Theory of Self-Process and Role Behaviour*. Houghton Mifflin: Boston.

Humphries, C. 1949. *Zen Buddhism*. London: Heineman.

Jourard, S. M. 1971. *Self-Disclosure: An Experimental Analysis of the Transparent Self*. New York: Wiley Interscience.

Kapleau, P. 1965. *The Three Pillars of Zen*. Boston: Beacon.

Kapleau, P. 1980. *Zen: Dawn in the West*. London: Rider.

Kennett, J. 1972. *Selling Water by the River: A Manual of Zen Training*. New York: Vintage, Random House.

Kennett, J. 1977/78. *The Wild White Goose*. Vols. 1 and 2. California: Shasta Abbey.

Kosho Uchiyama Roshi. 1973. *Approach to Zen*. Tokyo and San Francisco: Japan Publications.

Legett, T. 1985. *The Warrior Koans: Early Zen in Japan*. London: Arkana. London.

Lewis, M. and Brooks, J. 1977. Self Knowledge and emotional development. In M. Lewis and M. Rosenthal (eds.), *The Development of Affect*. New York: Plenum.

Ling, T. 1973. *The Buddha*. London: Penguin.

Love, J. 1976. *The Quantum Gods*. London: Compton Russell.

Lu K'uan. Yu. 1964. *The Secrets of Chinese Meditation*. London: Rider.

Mead, G.H. 1934. *Mind, Self and Society*. Chicago: University of Chicago Press.

Merrell-Wolff, F. 1973. *The Philosophy of Consciousness without an Object*. New York: Julian Press.

Pirsig, R. M. 1974. *Zen in the Art of Motorcycle Maintenance*. London: Bodley Head.

Sheng-Yen, Master. 1982. *Getting the Buddha Mind*. New York: Dharma Drum Publications (90–56 Corona Avenue, Elmhurst: New York.

Sullivan, H. S. 1955. *The Interpersonal Theory of Psychiatry*. London: Tavistock.

Suzuki, D. 1953. *Essays in Zen Buddhism*. London: Rider.

Tajfel, H. (ed.) 1978. Differentiation between Social Groups. *European Monographs in Social Psychology*, 14.

Thich Nhat Hanh. 1974. *Zen Keys*. New York: Doubleday.

Watts, A. N. 1957. *The Way of Zen*. London: Thames & Hudson.

Wetering, J. van. de. 1972. *The Empty Mirror*. London: Routledge & Kegan Paul.

Wetering, J. van de. 1974. *A Glimpse of Nothingness*. London: Routledge & Kegan Paul.

Chapter 14

Buddhaghosa, B. 1976. *The Path of Purification*. Berkley and London: Shambala. Trans. Bhikku Nyanamoli.

Glaser, B. G. and Strauss, A. L. 1975. *The Discovery of Grounded Theory: Strategies for Qualitative Research*. New York: Wiedenfeld & Nicolson.

Green, R. M. 1978. *Religious Reason*. Oxford: Oxford University Press.

Rahula, W. 1962. *What the Buddha Taught*. New York: Grove Press.

Reason, P. and Rowan, J. 1981 (eds.). *Human Inquiry: A Sourcebook of New Paradigm Research*. Chichester: Wiley.

Sumedho, A. 1983. *Cittaviveka. Teachings from the Silent Mind*. Chithurst: Chithurst Forest Monastery.

Chapter 15

Chögyam, Ngakpa. 1986. *Rainbow of Liberated Energy*. Shaftesbury: Element Books.

Chögyam, Ngakpa. 1988. *Journey into Vastness*. Shaftesbury: Element Books.

Chapter 16

Bateson, G. 1973. *Steps to an Ecology of Mind. Collected Essays in Anthropology, Psychiatry, Evolution and Epistemology*. London: Granada Publishing.

Chang, G. C. C. 1972. *The Buddhist Teaching of Totality: The Philosophy of Hwa Yen Buddhism*. London, George Allen & Unwin.

Govinda, Lama Anagarika 1969. *Foundations of Tibetan Mysticism. According to the Esoteric Teachings of the Great Mantra OM MANI PADME HUM*. London: Rider.

Selvini-Palazzoli, M., Cecchin, G., Prata, G., and Boscolo, L. 1978. *Paradox and Counterparadox*. New York: Jason Aronson.

Wilden, A. 1972. *System and Structure: Essays in Communication and Exchange*. London: Tavistock.

Wilden, A. 1980. *Changing Frames of Order: Cybernetics and the Machina Mundi*, in Woodward, K. (ed.), *The Myths of Information: Technology and Postindustrial Culture*. London: Routledge & Kegan Paul.

Wolf, F. A. 1985. *Mind and the New Physics*. London: Heinemann.

Conclusion

Abe, M. 1985. *Zen and Western Thought*. London: Macmillan.

Claxton, G. (ed.) 1986. *Beyond Therapy. The Impact of Eastern Religions on Psychological Theory and Practice*. London: Wisdom.

Index